ALSO BY HOWARD RUFF

How to Prosper During the Coming Bad Years

Survive and Win in the Inflationary Eighties

MAKING MONEY

*Winning the Battle
for Middle-Class
Financial Success*

Howard Ruff

SIMON AND SCHUSTER

NEW YORK

Published by Simon and Schuster
A Division of Simon & Schuster, Inc.
Simon & Schuster Building
Rockefeller Center
1230 Avenue of the Americas
New York, New York 10020

SIMON AND SCHUSTER and colophon are registered trademarks of Simon & Schuster, Inc.
Designed by Irving Perkins Associates
Manufactured in the United States of America

10 9 8 7 6 5 4

Library of Congress Cataloging in Publication Data

Ruff, Howard J.
  Making money.

  Bibliography: p.
  Includes index.
  1. Investments—United States—Handbooks, manuals, etc.
2. United States—Economic conditions—1981-   —Hand
-books, manuals, etc.   I. Title.
HG4921.R84   1984   332.6'78   84-5353
ISBN 0-671-50398-7

DEDICATION AND ACKNOWLEDGMENTS

This book is dedicated to the pioneers who blazed the trail I followed. These are the Thomas Paines of our time, the modern-day pamphleteers, the alternative press who serve up the things that would never come over an Associated Press wire. These men courageously broke from the traditional Wall Street view of the world to pioneer in popularizing inflation-hedge investments, combined with economic and political analysis based on the investment markets and sound-money economics.

I am proud to join the august company of men like Harry Browne, whose books deeply influenced my thinking in the early 70s; Vern Meyers, the crusty old curmudgeon of our industry, who was one of the earliest to recommend precious metals back when they cost a fraction of today's prices; Jim Dines, the "Original Gold Bug," one of Wall Street's finest analysts, who broke with Wall Street when he foresaw the debauching of the currency; Richard Russell, editor and publisher of the *Dow Theory Letters,* one of the first to popularize technical analysis, a man of great intellectual honesty; and Jim Blanchard, who brought the "hard money movement" together by founding the National Committee for Monetary Reform and his spectacular annual investment conference in New Orleans.

Then there are some of the finest thinkers of our time who slave away in relative obscurity but whose seminal work I continue to find stimulating, such as Dr. Gary North, editor of the *Remnant Review,* and R. E. McMaster, one of America's finest commodity analysts.

I would be ungrateful if I did not acknowledge the hours of drudgery and research by members of my staff, including my secretary and personal assistant, Joann Hebdon, who slaved over a hot word processor, along with the terrifically dedicated members of Target Inc.'s word-processing staff, Linda Parker and Pat McGriff.

Then there are my research and editorial staff and members of the Financial War Room, who contributed to the research, the making of the charts and the constant checking for accuracy, including Harvey Wilson, Robert Young, Sandra Broaddus (director of the War Room staff and chartist par excellence), Paul Eldridge (whose name graces the Eldridge Strategy described in the book), Fran Perry (who is responsible for Appendix II and monitoring of the firms we recommend), Susan Uhl-Esser, Kendra Broaddus, Sue Hahn, Peggy Hatley, Scott Hiner, George Resch and Lou Maraschiello.

Then there are long-time friends who contributed immeasurably, such as Terry Jeffers (computers) and B. Ray Anderson (taxes).

I deeply appreciate the wise counsel and good judgment of Fred Hills, my editor at Simon and Schuster, who had the patience to work through some pretty heated discussions with a hard-nosed, stubborn, maverick author. Because of him, this is a much better book.

Then there is Thomas Lipscomb, my agent and former publisher, who did all the things an agent should do.

Last of all (and best of all), there is my wife, Kay, and my family, who tolerated the incredible number of hours during which I needed to be isolated from the family so I could think and write. Kay's contribution was the greatest of all. She gave far more than she will ever get.

CONTENTS

HOW THIS BOOK CAN HELP YOU   9

INTRODUCTION: A RUFF LIFE   15

CHAPTER 1: THE MALARIAL ECONOMY   30

CHAPTER 2: FORECASTING THE FUTURE   39

CHAPTER 3: THE KING CANUTE SOLUTIONS:
             BALANCING THE BUDGET AND
             THE GOLD STANDARD   54

CHAPTER 4: LOSING MONEY   64

CHAPTER 5: MAKING MONEY   74

CHAPTER 6: THE GOLD AND SILVER LINING   83

CHAPTER 7: THE INCOME TRAP—AND HOW TO
             ESCAPE IT   110

CHAPTER 8: REAL ESTATE   117

CHAPTER 9: GOING FOR BROKE   130

CHAPTER 10: HOW NOT TO GET RIPPED OFF   162

CHAPTER 11: HOW TO ANALYZE INVESTMENTS   180

CHAPTER 12: TAXFLATION   195

CHAPTER 13: PAC-MAN TAKES ON THE
             MALARIAL ECONOMY   223

CHAPTER 14: BASIC SURVIVAL: THE WORST CASE   235

CHAPTER 15: THE SPIRITUAL ROOTS OF THE
             MALARIAL ECONOMY   243

8 CONTENTS

APPENDIX I: **HOW TO ANALYZE INVESTMENTS** **256**

APPENDIX II: **RECOMMENDED READING AND PRODUCTS** **272**

INDEX **289**

How This Book
Can Help You

A businessman was traveling east to Reno, Nevada, for an important engagement. As he began the long climb up I-80 from the Sacramento Valley over the Sierras, not only was he stuck behind a large diesel truck, but Ruff's corollary to Murphy's Law was operating: "Murphy was an optimist." The road was narrowed down to one lane because of construction, and the truck was in distress, going slower and slower up the hill until it struggled off to the side of the road. The businessman pulled up behind the truck to offer help. As he got out of the car, he was suddenly frozen by a frightening sight. The driver, who could have passed for an offensive lineman for the Oakland Raiders, was walking toward him, taking practice swings with a baseball bat.

The businessman jumped back in his car and started up the engine, ready to flee for his life, when it became obvious the driver hadn't even seen him but was pounding with the baseball bat on the back of the truck, which was covered with dents. Apparently this had happened before.

As the businessman watched with amazement, the driver suddenly stopped pounding and sprinted toward the cab, jumped in, started up and took off up the hill like a scalded cat.

It took our businessman two miles to catch up, and he followed the truck, hoping something equally interesting would happen.

Sure enough, on the next hill, the truck pulled off and the driver repeated his astounding performance while the businessman watched from a safe distance. After two more repetitions, the businessman's curiosity finally overcame his sense of self-preservation. At the next stop he pulled up beside the truck and confronted the driver as he stepped out of the cab.

"I've seen you do this four times. I want to know what's going on."

"Okay, I'll tell you if you promise not to tell anybody. I'm on my way to Reno with fifteen tons of chickens. This is a ten-ton truck, and if I can't keep a third of them flying, we're not going to make it up this hill."

Before my credibility is destroyed while this book is still on the launching pad, let me confess the story is apocryphal, but our imaginary truck driver had discovered the great truth that must govern investors through the bewildering Malarial Economy of the 1980s and 90s.

The old investment strategies no longer work. The things you will have to do to preserve your wealth, to take advantage of the new investment opportunities and avoid the yawning pitfalls that lie in wait for the unwary saver and investor, will be considered just as bizarre and unorthodox as the truck driver's single-minded concentration on getting his chickens to market.

Your personal truckload of chickens is the money you have set aside from your hard-earned wages or your hard-earned business profits, money you are trying to keep alive until you retire. If you don't utilize the unorthodox strategies detailed in this volume, you may well be stranded by the side of the road while your financial chickens die.

THE MIDDLE CLASS IN DISTRESS

The net effect of the wildly volatile economy which we have experienced in the 70s, and will see more of in the 80's and the 90's, is a shrinking middle class. The rich will get richer, and the poor will be poorer, and most of the middle class will join either of their ranks, mostly the poorer.

The royal road from the middle-class life into poverty is the same road traveled by your parents and grandparents from poverty to the "middle class." It is the road of "prudent" long-term saving and investing. Long-term is now six months to two years, and traditional "prudence" is the sure path to financial ruin.

Even more disturbing, the strategy required next year may be the complete opposite of what worked this year. This will appear to be totally perplexing to almost everyone, but part of a predictable pattern to those who have read this book.

America is the first nation in history to be dominated by a growing, relatively affluent, well-educated middle class, people who have saved and invested, and who live, not just from hand to mouth, but also from hand to savings account. They are the hard workers who are the depositors in the banks and savings and loans, the investors in the mutual funds and money market funds. They're the ones who buy the U.S. savings bonds and who occasionally take a flyer in the stock market. They are always the ones who get ripped off in the periodic scams and Ponzi schemes. Middle-class Americans aren't rich, but neither do they *always* have too much month left over at the end of their money.

This seldom-noted shrinking of the middle class is the most important economic trend of our times. It means no less than the gradual disintegration of the American Dream. The next decade will be a grim battle for middle-class financial survival. The Malarial Economy is the battleground, and there is no neutrality. There will only be victory or defeat.

Making Money will help you to understand the Malarial Economy Cycle, what it is doing to you now and how it can help you or destroy your future, depending on how you act.

The beginning of wisdom is to know that there are things you don't know. Not one American in ten thousand understands the realities of the Malarial Economy. Those who do will have an immense advantage over those who don't. I hope that because of this book, several million Americans will understand it. Probably 10 percent of them will have the courage to do what is necessary.

You can't stay neutral. All noncombatants will be victims. Those who understand and act will find it astonishingly easy to make real money, even after inflation and taxes. A few of the more aggressive and savvy who follow the rules of Chapter 10 may become genuinely wealthy.

Making Money distills the lessons I learned in more than twenty-five years of personal study, triumph and failure. In terms anyone can understand, it lays out an economic model which is the critical background for all your investment decisions. When you have studied this model, you will look at your investment portfolio and say to yourself, "So that's why I haven't done very well. How could I have been so foolish?" It works for big and small investors alike.

The theories and strategies in *Making Money* are continually tested and retested for their validity, and then refined and modified as experience dictates. Every recommendation is consistent with the basic strategy. I can't get 100 percent agreement in my own family, so I certainly wouldn't expect it from all of you; however, I hope you will accept the basic philosophy. How to apply the investment strategy and *when* to buy and sell are always ongoing dilemmas. Ultimately, your money-management decisions must be your own.

This book was originally conceived as a basic text for those who subscribe to my newsletter, *Howard Ruff's Financial Success Report.* We assumed that readers would have access to the weekly newsletter to stay current. Any financial book can be dangerous to your financial health if it is not intelligently re-evaluated in the light of changing conditions and new insights. However, many readers of this book will not be subscribers. You may buy the book several months from this writing, when the investment cycle will be at a different point from where it is now. The tax laws may change, or a government regulation may destroy the usefulness of a particular investment. A recommended investment may have gone up too high to continue to be a good buy. I have solved the problem of the nonsubscriber in two ways.

First, I have made the book a self-contained unit that can serve as a really useful guide for action.

Second, my staff has prepared and will keep current a free update on the book as changes occur, complete with a list of current "buy," "sell" and "hold" signals, and updates of any major changes in the strategies described in the book.

This is available to you absolutely free on a one-time-only basis.

Before you implement *any* of the advice in this book, please write to me at the address of the Howard Ruff *Financial Success Report,* listed in Appendix II. Ask for the current update on *Making Money.* You can use the coupon on the inside flap of the dust jacket. It is included in the price of the book. You've already paid for it, so please use it. It ensures that you will have a useful book that will not become obsolete.

Every well-known financial adviser is surrounded by people who will follow blindly anyone who looks like he knows where he's going. It's pretty seductive. Ego has been the downfall of many able financial advisers, as they begin to believe the constant ego stroking. Whenever I start succumbing, I just read my negative press clippings and remind myself that when Mozart was my age, he had been dead fifteen years.

I wince when people say to me, "I've canceled all other subscriptions to advisory services, and I only take yours. I do everything you say." That means they want me to do their thinking for them. A pedestal is a very dangerous place. Most people on pedestals are dead, and pigeons dump on them. My objective is to present a philosophy for you to accept or reject, with enough information and strategies to give you a knowledge base for making your own money decisions. They may or may not agree with mine. You shouldn't abdicate the responsibility for your finances to anyone—whether it be your broker, the trust officer at the bank, a financial planner or a newsletter writer. You have to live with the consequences of your decisions, good or bad, so you had better get a good education in order to make good decisions yourself.

HELPING THE MIDDLE CLASS

My first objective is *to help you stay out of financial trouble* without your becoming so paralyzed by "risk avoidance" that you neither advance nor retreat financially. As a student of my own rather impressive failures I am more valuable to you than if I had never had any. I know what causes failure and how to manage risk, and I will share that with you. I sometimes miss the boat, but since I started giving advice, I've never caught one that sank (although some took on water for a while).

Some very sophisticated people have lost a lot of money to scams, those too-good-to-be-true deals that prey on ignorant investors. I will teach you how to spot them.

I will teach you how *to determine the direction of the economy, and where we stand in the economic cycle.* This is by far the most important information any investor can have. If you get that wrong, then your investments will not work out. Will there be more inflation? Or less inflation? Is there a recession around the corner? Or an economic recovery? Will interest rates go up? Or down? First we must get those things right, or all else fails.

Once we know where we stand in the economic cycle, then we have *to learn how to invest in it.* I will teach you which investments move with each phase of the cycle and which do not. You must know which investments react favorably to inflation and which do not.

I will also teach you how to evaluate investment trends, how to increase profits while reducing risk, how to get rich in the 80s, and how to keep the tax man's hands off your hard-earned profits.

The occasional references to my newsletter aren't for the purpose of plugging the letter, but because many of the anecdotes that illustrate my lessons come out of my eight years of experience with my subscribers. It would be impossible for me to write this book without using those references, so please bear with me.

Almost every subject covered in *Making Money* has whole libraries devoted to it. Therefore I have tried to capture the essence, the core of what you must know to be inspired to try, and still avoid, most of the pitfalls.

If I've done my job well, you'll be motivated to read many of the books and other publications listed in Appendix II. (For most of you, they are tax deductible.) There is no more valuable asset for an investor than an unquenchable thirst for knowledge.

When I was on a talk show in Texas not too long ago, a woman called in to ask about one of her investments, which happened to be totally inappropriate for that stage of the investment cycle. I told her so and began to explain a simple alternative that would achieve much better results.

She interrupted me to say, "But I don't know anything about that." I was stopped dead in my tracks for about two seconds, but, never being at a loss for words for long, I said to her, "My dear, ignorance is a curable disease." And it is to that principle that this book is dedicated.

Introduction: A Ruff Life

"Life can only be understood backward,
but it must be lived forward."
      NIELS BOHR

Usually when you buy a financial book or newsletter, all you will ever know about the author are his professional qualifications. But because the advice and information that I dispense are highly personal, and encompass many far-reaching life-style decisions, it is only fair to share with you a brief personal history so you can understand what has shaped my attitudes, values and investment strategies. Then you can decide whether or not we are compatible.

If you already know more than you ever wanted to know about Howard Ruff, you can simply skip this introduction and go directly to the next. But if you're curious, read on.

First, I'm a practicing Mormon, a member of The Church of Jesus Christ of Latter-day Saints, and I intend to keep practicing until I get it right. Rest assured, I have no intention of imposing my religion on you, but this 153-year-old nineteenth-century American cultural phenomenon has deeply influenced my professional values, my attitudes and my advice. For the purposes of this book, it is important for you to understand some of what I believe.

Although my advice is directed especially to families, it also applies to the many single adults among my readers.

To Mormons, their roles as husbands or wives and as parents are the most important work they will ever do. Family responsibilities take precedence over business or even church responsibilities.

We Mormons believe that the family is an eternal institution, surviving beyond the grave. Whether or not that is theologically sound is not relevant. What is important to you is that this belief has caused me to take my fathering very seriously. I must prepare my children for the world in which they will have to live, so I constantly search for ways to make complex economic concepts simple and interesting so they can understand them and will want to know more. You will benefit from that simplicity.

You will find throughout my writings a deep emotional commitment to America, and particularly to its Constitution. Mormons believe that America is a Promised Land, and that those who wrote the Declaration of Independence and the Constitution were prepared by God to do so.

Consequently I have a deep, visceral love of constitutional government, and an equally deep faith in America that makes me optimistic about her ultimate future, even when the preponderance of the evidence says the road to Heaven may lie through the Valley of the Shadow of Death.

I believe that America's constitutional democratic republic is the closest the human race has ever come to God's plan of free will for man. I have been taught for as long as I can remember that free agency is God's gift to man, so I instinctively despise statism, regulation, government controls and socialism. I am deeply moved by Thomas Jefferson's glorious declaration, "I have sworn, upon the altar of God, eternal hostility toward any form of tyranny over the mind of Man."

The nineteenth-century Mormon pioneer heritage of self-sufficiency has affected me profoundly, and I have incorporated the pioneer practice of preparing in advance for a "worst-case" scenario into my basic financial planning. For me this is not a theological matter but a moral and cultural value which, when understood, makes sense in a volatile and uncertain age, as long as one maintains one's perspective and doesn't get carried away.

In the Malarial Economy, many breadwinners will lose their jobs, and many businesses will fail, as mine did years ago. For those people, the "worst-case" strategy outline in Chapter 15 will be a blessing. It was for me many years ago, as you will soon learn.

Mormon church leaders in their official church capacities in no way endorse my economic and political theories, my forecasts or my financial advice, although some of them are good friends and have been very supportive. I am probably as controversial among the Mormons as I am among the public at large. Of course, millions of non-Mormons share many of my values, and my corporate staff has been chosen without reference to religion and has included Catholics, Jews, atheists and Born-Again Christians. All I ask is that they share these values.

After my religion, the second most important influence on my life was poverty.

My father was a brilliant businessman and mathematician. He was one of the founders of the chain of stores that eventually became Safeway, and was its comptroller. He could add a long column of figures eight digits across by simply running his finger quickly down the entire column and writing the total at the bottom. He could go through a store, take an inventory in his head and record it on the train on his way to the next town.

Along with these extraordinary gifts, he had larger-than-life-sized flaws. He got caught up in the speculative fever of 1929, sold his stock in his company and took a small fortune to New York to speculate in the stock market, just before the 1929 peak. Sure enough, he lost everything, and his life disintegrated. He gambled desperately and unsuccessfully to try to recoup his losses, and began drinking compulsively. Eventually, when I was six months old, he put the barrel of a gun in his mouth and pulled the trigger.

My mother was left alone to raise two sons: my older brother, Jim, and me. We lived in Berkeley and later in Oakland, California. Mom was a great lady who had a sweetness that endeared her to everyone, a flinty, tough determination to raise her sons properly, and great skill as a seamstress. She took in sewing to support her young family. She was in every way a terrific mother. My childhood and youth, although "disadvantaged," was happy, probably because no government agency had officially explained to us that we were poor.

Early in life I learned that you had to adjust your "wants" to your resources. We had few resources, so I learned to be content with very little. When every other kid in the neighborhood had a bike, I didn't. We never owned a car or a TV set or a home, and we lived in walk-up two-room apartments. But we were never hungry.

By the age of seven, I had discovered that I was a boy soprano. My public musical debut was as Prince Charming in a school production of *Snow White and the Seven Dwarfs,* and I was hooked on music and performing. For the next twenty-five years, music was the focus of my life. I began planning a career in opera.

Jim got married when I was nine, and shortly thereafter Mom and I went to live for four years with my aunt and uncle in Reno, where I continued my singing career with six other boy sopranos, entertaining all over Reno, singing the songs of that World War Two era.

My musical career survived the vicissitudes of an adolescent changing voice (which changed halfway through a solo in church), and I landed a job in the chorus of a Gilbert and Sullivan repertory company in San Francisco at the age of fifteen. The boy soprano was now a boy baritone.

My musical career, however, was interrupted when, at the age of eighteen, I left to spend two years in the service of my church as a missionary, as is common among Mormon young people. They sent me to the heathens . . . Washington, D.C.!

My mission was one of the most influential times of my life. It forced me to be articulate and to think through those principles I had previously accepted only as a matter of blind faith. It also taught me to live with rejection—a darn good preparation for my controversial career as a financial adviser. Religion is about the world's most difficult "sell," and the experience was character-building, to say the least.

I also developed an insatiable thirst for learning. I had always been an avid reader, but mostly for fun. I became deeply interested in philosophy and current events, and my exposure to members of Congress, such as Senators Watkins and Bennett of Utah, who encouraged me, aroused my first interest in politics and economics.

My interest in business was awakened by church and social contact with J. Willard Marriott, Sr., the founder of the Marriott Corporation, who was a prominent Washington, D.C., church leader. I also got to know his son, Bill, who eventually became Chief Executive Officer of Marriott Corporation after his father stepped down.

On my days off, I loved to visit the Congress, and would listen to the debates for hours. At that time, I vowed I would someday change the world a little bit for the better. Although I didn't know it at the time, my music would one day take second place in my life, partly because of that vow.

Immediately after my mission, I went to Provo, Utah, to attend Brigham Young University, where I majored in music education and was featured in musical productions, operas and concerts. I also sang with the famed Tabernacle Choir, recording a lengthy solo on one of their biggest-selling albums.

After my freshman year I was required to pick a minor. Out of thin air, for reasons I still don't understand, I picked economics.

I don't remember much of what I learned about economics at BYU, although it was immensely interesting. I was deeply involved in music and dating, but a seed had been planted that was to bear fruit years later.

After three very happy years at BYU, I was broke, so I dropped out of school (temporarily, I thought) to make some money. I went home to San

Francisco, and sold cars by day and sang at night at Lacsadoro, one of the famous San Francisco nightclubs featuring all-night opera. I also was hired as a soloist in San Francisco's biggest synagogue, and was on call from forty different funeral homes, singing at an average of four funerals a day, at ten dollars a funeral. I also sang occasionally in the San Francisco Opera chorus, and performed in more than two hundred and fifty Gilbert and Sullivan performances with a local repertory company.

During that year, the most important event in my life took place. I met Kay, a lovely, serene and intelligent young woman, at church choir practice. She was everything I had ever dreamed about.

That dropout year cost me my student draft deferment, and suddenly I was called in for a physical, and I passed it. I was going to be drafted.

I remembered the Sunday night concerts of the Air Force Band and Singing Sergeants I had enjoyed on the steps of the U.S. Capitol Building in Washington, so I took a wild chance, called the Pentagon and got the phone number of the band. I called Colonel George S. Howard, commander of the band, and brashly announced my availability as his new baritone soloist.

To my utter amazement, he had an opening right then, as his soloist was leaving the service. I borrowed $150 from my brother and flew to Washington to audition. I was accepted, went home and promptly enlisted in the Air Force.

After only three weeks of basic training, I got orders to go immediately to Washington for an Air Force Symphony tour of northern Europe as soloist and announcer.

Kay had only two days' notice to quit her job so we could be married five days later in the Salt Lake City Mormon Temple. Our honeymoon consisted of a frantic cross-country drive to Washington, D.C., where I received my sergeant's stripes and left immediately for Europe for six weeks, while Kay got a job at the Library of Congress.

I had four terrific years with the band. We traveled about four months each year, all over Europe, Asia, South America, Canada and every state in the Union. We were always honored guests of the countries we were visiting, and we performed for and mingled with heads of state, prime ministers, high-ranking military officers and diplomats. I also appeared twice as a soloist on "The Ed Sullivan Show," and as a guest artist with major orchestras, including the Philadelphia Orchestra under Eugene Ormandy.

I soon found that singing with the band was not exactly a full-time job—it was government work, and I didn't have to show up too often. (You can only sing so many hours a day.) To keep myself occupied and supplement my Air Force pay, I took a full-time job with a stockbroker in Washington, D.C., and thus began my love affair with the markets.

The first lesson I learned is that markets don't always go up. If my judgment was poor, not only did my clients lose money, but so did I, because I always believed in my own recommendations and invested my commissions in them. I learned the hard way that you shouldn't invest based on faith alone. My investment losses almost equaled my commissions, and I was supporting my family on a meager sergeant's salary. Kay was now the full-time mother of Larry, Eric and David, who had come to us in rather rapid succession.

After my four-year Air Force hitch was up, I no longer wanted a professional singing career; I was tired of being away from Kay and the kids, and the markets were a lot more fun. In 1959 we moved to Denver to work for the same brokerage firm I had worked for in Washington.

After three years in Denver, my life took a sudden unexpected turn. I read an article in *Time* magazine about Evelyn Wood, who had successfully taught members of Congress and the White House staff to read thousands of words a minute. That night I couldn't sleep. I was on fire with the concept, so I called Evelyn to see whether or not there might be some place for me in their organization, Reading Dynamics.

She told me that their Denver office was being shut down and offered me the franchise. I bought it, paying for it with a $10,000 note, my first "nothing down" deal, and I confidently launched into selling fast reading. However, no one had told me they hadn't yet figured out *how* to sell speed-reading courses. That's why Denver was shutting down.

We went through a desperate financial period where every week we wondered if we could make our payroll—but I had discovered a new talent. I was a darn good marketer! I developed successful advertising and sales approaches that Reading Dynamics subsequently adopted all over the country, and I became a stockholder in the parent company. I eventually sold the Denver school and acquired the Northern California franchise so our growing family could go home to California, where I had been born and raised (Pamela and Sharon, numbers four and five, had now joined the family).

As the school became very successful, life began to be fun, and along came our sixth child, Ivan. But the greatest test of our lives was just around the corner.

During the three or four years of relatively easy money, we had lost our perspective and done some very foolish things. I had invested in several start-up businesses, all of which would eventually have been profitable, but which were now a money drain. I became dangerously overextended. We had become hooked on the easy celebrity that comes to people who like to spend money. I served on the board of the Oakland Symphony, and Kay and I were regularly featured in the society page accounts of Symphony social events. I enjoyed the ego trip. I had a boat in my garage and one at the Berkeley Marina. I had an airplane for my personal use and one for the business. But most of all, I spent money, and it was corrupting our kids.

Kay, however, kept her sense of proportion. She hadn't forgotten the lean days and was preparing for tough times, just in case. Although our church had always encouraged food storage, I was cool to the idea, because, as I told Kay, "If you have money, there is no problem. You can always see trouble coming and stock up, right?" She disagreed, and quietly began to accumulate storable food from the household budget. Her instincts were sounder than mine.

TROUBLE!

At the peak of our success in 1967 we had 10,000 students, and I planned for an even bigger 1968. I allocated a very large part of the budget to marketing, but did not set aside any cash reserves.

In March 1968, I planned a twenty-four-page advertising supplement to be inserted in the weekend papers. This was a huge expenditure for me—$40,000 to announce demonstration meetings all over the Bay Area at specific times and places during a two-week period. This one weekend of advertising would produce more than half of our students for the entire year.

Suddenly, after our inserts were printed, and on the night before our scheduled ads were to run, all three local papers were abruptly hit by a wildcat strike that lasted three months. I not only lost the $40,000 invested in the instantly-obsolete insert, but I had very little revenue and a huge overhead to maintain. I was in deep financial trouble.

Some months later, in June 1968, while we were still struggling to save the business, Kay and I had attended her brother's wedding in St. George, Utah, to be followed by a reception in Las Vegas. A phone call came to our Las Vegas motel just before the reception, and I went to the office to answer it. It was our bishop. Our twenty-one-month old son,

Ivan, had done two things he had never done before. He had climbed out of his crib, and he had opened the latch to the back door. He had fallen into the swimming pool and drowned.

I'll never forget that horrible moment when I went back to our room to tell Kay. But I will also never forget the peace and serenity that came shortly thereafter as we remembered that we were an eternal family, and would all be reunited. That, with prayer, made the pain endurable, and even helped us to comfort the hundreds of people who came to our home in a steady stream to offer their condolences or help, or to bring meals, which is customary in the Mormon community.

Six months later, my business, although still very sick, was beginning to improve, and the pain of Ivan's death no longer consumed all my waking thoughts. Then another bombshell hit us.

I had received verbal consent from Reading Dynamics (not from Evelyn Wood personally, who, although now a dear friend, had long since lost control of the company) to postpone my royalty payments and clean up my other business problems. I was asked to sign a note for the back royalties, which, I was told, was a matter of form.

I naively accepted the oral assurances at face value. I had stubbornly (and stupidly) kept supporting the money-draining peripheral businesses, despite the terrible cash-flow crunch. I had borrowed from banks, finance companies and friends to keep the business alive. I was racing checks to the banks, and the debts had been mountainous.

But the worst seemed to be behind us, when I walked into a meeting with representatives of the parent corporation and found my note had been called, my franchise had been canceled, my classrooms had been padlocked by court order, my bank accounts had been seized for repayment of loans, and I was broke, except for the $11.36 I had in my pocket. Unbeknownst to me, Reading Dynamics had sold my franchise to one of my employees for $500,000!

It was then that my present character, such as it may be, began to be molded. I decided that all this agony should not be wasted. It was time to make major changes in my life, and I began to face the many defects in my character, as well as the ignorance which had made me financially vulnerable. I did not like what I saw. I made up my mind to clean up my act, and never again forget what really mattered in life.

The twin shocks of that year were the pivotal events of my life. At times like that you find out whether or not your beliefs are bone-deep or skin-shallow.

Perhaps I could have fought a court battle to reclaim my franchise, and won, but I was tired—emotionally exhausted from Ivan's death and the months of financial struggle. I had some tough decisions to make.

First, I decided I wasn't going to dissipate my energies and resources on lawsuits. If I wallowed in past grievances for two or three years in the courts, I would never build a new future.

Second, I decided to learn everything I could from that experience so that it would never happen again—to me or to anyone else I could teach or influence. I spent months rubbing my nose in that mess, reconstructing the embarrassing story of my mismanagement, naiveté, ego trips, failure and, on occasion, only marginal honesty.

Third, even though I was forced to declare bankruptcy to get out from under the legal obligation for my debts—approximately $500,000—so I could make an unencumbered fresh start, I vowed that I would someday repay everyone, to the penny. Any bankrupt Mormon who makes no effort to repay his debts could find his church fellowship in jeopardy. That meant I had to become wealthy.

I never doubted I could come back, bigger than ever, largely because Kay's faith in me never wavered. I was the same guy who had made it once—I could make it again.

During those difficult months we lived in part on the stored food that Kay, despite my objections, had faithfully squirreled away. I became an enthusiastic convert to food storage. We also received some deeply appreciated help in the form of groceries from the church welfare plan, to which we had always contributed generously.

To start my comeback, I put together a new company in the education business, teaching a concentrated weekend course to prepare pilots for their written exam in Instrument Rating. This was modestly successful.

Then my new partner, Albert J. Lowry, and I launched a real estate investors' course. Eventually Al and I found that, although we were good friends and have remained so to this day, we were incompatible in business, so I voluntarily abandoned my interest in the business to Al. He eventually developed it into the immensely successful Lowry Real Estate Investor's course, and I am proud to have been in at the birth of that business. Al had the real estate expertise, and I learned much of what I know about real estate from him. I taught Al the marketing, sales and advertising end, which helped lay the foundation for his success.

I then started a distributorship with the Neolife Company, a multilevel Amway-type company, specializing in food supplements, cosmetics and biodegradable cleaning products. I started with only $50, but my past experience and skills paid off quickly, and I soon became the largest distributor for that company, with annual sales of more than a million dollars. We were well on our way back.

Two and a half years after Ivan's death, Timothy was born, followed by Deborah (numbers seven and eight, if you're counting).

All along the way, I had been working on my economic theories, trying to pull together everything I had learned from college, my business failures and my years as a stockbroker. The best thing I had retained from my Evelyn Wood days was the ability to read three thousand words per minute. I had become obsessed with economics, finance and the markets, and I was devouring books in case lots.

Despite my distaste for writing (I had managed to avoid freshman English during my entire college career), I felt compelled to write a book that argued the case for food storage. In *Famine and Survival in America,* which I published myself, I expounded on my concern for the coming inflation, which I had decided was inevitable.

It wasn't a very good book; it was overly simplistic and strident, and it overstated my case. It's no longer in print. What was important was that I was now a writer, with an evolving philosophy, and a growing ability to persuade and teach.

Because I loved teaching and giving advice more than selling products, I sold my Neolife business for a tidy profit, and I embarked with my partner, Terry Jeffers, on a new venture—a financial newsletter, which we called *The Ruff Times.* I gave financial advice based on the hard-earned economic, business and financial expertise I had developed while paying a high tuition at the school of very hard knocks.

We met with instant success, as measured by the rather nominal success standards of the advice biz. Five thousand subscribers was a big deal for those days, and we quickly attained that level—but it was far short of what we wanted.

We became very aggressive marketers, and we managed successfully to reach beyond the limited newsletter universe to the middle class at large. All the hard lessons of the past now paid off. My family orientation gave me a rapport with our typical middle-class subscribers, who shared most of my values. My fast-reading skills were also invaluable, as I was a one-man research team. My theories paid off with profits for my subscribers—and for me, as I always take my own advice.

This new business, like any new enterprise, had its learning curve. I was still paying off that $500,000 (it took twelve years), so money was scarce, but our family did without. It was the best thing that ever happened to our children. The years of struggle molded their characters, and each child who has reached young adulthood has sound values. Our five oldest children have all served as missionaries, and those who have married have established solid families of their own.

Before long I realized we needed a manual for our subscribers, a book to teach them the basics and to make the newsletter more useful. In 1978 I wrote *How to Prosper During the Coming Bad Years.*

The book sold more than 3,000,000 copies and was on the best-seller list for a year (usually second or third, after that #?!!@* *Scarsdale Diet*). It is still the biggest-selling investment book in the history of publishing.

I then launched a TV talk-and-interview show called *Ruff House,* which lasted three years, and was seen weekly in more than three hundred cities.

Eventually, as our organization grew and our services expanded, we had more than 150,000 subscribers, and it was time to translate my love of America into political action. In April 1980, we formed a political action committee, Ruffpac, and a lobbying organization, Free the Eagle. Our mission was to defend the investment free market and to fight inflation.

The theory was that if we could have an impact on elections with Ruffpac, Free the Eagle would have access to Congressmen and Senators between elections. We helped fend off legislation or regulation that could stand in the way of the inflation-hedge investor.

Free the Eagle has been in the forefront of some hot firefights in Congress, including opposing the 10 percent tax withholding on earned interest at the bank, and the $8.4 billion IMF/big bank bailout.

Ruffpac and Free the Eagle both maintain full-time Washington offices, and are my window on the Alice in Wonderland world of legislation and regulation.

We've also developed invaluable political intelligence contacts in congressional offices, congressional committee staffs, embassy staffs around the world and at the White House, with people who give us information that helps us to stay ahead of the game. It's a crucial part of our financial Early Warning System.

Late in 1982, we changed the name of the newsletter to *The Financial Survival Report,* to shed the unwarranted "gloom and doom" image that the title *The Ruff Times* seemed to foster in the media. As this is written, we have more than 170,000 subscribers, and our growth continues. We are the largest financial advisory service in the world.

Over the years, our free subscriber telephone consultation service had evolved into a Financial War Room, handling 300 to 500 subscriber phone calls every day, so we decided to bless it with that title officially.

We developed correspondents and information sources in every major market around the world—in places like Hong Kong, Johannesburg, Zurich and London.

Each of our telephone consultants was then required to develop a specialty in some investment area as well as being a competent "generalist." I was no longer a "one man band," but the leader of an orchestra of accomplished experts.

In 1980, although we kept the corporate headquarters in California, our family moved to a small town in Utah about fifteen minutes outside Provo, on ten beautiful acres. We swap one cutting of hay each year for a couple of calves, which we fatten for slaughter. We buy milk and eggs from neighboring farmers. We raise our own fruit and vegetables and have our own well. We are close to BYU, where I supply several scholarships each year for talented music students who find themselves in the same financial position that forced me to drop out. Starting these scholarships is something I had vowed I would someday do.

Five years ago, we adopted Patty (number nine), a lovely teenager, and she has since married and given us two of our seven grandchildren. Over the years we have shared our home with eight foster children, four of whom are living with us now. Fortunately for our sanity, Kay and I both love kids.

We have taught our family that when you prosper, you have a responsibility to share generously, that you don't just pray for God to bless the needy, but for Him to help *you* bless the needy, as Jesus taught.

Our lovely home, nestled at the foot of a gorgeous 11,000-foot mountain, has become an informal town community center. A steady stream of friends uses our swimming pool, our racquetball court and our tennis court. Our children's friends, many of them wholesome BYU students, use our place as a second home away from home. As a result, many of my best friends are under twenty-five, and our house vibrates with activity. We average about eighteen for Sunday dinner. Last Thanksgiving we fed thirty-eight. It's chaotic, but terrific!

With the help of a satellite dish, a telecopier and IBM word processors and computers, which tie into our mainframe computers in our corporate headquarters in California, I can monitor the world from Utah and work from home. I travel a lot and I work hard, but I spend more time in the home than most fathers. My wife and kids know they can count on me when I'm needed, and that they come first. I fish with my kids as often as possible, play racquetball with them daily, and spend my time doing the things I enjoy, such as reading, writing the weekly letter and flying. I let my staff do the rest. In California we have eighty-five employees, plus a full-service travel agency to service our 170,000 subscribers. I get to California about three times a month in my Beechcraft Baron.

Over the years, Kay has grown more beautiful and more serene and wise. She is the spiritual center around which our family rotates. If I am the head of the family, she is the heart. I make a good living, and she makes life worth living.

We have been blessed late in life (February 1, 1983) with a gorgeous baby daughter, Terri Lynn (number ten, and that's all!). This unexpected event sent our married kids on a frenzied search for baby "hand-me-ups," as Terri Lynn has five nieces and nephews older than she. Terri Lynn has to rank among the great miracles of my life. I adore her! And Kay is reborn, all aglow with youth and beauty. And if you think that sounds mushy, you should see what got edited out. Much of my political activity is aimed at ensuring that Terri Lynn grows up in a world as happy and as free as the one you and I enjoyed.

I owe an enormous debt to my incredible mother who gave me my values. I never missed not having a father.

I'm also grateful for my wonderful friends, our subscribers who have stayed with me when I have made stupid, costly mistakes, or temporarily have been on the wrong side of the markets. But over the years, as I have learned and refined my investment skills, the errors have become less costly, and the triumphs more frequent. I have never stopped learning, and I hope I never will.

If my life has taught me anything, it is how to live without fear. I don't fear criticism. I can live with rejection. I don't worry about losing money. I once lost it all, and it wasn't the end of the world. We were still happy. I don't fear failure. Failure is only a temporarily embarrassing setback. If I lose everything I own tomorrow, give me two years and I'll be better off than I am today, and the road back will be exhilarating. I believe in the words of Katherine Tingley, who said, "Fear nothing, for every renewed effort raises all former failures into lessons, all sins into experience."

I'VE BEEN THERE

As I reflect back over a rather unusual life, *I believe that the big reason for our publishing success over the years is simple: No matter where my readers are, I've either been there or I'm just about to arrive.* There is hardly any reader with whom I can't identify.

Young parents? Our Terri Lynn is only one year old.

Retired folks? I am only a bit more than a decade away from the traditional retirement age myself, although I have no intention of retiring until they cart me away dead, senile or incapable of communicating.

Up to your ears in debt? Broke? Here I can *really* identify. I grew up broke. I *know what it's like to have made it big, and suddenly lose it.*

. Are you prosperous, and worried about losing what you've worked so hard for? *I'm well off too, so I understand the frustration* of having to take precious time away from work, family or fun to cope with the mind-boggling complexities of protecting painfully accumulated assets from inflation, the IRS or markets that try to tear away from you the fruits of your labors.

A single parent? I've never been one, but my mother was. I have immense empathy for those heroic men and women, especially the women, who manage to be both effective parents and breadwinners.

Live in a big city? I grew up in one.

Live in a small town or on a farm? I live in a little farm community of 1,700 people, and I go fishing, to church and to Timothy's Little League games with people who come from generations of farmers.

I've been a small investor and a big investor. I've won big and lost big in the markets. *I've made every stupid, costly mistake there is.* I've succeeded in business and failed. I've been rich and poor (rich was better). I've been there!

HOW WE OPERATE

Let me tell you how I do my research, develop my theories and keep up with the markets.

Unlike most financial advisory services, which consist of one expert and a little clerical help, I work with a skilled team of researchers in the Financial War Room, which is located in 25,000 square feet of modern office space in Pleasanton, California.

Our two powerful IBM mainframe computers enable us to track all major industry groups and key commodities. They also produce our charts and any data comparison I can dream up.

I don't like to follow advice I don't understand, and I don't think anyone else should either. If God has given me any one gift, it is the ability to explain complex subjects in terms that anyone can understand, without sacrificing accuracy or completeness. I also use a mathematical formula called a "fog index" to actually compute the complexity of my writing style to make sure that anyone who reads well on a twelfth-grade level can grasp it, without insulting anyone's intelligence.

I often have my family read my books and articles prior to publication, to see if my explanations are clear. I have never written for the edification of great experts, and as a result, I have little status in the closed and somewhat incestuous economic community. I am not publishing econometric models for professionals. I just want to be helpful to real, live middle-class people.

I am an avid reader and feel undressed if I go on a trip without a pile of reading. For twenty-eight years my wife has been moaning at me every night to turn the light off, and with some justification. I spend three to five hours a day in reading, no matter what—at one thousand to three thousand words per minute.

I read all the latest significant books on economic theory and investments. I stay on top of all the major U.S. financial publications, the opinion-making, influential U.S. newspapers, many foreign financial publications, and mountains of clippings that my readers send in from all over the world—things I would never have seen otherwise. My staff monitors the Federal Register, the Congressional Record and government reports bearing on the subjects they know are of interest to me, as well as more than fifty economic and financial newsletters. We don't miss much.

Well, there it is folks, warts and all. As I look back on my life, I wouldn't change a thing. I still don't understand why I was so hard-headed that I had to learn so many things the hard way, but, all in all, I am a happy man. I wouldn't trade places with anyone.

THE MALARIAL ECONOMY

You can't make good investment decisions without a model of the economy, a theoretical structure that has stood the test of time. I have been developing, refining, modifying and testing such a model for ten years, and it works. I call it the Malarial Economy, malaria being a disease characterized by chills and fever.

THE MALARIAL ECONOMY CONSISTS OF ALTERNATING BOUTS OF INFLATION (FEVER) AND RECESSION (CHILLS), WITH EACH INFLATION PHASE REACHING NEW HIGHS, AND EACH RECESSION DEEPER THAN THE PREVIOUS ONE. As this is written, we are between phases and about to begin a new bout of fever.

Initially we became infected with economic malaria in World War Two, but we got a really massive dose during the Vietnam War, when Lyndon Johnson went for guns and butter at the same time, creating inflationary money to fund what were then considered to be huge deficits, although they would be penny ante stuff today.

THE ROOT CAUSE OF THE MALARIA IS INFLATION, WHICH IN ALL TIMES AND IN ALL PLACES HAS ALWAYS BEEN A MONETARY PHENOMENON—AN EXPANSION IN THE SUPPLY OF MONEY, AND/OR A DETERIORATION IN ITS VALUE, COMBINED WITH AN INCREASE IN THE SPEED WITH WHICH IT MOVES THROUGH THE ECONOMY.

The Germans experienced the most dramatic inflation in modern history when they began printing money in 1919 until, by 1923, it proliferated to the point where it wasn't worth anything.

The French tried to create wealth and prosperity by printing money in the 1790s. They too created a spectacular inflation which eventually resulted in the total destruction of the value of their currency.

The Romans created a massive inflation by increasing the number of coins in circulation, or by diluting their value when they added base metals or made them smaller. They eventually issued coins that were just made of base metals. They even tried wooden coins and ordered them to be accepted upon pain of death. Even then, the coins were rejected, and the disintegration of the currency, and the accompanying inflation, demoralized the Roman Empire and contributed to its final collapse.

Inflation can even be caused by gold. The Spanish conquistadors brought back huge quantities of gold from the New World. This more than doubled the money supply, which was strictly gold and silver coins. The resulting European inflation lasted a hundred years.

The mechanism is often different, but the *process* is the same. Inflation is not rising prices. It is diluted, shrinking money. It is watering the milk. The supply is expanded, and the value of each unit shrinks. And it almost always results from a desire to create wealth out of nothing by going into debt and "monetizing" that debt (printing money to cover it, a process I will explain in more detail later).

The Malarial Cycle is rooted in one basic fundamental—people want benefits that they are not willing to pay for now. They create debts that don't come due until the next generation, then monetize them and spend the money now. When my little girl, Terri Lynn, was born (February 1, 1983), she was $4,800 in debt—that was her share of the national debt. On her first birthday it was $5,500. Worse than that, if you add up all of the federal liabilities and guarantees for which she will probably be on the hook someday, her obligation is about $35,000. The government only guarantees those obligations which are not "bankable," which are relatively uncertain to be repaid.

If the Malarial Cycle should continue at an even pace, without accelerating, until Terri Lynn is of college age, four years of tuition, books and fees will cost her about $1,250,000. The federal deficits will be in the tens of trillions of dollars, and Terri Lynn's share of the funded national debt will be $121,200. The grand total for everyone will be almost $5,000,000,000,000,000. That's $5 quadrillion!

"MAKING" MONEY

How is money created? In fact, what is money? If you don't understand these two things, you can't grasp the concept of inflation.

Inflation, to most people, means "rising prices," which is like defining hurricanes as "falling trees." Inflation is not rising prices. Rising prices are only the consequence of inflation. Inflation is really badly mislabeled. It should be called "monetary depreciation."

We could have a bad crop year and the price of wheat might go up, but that is not inflation; it is only a temporary market phenomenon that corrects itself in a normal crop year. The creation of money, however, is an ongoing, self-reinforcing process, aggravated by rising expectations, and by the desire of people to have benefits from government for which they are not willing to pay. It is also fed by the willingness of consumers to go into debt to improve their standard of living, before they have earned the money to pay for it.

Once nations begin to expand the public and private debt base, and inflate the currency to monetize it, they create an almost rhythmic up-and-down cycle of inflationary fever and recessionary chills. Each round of inflation is higher than the last one, and each recession is deeper, more painful and more dangerous.

Ever since it was created, it has been the Federal Reserve's function to make sure there is sufficient money created through the banking system to accommodate everyone who wants to borrow and is "creditworthy." The Fed tries to keep the money supply expanding sufficiently to meet the demands of borrowers, and yet not so fast that it will create a runaway inflation, a tightrope act which, history has demonstrated, always—eventually—results in a fall. And under this particular high wire, there is no safety net.

Today, money is not generally "printed," but created through the credit system. However, I will use the term "print money" as a euphemism for the whole money-and-credit-creation process. Every penny of money that is created must be preceded by the creation of new debt by someone. As this concept is fundamental to many of the things I'll discuss later, let me explain how we "make money" out of nothing.

Let's say that I have just started a bank—the Howard J. Ruff Hip Pocket National Bank—and John Jones walks in to deposit $10,000 in my bank. When Jones walks out, if anyone asks him how much money he has, he says, "I have $10,000 in the bank."

Bill Smith wants to buy a boat but doesn't have the money to pay for it.

There are two kinds of people in the world: those who want the boat before they have the money, and those who want the money before they buy the boat. And these two kinds of people tend to marry each other. Smith's wife doesn't want him to buy the boat.

The argument is finally resolved, primarily because Smith has per-suaded both himself and Mrs. Smith that (1) "We're better off getting a loan and buying it now, rather than waiting until the price goes higher and paying cash"; and (2) the ultimate argument, "Besides, dear, the interest is tax deductible. We need the tax shelter."

Smith then comes to my bank for a loan. How much of the $10,000 in my bank can I lend Smith? Of my $10,000 in reserves, I'm required (by current regulations) to put $1,200 (12 percent) of Jones's money in a non-interest-bearing account in the Federal Reserve Bank, just in case Jones comes in and wants $1,200 of his money. (Experience has shown that, in the aggregate, depositors don't at any given time ask for more than 12 percent of their money.) *I can lend Smith $8,800.*

Rather than giving Smith his $8,800 in cash, I just open a checking account for him, and deposit $8,800 to his account.

But just a minute! According to his financial statement, Jones has $10,000 in the bank. Smith has $8,800 in his account. There's now $18,-000! Did we print any money? No. Only deposit slips.

Then, Miller comes into my bank to borrow some money. I've lent Smith all of Jones's money that I'm allowed, but don't forget, I now have a new depositor: Smith! I have another $8,800 in reserves. I lend Miller 88 percent of Smith's deposit of $8,800 ($7,744) and deposit it to his account, further increasing my reserves by $7,744. Smith and Miller write checks on their accounts to people who deposit that money in their banks, even before it's cleared my bank—which creates new reserves against which those banks can lend money, ad infinitum. Eventually Jones's $10,0000 will have grown to $65,000 in money, credit and money substitutes—real purchasing power. The money multiplies like hamsters, and the Fed has the power to determine how much money my bank can create by determining how much it must hold in reserve at the Federal bank (12 pecent in our example). If they increase the requirement, less money can be created. If they reduce the reserve requirement, more money can be created. Under the Monetary Control Act of 1980, the Fed fought for and won the power to reduce the reserve requirements to zero if necessary. They were awarded an incredibly inflationary power, while posing as our protectors against inflation!

Our money is not backed by gold, as it used to be, but by debt. In our example no new money was created until a consumer was willing to go into debt. The initial $10,000 came from the Fed, and even they couldn't create it until the Treasury created a new debt instrument, such as a note, a bond or a bill, which they sold to the Fed. They authorized the Fed to go to the Bureau of Printing and Engraving and order money printed, which they used to buy that debt instrument—and charged the Treasury interest. Not a bad deal—for the Fed!

The initial money comes from federal debt resulting from federal deficits. The subsequent money growth, building on the initial debt, results from consumer, corporate, state, municipal and foreign debt, created through the banks, and manipulated by the Federal Reserve. Less debt, less inflation. More debt, more inflation. It takes from twelve to twenty-four months before a federal deficit works its way through the credit-creation process, and the resulting increases in purchasing power finally are reflected in rising prices.

Chart #1 graphically displays the Malarial Economy chills and fever. Don't worry if you don't understand the chart completely. Just look at the big picture . . . the peaks and valleys. The shaded areas are recessions. This is the cycle that can make you rich.

Inflation peaked in 1970, 1974 and 1980. It bottomed after recessions in 1972, 1976 and 1983. Those recessions were characterized by high unemployment, rising bankruptcies, falling corporate profits, and universal assurances by conventional economists that inflation was dead. They were wrong in 1972 and 1976, and they will have been wrong in 1983.

In 1970 the inflation rate rose to an unprecedented 6 percent, which panicked "conservative" President Nixon so badly that he imposed wage and price controls in 1972, even though by then inflation had come down to about 4.9 percent. Those were the good old days, when 4.9 percent inflation was considered so dangerous. It now looks like a tiny blip on the inflation chart, compared to what was to follow. After soaring to 12.2 percent in 1974, inflation came way back down in 1976 to 4.8 percent, a bragging point for President Ford in that election year. Ford's bragging point had been Nixon's nemesis only six years earlier. Then inflation climbed in 1980 to a high of about 15 percent, before retreating to the 1983 lows of 3 percent to 5 percent.

The above inflation figures are based on a moving twelve-month period, with the peak in 1980 at about 15 percent. I prefer to annualize the monthly inflation rate, which is a much more sensitive indicator. By that measure, the 1980 peak was around 18 percent. In the next bout of fever, using the same measure, we project that inflation will hit *a peak of about 25 percent,* probably before 1987.

CHART #1

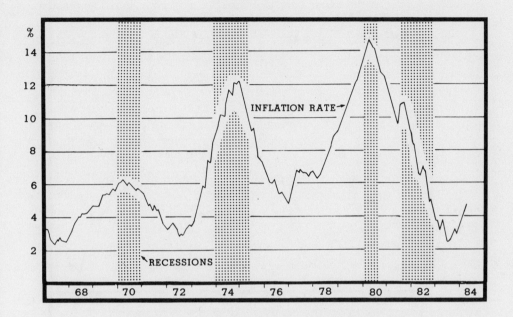

SNAPSHOT OF THE MALARIAL ECONOMY

The jagged line represents the inflation rate on a moving 12-month basis. The shaded areas are recessions. Business activity tends to rise and fall with inflation, as do interest rates. Unemployment and bankruptcies move in the opposite direction, shrinking as inflation rises, and rising as inflation shrinks during recessions. The most important lessons of this chart are: 1) Each inflation peak causes a recession; and 2) each recession lays the foundation for renewed and higher inflation.

INFLATION AND INTEREST RATES

Interest rates are dragged up by inflation rates. Institutional lenders look at the rising inflation rate and raise their lending rates to keep up. Even so, interest rates tend to lag behind the inflation rate on the way up. During the fever phase of the Malarial Economy, rising interest rates are strictly an inflation phenomenon. During the chills, they are a Federal Reserve tight-money phenomenon. (See chart #2.)

CHART #2

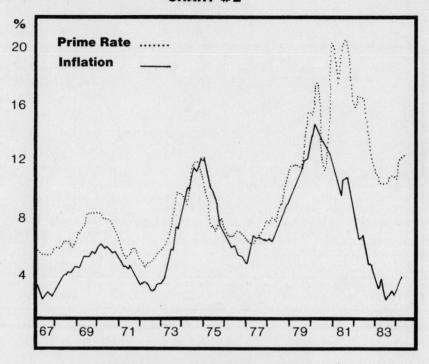

INFLATION & INTEREST RATES

The solid line is the inflation rate, the dotted line is the bank prime rate. They generally parallel each other, although after the 1980 inflation peak, interest rates were kept artificially high by the Federal Reserve, and as of this writing (Feb. 1984) have not yet declined so far as in past recessions. The lesson of this chart is that inflation and interest rates are related events.

Near the peak of the fever, however, the White House and the Federal Reserve finally decide that inflation must be fought, because the natives are getting restless and inflation is in the headlines.

The Federal Reserve represents the American banking system. It is controlled by the member banks, and its board members are former bankers. The banks like a little bit of inflation, as it stimulates the economy, but they don't want too much.

The bankers also like *some* deficit spending, because when the government spends more than it takes in, it creates lots of new notes and bonds and bills, which are a safe, secure investment for the banks. Large amounts of bank revenue come from funding deficits for cities, states and Uncle Sam.

Also, as newly created money is spent and loaned into circulation, its new purchasing power stimulates business. However, this gives a false sense of euphoria and prosperity, until inflation starts to get out of control, which it did in 1980. (See chart #2.) Then the Fed decides to tighten up the money supply to "cool off the economy" and keep price inflation from running wild, which causes even higher interest rates.

High interest rates do decrease inflation. If people suddenly can't qualify for a car loan or a mortgage because the payments are too high, prices stop rising as buying demand falls. At the peak of the fever, just as the price-inflation rate begins dropping due to reduced economic activity and price competition, interest rates climb further because of the Fed's tight-money policy. Prices in general don't actually fall, but the rate at which prices are increasing is reduced. Prices are still going up, albeit slower. Price inflation is not really dead, just resting.

The fever turns to chills, and the economy slides. The recession has begun.

Any doctor will tell you that if you clean out an infected wound but leave one little pocket of infection, as soon as you stop the therapy the wound will be reinfected. The Fed's efforts to stop inflation finally run out of steam before inflation is truly dead, because the price of stamping it out entirely by persisting in the tight-money, high-interest-rate policies would be at least a major depression. In fact, in 1982 the Fed led us to the brink of depression. Going over the brink, however, was politically unacceptable, even for the so-called "independent" Federal Reserve, so they were forced to expand the money supply at the highest rate in history to stave off a potential disaster.

The very effort to control inflation had created fertile conditions for the remaining pocket of inflationary infection (3–5 percent) to fester again.

As the economy erodes because of high interest rates, cities and states start running out of welfare and unemployment funds. As unemployment rises, tax collections fall. Taxable corporate profits erode, and personal and business bankruptcies proliferate, so Uncle Sam has to come to the rescue. He makes "off budget" loans and expands the eligibility for "entitlement programs," which creates huge federal deficits to be monetized, and money must be "printed" to pay for it. Tax collections continue to fall while the social burden is still increasing, so a new massive injection of the inflationary virus is received, even as the statistics tell you that inflation is falling. The incubation period is twelve to twenty-four months.

Eventually and inevitably, falling interest rates and falling inflation rates stimulate new business activity. People realize that their old clunker is now two years older and it needs to be replaced, and that the cost of a new car loan is down. The number of cars on the highway that should be junked has increased by now, and there is a great surge of pent-up, postponed demand. People start buying automobiles—and borrowing to pay for them.

During the last high-interest-rate period, home sales and new construction collapsed. For two years the supply of new housing did not keep up with the pent-up, postponed but ever-increasing need for housing. In the recovery, housing construction picks up, and so does mortgage borrowing.

The recession is ending. The chills are over. Business generally starts to get better, consumer spending improves and unemployment begins to fall. For the businesses that have survived, happy days are here again, and we feel very good for the year or so in which the chills are behind us and the fever has not yet begun. As this is written (February 1984), there's not yet enough inflation to really worry us, and it feels pretty healthy. Boat and refrigerator sales are booming, cruise ships fill up again, tourists are traveling, automobile sales are up 36 percent over the same period last year and housing sales are soaring. However, underneath the euphoria lurks a fully monetized monstrous federal deficit of almost $200 billion dollars, whose inflationary effect has not yet been felt, but will be in a year or two, as public and private borrowing are on the rise, with the inevitable price inflation around the corner.

Our political/fiscal behavior is about the same in each cycle as in previous cycles. Breaking the cycle would require major changes in private and public psychology and political behavior.

If the Malarial Cycle does not repeat itself, you would make terrible mistakes investing in the things that worked the last time at the same point in the cycle. If it does happen again, you could make terribly costly mistakes if you believe the conventional seers' claim that inflation is dead, and invest accordingly.

Remember, there is a one-to-two-year time lag before an inflationary event (a deficit, with expansion of the money supply) reflects itself in the Consumer Price Index (CPI). The huge increase in the money supply from late 1982 through mid-1983 was at a much higher rate than in the last similar stage of the Malarial Cycle (1976).

2

FORECASTING THE FUTURE

WASHINGTON DC (UPA)—"Last night, at a surprise press conference in the Rose Garden, President Ronald Reagan and House Majority Leader Tip O'Neill announced a joint agreement for eliminating federal deficits for fiscal 1984. President Reagan, speaking for both of them, said,

" 'Government spending will immediately be reduced by 30%, ceilings will be put on all entitlement programs, and all subsidies to politically powerful special-interest groups will immediately be terminated.'

"In an extraordinary evening session, both houses of Congress passed unanimous resolutions endorsing the agreement without debate.

"In a related incident, hell froze over."

It's an unlikely scenario. Will the Malarial Cycle continue unchanged? All the signs say yes, unless something changes radically. We thought there might be radical change when we elected Ronald Reagan. Ronald Reagan hates big spending, he hates deficits, he hates taxes and he hates inflation, but he found out to his dismay he was only elected President, not Emperor nor King nor God. Tax and fiscal policy is still made in the Congress, and monetary policy is made by the Federal Reserve Board, not in the White House. The White House can slow a trend or accelerate it, but it cannot reverse it.

So, we have the spectacle of a President who, philosophically, has a

39

greater repugnance for deficits and inflation than any President in recent memory, presiding over the biggest budgets and deficits in the history of the known universe. In fact, the Reagan deficits are just slightly less than the *combined* deficits of all of his predecessors since George Washington.

We see a President who hates giveaways and "bailouts," nevertheless bailing out the International Monetary Fund (IMF), because he has been persuaded that if he doesn't, the end of Western civilization is a distinct possibility.

If Reagan can't or won't reverse the process, who will? Walter Mondale? George Bush? Jesse Jackson? Bob Dole? None of the above?

History shows us that at the bottom of each recession we do precisely the wrong things and lay the foundation for the next round of even higher fever. At the peak of each inflation we again do exactly the wrong things and bring on and even deepen the inevitable recession. In 1981–83, we have done all the same stupid things we did in 1975–76, only more so. We did not stay the course. We took some of the medicine, but before the infection was cleaned out, we decided the therapy was too painful and went for relief. How do you spell relief? P–R–I–N–T M–O–N–E–Y!

Our projections tell us that the next inflation peak (the annualized monthly rate) will be approximately 25 percent and that the next prime rate peak will be approximately 30 percent. There are two chances in five that this is the Killer Wave that will break away into hyperinflation. The things we did to keep the last recession from breaking through the bottom into a depression have pretty well guaranteed that inflation will start up by mid-1984, ensuring a continuation of the cycle.

MONEY JUNKIES

Every effort by the Federal Reserve to slow down the debt-creation process by refusing to monetize that debt (expand the money supply to fund it) has resulted in a recession. Cutting federal spending would just mean more hardship to all those who are now dependent on it. Tightening up on money results in rising interest rates and falling sales on "big ticket items" such as cars, boats, stereos, refrigerators and so on. Then we have rising unemployment and more business bankruptcies. Even slowing inflation, let alone curing it (which we haven't tried), is a messy, almost universally painful process that gives rise to the specter of "depression," and recalls images of the 1930s, a still painful memory for almost 50 percent of Americans. In a democracy, that means trouble for the "ins," the incumbents who are intent on retaining power.

Recent history says we are not willing to endure the pain or the discipline necessary to end inflation. We are money junkies, and we have repeatedly demonstrated we will not voluntarily go through painful withdrawal symptoms when the needle is within reach and "Uncle Feelgood" is only too willing to be our connection. By what stretch of imagination will we be so self-disciplined that we will not pick up the needle? History records not a single example of a democracy controlling its inflation by such an act of self-discipline.

If money is created only to fund new debt, and if inflation is caused by creating money, and if we want to stop inflation, why don't we just stop creating money? Ronald Reagan swept into office in a landslide, propelled by his pledge to control inflation, cut spending and eliminate deficits. Why didn't he? Partly because Congress wouldn't let him. Who tells Congress what to do? You do!

Most of us want to see the end of inflation. But our desire is unfocused. There is a very specific, very focused desire, however, to preserve and add to specific programs that in the aggregate create the debt which is the cause of inflation. The average American approaches the problem with the conviction that *"Your* benefits from government are inflationary . . . mine are merely social justice." Congress continues to create huge deficits, while giving the President all the blame, of course. Ronald Reagan found out he could only accomplish what he could coerce or persuade Congress to do; and besides, he felt we needed a big increase in military spending. Congress and the President were only doing what they thought you wanted them to do.

Washington politics bring to mind a sign in the office of one of my employees: "Did a crowd of people come through here? How many were there? Which way were they going? I must find them. I'm their leader!"

The only way the consumer has been able to maintain his standard of living is by increasing his levels of debt. There's been a persistent rise in the American consumer's percentage of debt in relation to his assets and his income. Even in the depths of the last recession, there was very little contraction in the debt level, and now it's increasing again. At the risk of boring you by repetition, let me again pound home the central fact of inflation: *All debt must ultimately be monetized!*

At the bottom of recessions, economists are always saying things like "There is slack in the economy"; "We can expand the money supply without creating any inflation"; and they are correct—for twelve to twenty-four months! It is like a water-skier starting out ten feet behind his boat with the rope all piled up in the water and yelling at the driver of the boat, "Hit it! There's slack in the rope."

Inflation is already in the pipeline (February 1984). There is no way, short of military dictatorship or a politically unlikely total collapse of the debt structure, to prevent the next round of inflation. It is ordained. Politically, in fact, we must inflate or die!

BUILDING INFLATION

The foundation for the unprecedented inflation of 1977–80 was laid during the recession of 1975–76. The foundation for the coming inflation of the mid–1980s has been laid during the recession of 1980–82. What is the difference between 1975–76 and 1980–82? Very little! It is generically the same, only more so.

In fiscal 1976, before the last fever cycle, the federal deficit was only $60 billion.

In fiscal 1983, it's $220 billion!

In the mid-70s the government bailed out sick Penn Central and Lockheed and New York City by lending them billions.

In 1983 it's Mexico, Argentina, Poland, Brazil, Yugoslavia, eventually nuclear power plants in the Northwest which have defaulted on $2.5 billion in bonds, and the whole international banking system. This could add up to *hundreds* of billions, all new debt to be monetized.

Then there's Social Security. The recent Social Security compromise bailout plan depends on the Treasury, and tens of billions of dollars of new money must be created. Social Security has $7.5 trillion in unfunded liabilities that will have to be monetized. This alone guarantees exploding inflation.

The Federal Reserve's options are more limited than most people realize. If the government runs a $200 billion deficit, the Fed has no choice but to increase the money supply enough to accommodate Uncle Sam's borrowing. From late 1980 until late 1982, the Fed tried tying down the safety valves (tight money) on the boiler (the economy) to slow down inflation. They refused to increase the money supply to accommodate borrowers, which drove up interest rates to unprecedented levels (21½ percent prime rate). At the same time, Congress was turning up the heat under the boiler by voting for huge deficits. Ultimately the Fed had to open up the safety valve to accommodate the heat, or the boiler would have blown apart. They had to surrender in order to avoid breaking the back of the economy. That surrender resulted in the aforementioned money-supply explosion. As it was, the prime rate of 21½ percent would have caused a monumental depression if the Fed had persisted a few months longer. We escaped by the skin of our teeth, and the prime rate crashed to 10½ percent, as of this writing. I expect it to fall further, at least temporarily, before beginning a new upward spiral.

CONTRARY EVIDENCE?

If monetized debt is the root cause of high inflation and high interest rates, why do the Germans and the Japanese have lower inflation and interest rates, despite having larger government deficits, as a percentage of their budget and their GNP? The answer is in their savings rate. They save 15 percent to 19 percent of their income. We save less than 5 percent of ours. When they run deficits, they can borrow in their capital markets without printing a lot of money, because the pool of savings is growing fast enough to accommodate both private and public borrowing. They print some money, but not a whole lot. The rate of growth of our capital pool (savings) is totally inadequate, so we have to create new money.

Why do they do it right and we do it wrong? Mostly because of tax policy. Our tax policy encourages debt, theirs doesn't. Washington wants you to go into debt. An increase in consumer debt is considered a "positive" economic indicator. If you decide to buy a boat, you withdraw your savings and use them as a down payment. You don't leave your money in the bank to become part of the pool of capital available for forming new businesses and modernizing plants and equipment. You go into debt for three reasons.

(1) The interest earned on your savings is taxed (in this country we are thus fined for saving), reducing the reward for saving below the level that beats inflation—so why save? (The Germans and the Japanese don't tax interest.)

(2) The interest on the boat is tax deductible, so that you are rewarded for going into debt. (The Germans and the Japanese don't allow tax deductions for interest paid on consumer borrowing. Our tax policies provide precisely the wrong incentive.)

(3) You want this boat. We are suffering from a national epidemic of

an infantile inability to postpone gratification. The result is less capital formation, higher interest rates and less money available to start new businesses. The creation of new jobs will not come from General Motors, U.S. Steel and IBM. More than half of the new jobs created in the USA come from businesses with less than 100 employees. With insufficient savings to fund new businesses, there will be less of them, and unemployment will become more deeply embedded, because there are more people needing new jobs than new jobs needing people. This results in higher government spending to alleviate economic distress, more government debt and more inflation.

Lack of capital is a major factor in business failure, so the bankruptcy rate will be higher. Thus we have more "structural unemployment" and a greater, more expensive public social burden, creating bigger deficits and adding more fuel to this fire.

Under our present tax structure, inflation and high interest rates are assured. We keep sending the malaria victim more mosquitos.

If we were to eliminate the tax on earned interest, savings, dividends and capital gains, there would be tremendously more money saved and invested.

If we suddenly emulated the Germans and the Japanese, however, there would probably be a short-term business depression, since debt-financed consumer purchases would decline for a while—but the explosion of savings would be sowing the seeds for a powerful, noninflationary recovery in eighteen months or less. The short-term price we would pay in a brief depression would be worth it.

THE END OF THE ROAD

How about the future? How will it all end?

If we refuse to make basic structural changes, and persist in our present policies and practices, the Malarial Cycle will accelerate, the chills of recession will be worse each time and the fever of inflation will peak at higher rates each time. Eventually, we will (1) either break loose into a runaway hyperinflation near the peak of an inflation cycle, or (2) crash into a depression at the bottom of a recession. Both alternatives would be miserable experiences for people who aren't prepared for them. Unfortunately, real structural change doesn't seem to be just around the corner. We are moving further from reform, not closer to it.

Let's look at both possibilities.

THE HYPERINFLATION SCENARIO

Money is supposed to be "a store of value and a means of exchange."

There is a point somewhere beyond a 25 percent inflation rate where people look at the rate at which money is losing utility as a store of value and say, "When I am paid, I will get rid of my money as fast as I can. I'm going to spend it before prices go up." Inflationary psychology now becomes a big factor. People start stockpiling things, creating shortages, driving up prices, accelerating the panic.

The speed, or velocity, at which money is spent accelerates. A dollar spent twice in a week is twice as inflationary as a dollar that is only spent once in a week. One of the most common phenomena of a hyperinflation is people frantically getting rid of their money as fast as they can. As inflation erodes money's attractiveness as a "store of value," it becomes even more important as a "means of exchange." During the German inflation of the early 1920s, workers were paid four times a day, and their wives waited outside the office or factory windows to get the money and rushed out to buy something before prices went up.

Businessmen also stop giving thirty-day credit. "Twenty-five percent a year inflation? I'm losing two percent a month on my accounts receivable. I can't afford that. I want cash!"

As the demand for cash continues to rise, the Fed has to print even more.

As the velocity of transactions increases, along with the rising demand for cash, more money must be printed to serve as a means of exchange, and our credit economy rapidly evolves into a printing-press economy.

Today, printed money is only 5 percent to 6 percent of the total money supply. The rest is credit. If, however, people no longer want to extend credit, but demand cash, the printing presses will run overtime, and that percentage will soar.

Historically, a Malaria Cycle never ends in a soft, painless landing. Most nations experiencing uncontrolled inflation turned in desperation to dictatorships of either the left or the right. Such governments dominate every aspect of people's lives, beginning with wage, price and rent controls, which substitute shortages for "official" inflation. The underground economy expands, as a black (free?) market continues to provide goods and services at free-market prices, which, of course, are more inflated than they would have been without the shortages caused by controls.

Economist Gary North whimsically but accurately refers to the black market as "alternate zones of supply."

I'm not saying a less disastrous outcome is impossible. My hope springs eternal, but historically the landing has always been hard, and in the crash, freedom is usually the first casualty.

THE DEFLATION SCENARIO

Is hyperinflation the only possible scenario? No. There's another serious but less likely possibility.

In this case, the inflationary fever will drag up interest rates, just as it did in past years, which will again slow down the economy, probably in 1986 or 1987. The next recession, if deeper than the one we just endured, could break the back of the economy so that it does not recover, but crashes through the bottom into a real deflation and depression.

For that to happen requires a major financial accident, Federal Reserve miscalculation and a lot of big bankruptcies. Just as the *explosion* of debt is at the heart of inflation, the sudden *implosion* of debt through bankruptcies and debt repudiation is the essence of deflation. Deflation and depression are synonymous. Imagine that Brazil and Argentina collapse politically and the new governments default on $150 billion of foreign debt, causing a major bank, which holds overnight obligations to other major banks, to go under. Banks lend each other money overnight, fully expecting to have those funds back the next morning so they can function. They do it to earn money overnight on their cash reserves. A major bank collapse could create a chain reaction, not just nationwide but worldwide, if the Fed were too slow in coming to the rescue.

I just read a study, as a measure of bank vulnerability, commissioned by the California banks, asking what would happen if a really big earthquake hit Southern California and put Bank of America, Security Pacific and other big banks out of business for a week. They concluded that the monetary system of the Western world, in such a case, would probably come down around our ears, because the California banks would not be able to meet their obligations to other banks, which would in turn find themselves insolvent. Seismologists tell us that there will be a major earthquake in Southern California—we just don't know when. The banks have not taken adequate steps to see that their records are all earthquake-safe. They are completely computerized. Banks deal with each other by electronic transfer, computer to computer. If their computers are damaged or destroyed, or the tapes inaccessible, or there is no power, they can't meet their obligations.

I'm not forecasting earthquakes. I'll leave that to Joe Granville. I merely wanted to illustrate bank interdependence and intervulnerability.

I place less than a 25 percent probability on the deflation/depression scenario, but it is possible.

Actually, there is a third possible scenario for ending the Malarial Cycle.

Sometime late in the inflation cycle we get so disgusted with inflation that when some charismatic "strong man" comes along and says, "I will save you, just give me power, I only need it temporarily," we give it to him. Unfortunately, democracies besieged by inflation have usually turned to that dubious solution. We have only to look at Argentina, Chile, Brazil. The great inflations of China after World War Two, France in the 1790s, and Germany in the 1920s gave us Mao Tse-tung, Napoleon and Hitler.

The cry usually begins with demands for wage, rent, price and currency controls—the first step toward dictatorship. Diocletian, the Roman Emperor, was a well-intentioned man. There's no evidence that he really wanted to be a tyrant. But after he introduced controls, he eventually found that a growing web of new regulations, rules and laws was necessary to enforce the controls, and he created the most all-pervasive dictatorship in history, regulating virtually every phase of people's lives. Violation of the controls was a capital offense. Off with their heads!

Despite the harsh punishments, the Roman economy collapsed, because people just went underground and created a huge nontaxable underground economy; and a demoralized Rome was conquered by an inferior invading force.

We escaped controls by the skin of our teeth in 1979 and 1980 when Teddy Kennedy and other Democrats were demanding them. Jimmy Carter, who previously had spoken favorably of price controls, suddenly reversed his position and decided against imposing them by executive order, probably because Kennedy, his chief rival for the 1980 nomination, was for them.

The media gives the impression that loss of freedom is purely a right-wing phenomenon. Actually, it is just as likely to come from left-wing "liberals," who seem to turn to government for the solutions to all problems, as it is from an extreme right-wing military coup. Both kinds of repression are equally hateful, but in the Malarial Economy, the left is politically more dangerous, because of its attitude towards controls. Ted Kennedy, if ever elected President, could become the modern Diocletian, despite his good intentions.

Is a great depression or a hyperinflation the end of the world? I have about as much enthusiasm for either one as I do for root canal work; but in the 1930s this nation demonstrated that it could not only survive a depression but could come out of it with a stronger character than when we went into it. I'm a great believer in the beneficial lessons of adversity—I've benefited mightily from my share of trouble—although neither wealth nor the lack of it has much to do with how happy we are. I believe we must try with all our might to modify the Malarial Cycle and to create stability, even though the odds are against us. We must also prepare to live with what happens.

A depression is not the ultimate tragedy. Bondage and the destruction of freedom are the ultimate tragedy. But whatever the outcome may be, while working to try to change things, I also invest in what is most likely to generate profit. Wealth can't buy happiness, but it can open up a lot of options and buy a lot of protection in a difficult world.

BLOOD OUT OF BURIED TURNIPS

There's another force at work in our economy that deserves mention. No modern nation has ever successfully taxed away more than 40 percent of its people's income for a prolonged period. When you pass the 40 percent level, money is driven underground, creating an underground economy, complete with tax-protest movements and tax evasion, which is a form of passive revolution. We are now almost at the 40 percent level.

Italy is now collecting a little over 40 percent of its citizens' income in taxes, but cheating is so widespread that in order to collect it, the various taxes for the highest wage earners total about 120 percent. It takes a 120 percent tax rate to actually collect 40 percent, because even patriotic, law-abiding citizens suddenly lose their sense of obligation above 40 percent! Sophia Loren had to go to jail when she got caught.

In the United States, rising evasion, tax rebellion and tax sheltering have prompted counterefforts to "plug loopholes," to "increase compliance"—measures which are really tax increases. This has also prompted a political battle to repeal the indexing provision that was built into the 1981 tax law. Substantial tax increases on top of the already dangerously volatile Malarial Cycle ensure that the intermittent recessions will be deeper. Tax increases will also increase considerably the risk that the "chills" part of the Malarial Cycle will turn into the long winter of a great depression.

Under the tax structure prior to the indexing provision (which is scheduled to take effect in 1985), if your employer gave you a cost-of-living raise because of inflation, you would probably find yourself in a higher tax bracket because of the graduated income tax. Where they were taking 30 percent, now they might take 35 percent ("bracket creep"), which probably eats up your raise, and then some. The Congress will have avoided the political embarrassment of having to vote for a tax increase to get more revenue with which to buy votes. They get it automatically. Because the rising inflationary tide raises all boats, all levels of income tend to rise, so middle-class Americans naturally rise to higher tax brackets, eventually paying tax rates that were originally intended for the Rockefellers.

Under the tax-indexing provision (if it isn't repealed), after 1985 the income levels at which you move into higher tax brackets will be adjusted upward with inflation, so you can't get an automatic tax increase just because your income has kept up with inflation. I'm for it.

Indexing was voted into law when Reagan was at the height of his political influence. Now the big spenders in Congress want to repeal indexing so politicians can continue to get their hands on those automatic tax increases, which means more money to buy votes through the usual pork-barrel programs, subsidies and government programs for the benefit of constituents. Congress uses the huge federal deficits, which were caused by Congressional spending, as the excuse to repeal indexing. At the same time, the big spenders pose as responsible, born-again budget balancers.

Their most effective political argument is that tax indexing "benefits the rich," an almost risk-free political slogan. That's bull! The rich are already in the highest tax brackets. Indexing would benefit the middle class by keeping the tax laws from doing further damage. The worst victims of bracket creep are society's middle-class workers, savers and producers. Without indexing, bracket creep will give the government $1.25 in tax revenues for every dollar of increased taxpayer income.

Huge deficits, low savings and big spending guarantee the inflationary fever. Rising taxes and high interest rates guarantee the periodic chills of recessions. Together, they perpetuate the Malarial Cycle.

ECONOMIC FORECASTING IN THE MALARIAL ECONOMY

The most important service I can perform is to teach you how to tell when the chills are about to turn into fever, or when the fever is about to turn into chills. Through twelve years of trial and error we have identified several indicators that, taken together, tell us whether or not the present trend will remain in motion or whether it is running out of steam.

I watch markets. They have been far more dependable for me than the "Index Of Leading Indicators" has been for orthodox economists. The commodities markets, along with certain stock industry groups, almost invariably forecast inflation trends well in advance of changes in consumer prices.

For example, when gold, silver, copper, platinum, gold-mining shares and silver and copper-mining shares all begin to show certain formations on my charts that in the past have preceded bull markets, I know that the chills are behind us, that the recession will end in a few months and that we have seen the worst. I don't have to see all of them lined up in bull-market formations—just the majority, with the others moving in the right direction.

I also watch the Commodity Research Bureau Index (CRB), which is an index of the price movement of all commodities, in much the same way that the Dow Jones is an index of 30 leading industrials. When that begins to show a bull-market formation, signifying that the long-term trend has turned up, that's another indication that the economy is about to turn up. Near the peak of inflation, we also watch for technical weakness in the same commodities in anticipation of the chills.

I will discuss how to read these charts in Chapter 11 and Appendix I.

All of these signals tend to become clear long before the "leading indicators" can be used to predict the direction of the economy.

THE CLEAREST CRYSTAL BALL

The best indicator, which has been close to infallible ever since the birth of the Malarial Cycle, is the relationship between short-term and long-term interest rates.

Historically, long-term interest rates are higher than short-term interest rates. The rationale is pretty simple.

If you're going to lend money for ninety days, you're not so concerned about protecting yourself against inflation because inflation tends to be relatively predictable over short periods. If, however, you are going to lend money for twenty-five years, you demand a higher rate to give you a margin of safety against the uncertainties of the inflation rate. The longer the term of the loan, the higher the interest rates. The difference is called the "inflation premium."

In a relatively stable world, mortgage rates will be higher than the bank prime rate, and ten-year U.S. Treasury bond rates will be higher than thirty-day Treasury Bill rates.

As long as that "inflation premium" exists, the economy is not headed for a major downturn.

It is important that you understand this clearly. *As long as the short-term interest rates are safely below the long-term interest rates, the economy is safe.*

If, however, short-term interest rates begin to approach the long-term interest rates, and the inflation premium shrinks, I begin to watch very carefully. If the short-term rates rise above the long-term rate and persist in maintaining that inversion so that the inflation premium disappears, I can tell you with virtual certainty that we are a few months at most from plunging into a recession. The length and severity of the interest-rate inversion is a good measurement of the length and severity of the coming recession.

Later on, no matter how deep the recession, when short-term interest rates fall below the long-term interest rates, restoring the inflation premium, I can state with virtual certainty that this recession will not plunge into a depression, but that a recovery is only a few months away. The size of the inflation premium is a good indicator of the strength of the recovery.

The chart on page 52 illustrates this very clearly:

The shaded areas of the chart are recessions. We have used short-term Treasury bill rates against long-term U.S. Treasury bond rates.

Note that a few months prior to each recession, the short-term rate (dotted line) has climbed above the long-term rate (solid line). Note that near the depths of the recession, the short-term rate has fallen below the long-term rate, and a recovery followed.

Although 1980–1982 is a bit different, it is still a good illustration of the principle. Most economists treat that period as two recessions, one occurring in 1980 and one from late 1981 through 1982. Although we did have a short-lived, though fairly strong, recovery in the middle of that re-

INTEREST RATES

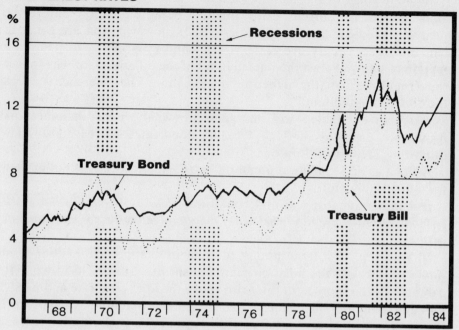

This chart shows how interest rates can forecast recessions and recoveries. Just before recessions, short-term interest rates (T-bills—dotted line) rise above long-term rates (T-bonds—solid line). Just before recessions end, the short-term rates fall below long-term rates, announcing recovery is imminent. This has been a near-infallible indicator for 20 years.

cession, I believe it was simply a W-shaped recession with the second downstroke of the W being deeper and longer than the first. The first "recovery" was preceded by a decline in the short-term rates below the long-term rates. However, when the short-term rate shot back up above the long-term rate, I published a warning in Novemer 1980:

"Now comes the real recession. Businessmen, pull in your horns. Reduce your inventories and get cash rich. Tough times are ahead."

When the short-term rate fell below the long-term rate to stay in late 1982, we knew the recession would soon end, and we called the bottom of the recession for the last quarter of 1982.

This one indicator will give us our most dependable and decisive measurement as to whether or not the inflation is about to turn into a recession, or the recession is about to end, triggering a new round of inflation.

OTHER INDICATORS

We fine-tune our timing by watching even more closely the performance of gold, silver, platinum and copper. Gold is the most sensitive indicator of inflation. Silver, platinum and copper are part of the bones and sinews of our industrial society. Copper is used in practically every industry, and platinum, a major component of catalytic converters, gives you advance notice as to the health of the automobile industry.

We also watch plywood, lumber and heating-oil futures. Rising prices are indications that contractors are buying in anticipation of more construction and more energy use.

If you want to track the indicators, look in *The Wall Street Journal* every day, where the various interest rates are reported, and carefully track the performance of Treasury bill interest rates against Treasury bond rates. When the gap starts to narrow, watch out! When short-term rates fall below the long-term rates, it is time for an aggressive businessman to begin to expand his plant capacity and production and prepare for several years of good times ahead. It's also time for the inflation-hedge investor to prepare for a new bull market.

When the short-term rates rise above the long-term rates, the businessman should reduce his inventory and build cash revenues. That's also the time for investors to consider bonds, and unload inflation hedges, if they haven't already done so.

THE KING CANUTE SOLUTIONS: BALANCING THE BUDGET AND THE GOLD STANDARD

You've all heard the legend of King Canute, who became so convinced of his godlike powers that he believed he could command the tide not to come in. When he went to the beach to demonstrate his power over the sea, someone forgot to tell the sea, and the King got his feet wet.

There are two solutions to the root causes of the Malarial Economy that are often proposed by well-meaning conservatives: a "Balanced Budget Amendment" and the reinstitution of the gold standard, both prime examples of the political and economic King Canute principle.

I'm not arguing that these are not worthy objectives, but I am dubious about their practicality in the current world of tough economics.

THE BALANCED BUDGET AMENDMENT

A Balanced Budget Amendment would require that the federal budget be balanced so there would be no way government could spend more than it collected in taxes. Consequently, there would be no deficits to be funded and no inflation, because the Constitution would forbid it.

People touting this amendment, including some of my best friends in Congress, have a touching faith in the willingness of elected officials to abide by the Constitution, even if it flies in the face of most people's vested interests. They fail to consider that there are numerous examples of institutionalized disobedience to the Constitution.

For example, the Constitution mandates that a man is innocent until he's proven guilty, and that if he is accused of a crime he is entitled to a trial by "a jury of his peers." Yet if the IRS alleges that you have not paid your taxes, they can arbitrarily seize your bank accounts, which could destroy you before you are proven guilty and they can then force you to prove your innocence. You are guilty until proven innocent, despite the Constitution.

For example, you have the right to "trial by jury" if a case is brought against you in the criminal courts, but there is a whole fourth branch of government, the regulatory branch, in which that is not the case. The Supreme Court ruled eight to zero (one justice was absent) that in an "administrative procedure" brought against you by federal regulatory agency judges, who are creatively titled "Administrative Hearing Officers," you have no right to a jury trial.

"Administrative procedure" is legally different from a criminal action, but I fail to see the practical difference when the penalties can be every bit as severe as when criminal charges are brought against you. In these cases the Constitution has been neatly circumvented.

Also, the Constitution provides for unqualified freedom of the press. The government is supposedly not allowed to interfere with or regulate the press in any way.

I'm the publisher of a newsletter, which is clearly "the press." It is no different generically from Tom Paine's *Common Sense,* published prior to the American Revolution.

The Investment Advisors' Act of 1948 requires that all financial newsletters be registered with the SEC, and the publishers are subject to stringent restrictions—restrictions which *The New York Times* or *The Wall Street Journal* wouldn't sit still for—but to which I am subject nonetheless. By SEC fiat, I'm not allowed to quote testimonials as to the effectiveness and validity of my service, nor am I allowed to buy securities for my own account without first notifying all my clients of what I'm doing. In the newsletter industry, freedom of the press is a myth.

The Constitution also provides that "lawful money" consists of gold and silver coins of a carefully defined weight and fineness. That doesn't prevent the government from taxing you on the receipt of Federal Reserve notes, which are "legal tender for all debts public and private," in a way that is clearly unconstitutional.

So much for the Constitution when it conflicts with "public policy."

Now let's see whether or not a balanced-budget constitutional amendment could or would be honored.

Federal budgets are drawn up more than a year in advance of that fiscal year. (At least, that's the way it's supposed to be. In recent years, because we have not been able to resolve the budget conflict between the President and the Congress, we have been operating under a series of "continuing resolutions" where there is no formal, comprehensive budget.) The budget projections, which involve forecasts of revenues and expenditures, are prepared by the Office of Management of the Budget (OMB). The Congressional Budget Office (CBO) also makes its own projections. Those "budgets" have been within 25 percent of reality only once in the past twenty years!

The state of the government's economic forecasting is such that its economists can't even get it right during the first six months of the fiscal year they are trying to forecast.

Now let's say we have a Balanced Budget Amendment, and Congress prepares the budget for fiscal 1985 sometime in fiscal 1984. After all of the political posturing and compromises, Congress arrives at a figure for tax revenues. This involves a battle between the "ins," who have a vested interest in rosy forecasts about business activities and tax collections, and the "outs," who are arguing that we're probably headed for a big recession because of the actions of the "ins."

Eventually a compromise will be reached. Compromises are wonderful ways to get agreement, but they are a terrible way to arrive at truth, so the resulting projection of income has nothing to do with reality.

We really enter Alice's Wonderland when they begin budgeting expenditures.

The big spenders, who depend for their own jobs in Congress on dispensing money to politically powerful pressure groups, have a vested interest in grossly understating the amount of money that will be spent on the "entitlement" programs. The conservatives, who oppose these transfers of wealth, tend to overstate the estimates, but they eventually compromise. The compromise decision has nothing to do with the amount of money that will actually be spent, because there is no ceiling on entitlement programs. The term "budget" is a farce when applied to entitlement programs, because Uncle Sam is not bound by any legal requirements. In fact, to the contrary, any eligible person can draw on the entitlement programs. The compromise that is arrived at is only a guess, and a politically biased one, about how much will be spent.

Eventually the Congress, having met its constitutional responsibility to "balance the budget," congratulates itself and goes home to brag to the voters.

Now the real world gets in the way. An unexpected recession occurs, inflation causes higher-than-expected interest rates, and the amount of interest paid on T-Bills is billions of dollars more than was expected. Expenditures rise and tax collections fall. *Voilà!* Deficit!

Theoretically, there's also a chance of overstating revenues and understating expenditures, but it never happens that way. In government, the opposite is always the case.

The end result is that we don't know that the budget will produce a huge deficit until late in the fiscal year, and by then it is too late. The law requires that the entitlement programs disburse money to everyone who is "entitled," and you can't change the tax laws in the middle of the year to produce additional revenue. Taxpayers simply wouldn't sit still for that. So we have another deficit, and all Congress can say is, "Oops! How were we supposed to know? We did the best we could."

The Constitution has been violated. What are we going to do? Arrest Tip O'Neill? Indict Howard Baker? Fine Ronald Reagan? Incarcerate David Stockman?

The Balanced Budget Amendment has three problems: (1) There is little chance that it will ever get passed; (2) It can't be enforced; and (3) It will take about eight years to be approved by the states if it is passed. By then it will be too late. We will probably be in a hyperinflation. It fails the test on both practical and political grounds.

"Just a minute," I hear you cry. "A lot of states have mandatory balanced budgets that work. Why so cynical? Washington could do it too. Don't forget Proposition Thirteen in California."

You're right. The states make balanced budgets work. Why? Because they are handing more and more of their burdens to Washington. They get grants, "matching funds," and so on.

Who is going to give Uncle Sam grants or matching funds?

And don't forget that several states have run deficits in recent years, including California, despite the State Constitution.

Would I vote for a Balanced Budget Amendment? Sure I would. It's an important symbol. It's the right thing to do. I just wouldn't bet my farm (all ten acres) that it would work.

THE GOLD STANDARD: SAVIOR OR FANTASY?

One of Ronald Reagan's campaign promises was to return the U.S. to the gold standard. "No nation can survive a fiat currency," he declared, offering the gold standard as his major weapon in his fight against inflation.

Shortly after he took office, Reagan appointed a bipartisan gold commission to study the question.

The commission, consisting of thirteen members, had two members who favored a gold standard, two who might be persuaded, and the rest were either indifferent or violently opposed.

After meeting for more than a year, the commission finally made a halfhearted recommendation that the government consider minting a few gold coins, but the rest of the report, predictably, turned thumbs down on a gold standard. A minority report was issued by Congressman Ron Paul, one of my personal heroes, who was in favor of a true gold standard, but there was no real progress made.

A gold standard is an example of the "toothpaste out of the tube" theory. One of the reasons the Malarial Economy is plaguing us is that we got rid of the gold standard. But now that the toothpaste is out of the tube, is the answer simply to put it back in?

Before we consider that question, perhaps it might be instructive to relate how we went off of the gold standard.

As recently as 1928, the government was printing "gold certificates." On the front of the certificate there was a statement that read, "This certifies that there has been deposited in the Treasury of the United States of America $10 in gold, payable to the bearer on demand."

With that kind of promise, the government had to be careful about how many of these claims against our gold they created. If they printed too many of them they could lose all their gold to claims against it. This had an immense restraining influence on politicians who had been inclined to print money to buy votes. As long as they acted responsibly, no one would ask for their gold.

At that time, paper money was essentially a printed warehouse receipt for gold, an American gold certificate. Because of that, the certificates were universally accepted. They were an acceptable "means of exchange," precisely because they were a sound "store of value." In fact, paper money was created because citizens found gold and silver too bulky to carry around. Paper money was a proxy for gold. These certificates were "as good as gold" because they were backed 100 percent by gold.

A somewhat similar Federal Reserve note was also issued in 1928. It said essentially the same thing: "The United States of America will pay the bearer on demand $10 redeemable in gold at the United States Treasury." That meant you could exchange your Federal Reserve note for American gold certificates, which could then be redeemed at the Treasury. However, at this crucial point in our monetary history, the Federal Reserve concluded that because it was unlikely that everyone would ask for gold at the same time, they could issue more currency than there was gold on deposit. At that time, they were required to maintain only 40 percent as much gold as there were certificates in circulation, which meant they could issue 2½ times as many Federal Reserve notes as there was gold to back them up. This represented a potential 250 percent dilution of the currency.

There was an important difference between the 1928 Federal Reserve note and the Treasury gold certificate. While the $10 gold certificate was a *certificate of deposit,* with $10 in gold coin at the Treasury which the bearer could claim on demand, the Federal Reserve note was just what it said—a *note*—an obligation of debt. There was not $10 in gold coin on deposit, but only $4. The "bearer" could only claim his $10 provided that no more than 40 percent of the people wished to do so at any one time.

The dollar evolved further until the series 1950 Federal Reserve note, which promised, "The United States of America will pay to the bearer on demand $10 redeemable in lawful money at the United States Treasury." Also, the wording, including the promise to "redeem for lawful money," was reduced in size so it was more difficult to read. Notice the subtle difference between being "redeemable in gold" and "in lawful money." Now, theoretically that's the same thing, because the Constitution defines gold and silver coin as lawful money, but it was a subtle departure. These notes did not yet claim that the currency itself was money.

Now we come to the series 1963 Federal Reserve note, when the debauching of the currency was complete. There was no promise to pay the bearer $10 in demand. There was no promise to redeem for anything of value. There were no promises at all. All pretense that our paper currency was redeemable for lawful money was dropped. All it said was, "legal tender for all debts, public and private." Gold certificates were discontinued in 1933 and silver certificates in 1962, leaving only Federal Reserve notes in circulation. With the printing of these notes more than twenty years ago, all promises were abandoned. The Fed simply declared that this piece of paper, by some mystic process, was $10 all by itself. This is called "fiat" money—currency by government order, or "fiat."

Until 1964, our dimes, quarters and half dollars were required by law to contain 90 percent pure silver. In 1965 all silver was removed from quarters and dimes, and the silver content of half dollars was reduced to only 40 percent. By 1971, even that final 40 percent link with lawful money was done away with. Now the currency merely tells us that our backed-by-nothing currency is "legal tender for all debts public and private."

All is not lost, however, because the paper money also says, "In God we trust," although I can find no public record of God's having agreed to back our money with the help of a gold standard.

The Federal Reserve carries all Federal Reserve notes on its balance sheet as liabilities of the United States government. A "liability" means you are required to give somebody something in return for the paper you hold. If I hold your note, it says you are going to pay me on maturity. You have a liability. The liability aspect of money is a laughable farce, because the notes do not specify the form of payment and have no maturity date. As I understand it, a note is a promise to pay. So take your Federal Reserve note to the Federal Reserve Bank and ask them to pay you. They will ask you what kind of change you want, and they will give you more fiat money.

Here is the more startling fact in this whole sad scenario. None of these crucial changes were brought about by legislation! The Federal Reserve, acting arbitrarily, is responsible for the whole process. How does that grab you?

Despite all these legal definitions, in the real world, money is worth whatever goods and services someone is willing to give you in exchange for it. Money is whatever people are willing to accept as a means of exchange and a store of value. As of now, people are willing to give you valuable things in exchange for currency, so it has value. However, the creeping awareness of the dilution of our currency and the nonmonetary nature of our currency is reflected in the inflation rate. If prices rise 15 percent within a year, it means that the purchasing power of money has shrunk by 15 percent because there is 15 percent less confidence in the money than there was a year ago.

As the government supply of unbacked currency increases, diluting the value of all the existing dollars, a landslide can develop, as it did in all of the modern countries that have inflated their paper currency—Germany, Argentina, Peru, Chile, Brazil, China, France. Eventually the basic structural factors that keep inflation reasonably under control are overwhelmed by an accelerating, panicky loss of confidence in the currency.

Eliminating gold backing of money is like opening the door for a lion who has lived in a cage all his life. It takes a while before he goes out and runs wild, and it takes time after the money is unchained before inflation bursts out, but history says it always does. Fiat money always self-destructs.

Rising prices create their cannibalistic demand for more money, and cause and effect become blurred. When the gold standard dies, there is no restraint on the printing press.

The basic principle is simple. When gold is real money, and paper is merely a warehouse receipt for the gold, then governments have to be careful about how much paper they print. Otherwise they will lose all their gold.

A PEOPLE-BACKED STANDARD

A gold standard is only as ironclad as the willingness of the people to accept its discipline. It works only as long as the people in the society as a whole are willing to submit voluntarily to the disciplines that keep us within that framework. We have to demand balanced budgets and refrain from demanding special benefits, which collectively add up to deficits. We killed the last vestiges of the gold standard when President Nixon "closed the gold window" and no longer allowed foreign governments to exchange their dollars for gold. We did it because we had printed too many dollars and were ignoring the gold standard anyway. The gold standard had no value in the absence of the will to refrain from government deficits.

Now, back to the "toothpaste out of the tube." If our problems are caused by abandoning the gold standard, then our problems would be solved by going back to the gold standard. Right? I am not convinced, at least for now. In the absence of a willingness to balance the federal budget, a gold standard wouldn't work. It would be abandoned again, just as it has been in the past.

Many hard-money fans have proposed that we go back to a genuine gold standard, which means gold and silver coins as a circulating medium, allow the money to be issued by the banks and get the government out of the money business. Now there's a real gold standard. It has also been proposed by Austrian economists like Friedrich von Hayek and Dr. Hans Sennholz that money be freed up to "compete."

If the Bank of America wants to issue bank notes with 20 percent gold backing, and Citibank wants to issue bank notes with 40 percent gold backing, let the free market determine which money the people want! Take the whole monetary manipulation process out of the hands of the politicians and let the free market determine it.

This is, theoretically, the soundest of gold standards, but the sheer reality is that the politicians will never take their hands off the money throttle until hyperinflation has thoroughly discredited them.

Most of the gold standard proposals are really "gold veneer" standards, to use Dr. Sennholz's term. What kind of gold standard? Would you back our dollars 100 percent with gold? That would mean a gold price of over $1,000 an ounce. How about 40 percent, as proposed by economist Art Laffer and approved by President Reagan? Then gold would be worth $400 an ounce.

"How about our ability to expand the money to accommodate economic growth?" the monetarists ask. Loosely translated, that means, "How can we have a gold standard and still inflate?"

They say we're not mining gold fast enough to meet the demands of a dynamic society. The world's largest gold producers, South Africa and the Soviet Union, would then have control over the world monetary system, because of their ability to produce gold or withhold it from the marketplace. We would "be at their mercy."

None of these arguments works.

If we ever had a true gold standard with teeth in it, it would end inflation, and the price of gold would disastrously plummet as inflation-hedge investors rushed in panic to liquidate. This would be bad for Russia and South Africa, and would create terrible fluctuations in the market as speculators tried to guess how much gold backing the dollar would have, and at what price gold would eventually be pegged.

This idea of returning to the gold standard does create a conflict of interest for all of us who now advocate gold as an investment, but also work for a gold standard. However, I would much prefer for the sake of my children and grandchildren that our money be backed by gold. I can always find other appropriate investments. Unfortunately, I don't believe we will have a gold standard any time soon because the disciplines involved are absolutely unthinkable to those who control public policy.

Only when inflation has devastated the currency, caused a constitutional crisis and totally destroyed money as a store of value, then and only then will this nation be willing to accept the discipline of gold. We did so after the Revolutionary War and the Civil War, when inflation had prostrated our economy. It will take a lot more than the relatively minor lack of confidence in money that we call inflation at the rate of 5 percent or 10 percent. Remember, too, that the only thing politicians hate more than rising prices is falling prices, which affect the income of their constituents. When you begin to hear a chorus of demands for a real gold standard from establishment circles, then it will be time to get rid of your gold, sell your speculative real estate, your diamonds, your coins, your stamps and your colored stones. In fact, then you will be able to abandon all of your inflation hedges and invest in cash money, preferably hidden in the mattress, as deflation can destroy banks. An actual end to inflation will be messy, as the toothpaste is out of the tube (in terms of inflation), and there is no way to put it back in without doing serious damage to the tube.

The gold standard is currently looked upon with scorn by most of those people who have the power and influence to establish such a standard. It stands in the way of politicians printing money. It stands in the way of the entitlement programs. It stands in the way of official "compassion." Politicians and the Fed don't want to relinquish their iron-clad grip on the printing press, their principal tool for rewarding their constituents and ending recessions.

I predict that someday we will have a gold standard, but only when the currency is in tatters at our feet and all else has failed. You may remember that the Germans finally went to sound, gold-backed money in 1923 only when their currency had become totally worthless, and long after a demoralizing depression was assured. After all, if there is no longer any monetary system, why not start a good one? As long as the present monetary system seems to be working politically for the benefit of the powers that be, why meddle with it?

A lot of things could end the Malarial Cycle—runaway inflation, or an implosion of the money supply caused by bank collapses, or nuclear war. They are all much more likely to happen than a gold standard or a Balanced Budget Amendment, both of which require a collective act of moral strength. The other events merely require collective stupidity and an unwillingness to face reality. Given our recent political history, I'll bet on stupidity, until we have no more choices.

CHAPTER
4

LOSING MONEY

One of the best ways I know to avoid losing money is to study how others have lost theirs. Only when you thoroughly understand the pitfalls can you avoid them. Because most people give no thought to the nature of the Malarial Cycle, and because it has never even occurred to them that inflation is not rising prices, they willingly construct their own traps, walk into them, lock the doors behind them and resist all efforts to rescue them.

THE SECURITY TRAP

There are some very popular ways to lose money during the fever. The things that get you into trouble are the same ones that motivate the most conservative middle-class members of our society: the desire for safety and income, which will destroy you during the fever phase if you don't know what you're doing.

Let's look first at the typical certificate of deposit (CDs) at the bank. You lend the bank $10,000; they promise to give you 10 percent interest for three years. The government guarantees the money in case the bank goes broke, so it is riskless. What could possibly be wrong with that? Nothing, except it's all based on the lie that the money has stable value.

Inflation is the neutron bomb of the financial world. The neutron bomb doesn't blow up buildings; it just kills the people in the buildings. Inflation doesn't destroy your bank account; it just silently gnaws away at its purchasing power. The numbers don't change. The bankbook says you're making a profit, but you're not.

64

You thought the only risk you took was whether or not the bank would go broke, and you counted on Uncle Sam to protect you from that unlikely event. You ignored the question of whether or not the money would go broke.

What happens to the real value of that capital?

During the fever phase of the Malarial Cycle, any fixed-return investment that does not give you a high enough return to offset the rate at which the money is going broke, plus taxes, plus 2 to 4 percent, isn't worth buying. If you spend more than the 2 to 4 percent real return, and do not reinvest the rest, you are consuming your capital. You go broke, slowly but steadily, during an inflation cycle, while, ironically, you are generating taxable income.

Let's assume you had 10 percent per year inflation during the life of your three-year CD. Ten percent inflation, compounded on $10,000 for three years, is about a 33 percent loss of purchasing power. Your $10,000 would then have the purchasing power of only $6,700.

Let's assume you did not spend any of the interest but reinvested all of it. You earned about $3,300 (10 percent compounded for three years) in interest, against $3,300 in purchasing-power losses. You broke even, right? Wrong—unless you are not required to pay taxes. You probably paid between $700 and $1,600 in taxes on your $3,300 in interest, depending on your tax bracket. The net effect was a 7 to 16 percent loss of purchasing power on a 10 percent investment in three years. During the fever, taxes on earned interest are really the systematic confiscation of your capital. Ultimately they will impoverish middle-class savers. The fever phase of the Malarial Cycle specifically attacks people on fixed incomes and those who make fixed-principal, interest-earning, fixed-return investments, especially if they live on the income.

Here is a table to help you figure out whether any interest-bearing instrument makes sense for you. The table assumes you need a "real" 5 percent return after inflation and taxes. Whether or not a CD is a good deal depends on the inflation rate and your tax bracket. Find your tax bracket on the left and move to the inflation columns to discover the rate of interest required for a "real" 5 percent return. The real structural inflation rate (February, 1984) is about 5 percent.

As you can see, even with lower inflation and high rates, it is still difficult to get a "real" return. Compare your current rate of return on your CD or money fund with the chart. It's eye-opening.

A true positive-interest yield happens only every five or six years, during the chills, when the inflation rate is temporarily retreating and interest

INCOME TAX BRACKET	INFLATION RATES						
	0%	2½%	5%	7½%	10%	12½%	15%
25%	6.667%	10.000%	13.333%	16.667%	20.000%	23.333%	26.667%
30%	7.143%	10.710%	14.285%	17.857%	21.429%	25.000%	28.571%
35%	7.692%	11.538%	15.385%	19.231%	23.077%	26.923%	30.769%
40%	8.353%	12.500%	16.667%	20.833%	25.000%	29.169%	33.333%
45%	9.091%	13.636%	18.182%	22.727%	27.273%	31.818%	36.364%
50%	10.000%	15.000%	20.000%	25.000%	30.000%	35.000%	40.000%

rates are temporarily high. Only then can you get a true and honest yield after inflation and taxes. Many of you who nailed down 15 percent to 18 percent CDs at the peak of interest rates in 1981 made real, spendable income—assuming of course, that the banking system hangs together, which is another subject that needs exploring, and assuming you don't count on this positive yield to be a permanent condition. I sometimes think the purpose of the chills is to suck you in so inflation can rip you up later.

Each peak in the inflation rate so far has been higher than it was the last time. During the fever, interest rates, even though they're on the rise, gradually become more and more inadequate for the investor because his true profit turns negative. He is a loser, but still being taxed like a winner. This fact gives rise to Ruff's Theory of Inflation Relativity, which is alive and well in Argentina.

There was a time in the late 70s when the Argentine National Bank was offering 120 percent interest on CDs. Sounds terrific, doesn't it? Except that the inflation rate was 800 percent! Give me zero inflation and I'll happily invest my money at 4 percent. But offer me 100 percent interest against 150 percent or 800 percent inflation, and it's a fool's game.

MONEY MARKET FUNDS

In the last fever cycle, as interest rates rose in 1979 and 1980, we saw the explosive growth of money market funds to more than $230 billion in assets. The MMF was a truly wonderful new invention. It was a great place to park funds while looking for a better place to invest them, and it offered something the banks could not offer—liquidity combined with high yields. If you wanted liquidity at your local bank or savings and loan, you had to settle for a 5–5½% passbook account. If you wanted a high yield, you had to tie up your money in a CD for one to three years, and accept heavy penalties for early withdrawal.

The Money Market Fund is simply a mutual fund which invests in money market instruments and passes all the yield on to you, the stock-holder. It enables little people to pool their money with other investors to get the same high yields that buyers of jumbo CDs can get at the bank. Because you can write checks against your money market account, the MMF gives you the same liquidity as a bank checking account.

From an investment return point of view, however, most of the time it was a disaster.

As you can see from this chart, most of the time the money market fund didn't even come close to our standard of a 2 to 4 percent return after inflation and taxes. Until 1981, the negative yield was never less than −1 percent, and reached a negative peak in early 1980 of more than −10%. That assumed a 35 percent income-tax bracket, and follows our formula of deducting the inflation rate and the tax rate from the nominal (stated) interest rate.

I was one of the first people in the investment community to tout these

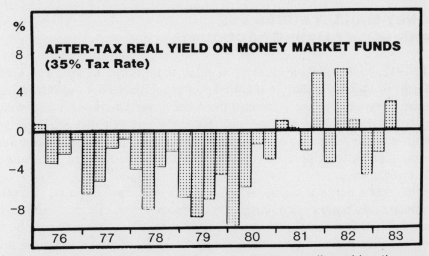

This chart will help you tell whether or not you are really making the money you think you are when you invest in a money market fund. The percentages are figured by deducting the inflation rate and your taxes from the fund's yield. We have assumed you are in the 35% tax bracket. When the bar is above the line, you are making real money. From April 1976 until January 1981, you lost money. From January 1981 through June 1983, you generally made money.

funds as a useful invention, but I repeated over and over again that it was not an investment, but merely the safest, most liquid, best-yielding temporary parking place while you were looking for an investment that would beat inflation.

The chart shows us that money market fund yields began to turn positive during the chills in 1981 as we moved into a recession. Interest rates stayed high while the inflation rate came down. For the first time, the money market fund became a sound investment. You could get an honest after-inflation return, along with the liquidity that enabled you to get out when either the economic cycle or your personal needs dictated. You did not have to tie up your money for some specified period, as with a CD.

Later on, we will say more about the money market fund as an investment during the chills, but for now, there's one lesson you need to learn from this example: You can't beat inflation with interest, most of the time. It's a loser during the fever. A terrific investment during one phase is almost always a loser during the other phase. Only one investment (an exception I'll explain later) works in both phases of the economic cycle.

MONEY MARKET FUNDS VS.
BANK MONEY MARKET ACCOUNTS

In 1982, banks asked for and got regulatory authority to issue new Certificates of Deposit called "money market accounts." This was a banking industry response to the competition of the money market funds, which had drained $230 billion of savings that the banks felt they would have gotten had they been able to compete effectively. The banks made numerous efforts to cripple the money markets funds through legislation and regulation.

Utah was a major test case. A bill which would have imposed onerous financial and regulatory requirements on money market funds and make them far less attractive to investors sailed through the state Senate by a huge margin. When it got to the state House of Representatives, Free the Eagle (our citizens lobby) and I got involved. A lot of Utah legislators are Financial War Room subscribers, so I went to work to educate them on this special-interest, anti-free-market bill. Subsequently I was asked to address the full House of Representatives just prior to the vote, and I did so. We managed to switch four votes, and won by three.

I later testified before the U.S. Senate Banking and Finance Committee, and we were able to get some significant changes in proposed banking legislation by working closely with Committee staffers. We also won battles similar to our Utah fight in three other states.

Shortly thereafter, rather than crippling the money market funds, the regulators freed the banks to compete for savings, and the bank or savings and loan "money market account" was the centerpiece of that competitive effort.

What are the advantages and disadvantages of money market fund vs. a "money market account" at the bank?

In the first place, the "money market account" at the bank is deceptively labeled. It's not really a "money market" account.

A money market fund invests in money market instruments, such as short-term CDs issued by banks, Treasury bills, bankers acceptances, commercial paper and so on. The fund actually owns these money market instruments, just as any mutual fund would invest in and own stocks or bonds. All earnings are passed on to you, less a small management fee, usually .5 percent of the fund's annual assets.

The banks' so-called "money market account" is simply a CD. They profess to pay a yield which is based on going interest rates in the "money market." It differs from your money market fund in that it is invested in anything the bank chooses, including long-term mortgages, or loans to Brazil—not necessarily in short-term money market instruments. The earnings aren't passed on to you; you get only the agreed-upon interest, regardless of how much profit the bank makes investing your money.

A money market fund passes all the investment earnings through to you. The profits are not taxed at the money market fund level, but you are taxed on the earnings distributions.

How do the relative merits balance out?

Either one might pay a higher interest rate at any given time. No edge here.

The bank account is insured by the FDIC. The money market fund is not. Edge to the banks.

The money market fund, however, has an equivalent safety factor in that the typical money market fund portfolio is diversified across hundreds of separate investments, and if they needed to liquidate their entire fund, they would just wait until everything matured, generally in thirty days or less. Investments in their portfolio mature every day. Because of this, the money market fund offers total liquidity. You can even write checks against your account. Edge to the MMF.

If the banker needed to raise the money to pay back all of his "money market account" investors, he'd have to sell off his mortgages or other investments, possibly at huge losses.

Liquidity and safety are somewhat synonymous in this volatile world. Most money market funds are as safe as the FDIC-insured bank account, and far more liquid.

I use a money market fund only for money I need to keep totally liquid, and for a six-month cash emergency reserve. It is a "cash equivalent." The money market fund is better for that purpose than a bank CD.

Financially speaking, sometimes I like to wear a belt and suspenders to keep my pants up. For supersafety, I prefer to use a money market fund that invests only in Treasury bills. Uncle Sam wouldn't dare default on his T-bills, or he could never borrow again. The only fund I know which is 100 percent in T-bills is Capital Preservation Fund I (see Appendix II). They will pay a slightly lower yield than some other funds, but I'm willing to take a little less yield in return for that perfect safety and liquidity.

How about owning a T-bill rather than investing in a money market fund that invests in T-bills?

The main problem with owning a Treasury bill is that if you suddenly need the money you would have to sell your T-bill, probably at a discount. If you have to suddenly liquidate a money market fund account, you just write a check.

Also, if you own T-bills, you have to roll them over when they mature every 30 to 180 days, which takes your time and attention.

There's nothing wrong with owning T-bills at the right time in the cycle. It's just that a T-bill money market fund gives you greater liquidity and convenience. You just call the fund, or send them a wire, or write a check against it. Also, money market funds buy in "round lots" of $1,000,000. If you don't have $1,000,000, you will have to buy T-bills in "odd lots" of $10,000 or $100,000. That costs more. Even after the fund charges its ½ of 1% of the assets as a management fee, you're probably ahead of the game, because it buys more cheaply.

BONDS AND MORTGAGES

Most people buy bonds for income and safety. Conservative trustees consider them appropriate for "widows and orphans." Municipal bonds even pay tax-free interest. And obviously U.S. Treasury bonds are "safe."

That would all be true if there was no malaria, but what happened to bonds as a result of the last fever cycle, from 1977 through 1982? Investors earned interest all right, but inflation was eroding their principal faster than they were earning interest. That was hard enough, but on top of that, the market value of all bonds, including U.S. Treasuries, plunged as much as 55 percent. If you bought a $1,000 bond in the 1970s, you might have been able to sell it for $550 or $600 in 1982. Why? As interest rates go up, the market value of a bond goes down, because its interest rate is fixed and cannot rise to be competitive with newly issued bonds paying higher rates, so the bond becomes less valuable. The market price then falls as the marketplace renders its very astute verdict.

The same thing is true of second mortgages. Even if the borrower pays as agreed, if you wanted or needed to sell the mortgage, you could do so only at a huge discount if market mortgage-interest rates had subsequently risen to higher levels than your mortgage pays.

As interest rates go up, the market value of any fixed-return security goes down. As interest rates fall, the market value of the same security will go up. The only way to make real inflation-and-tax-adjusted money in bonds is to buy them when they are depressed because of high interest rates, and sell them at higher prices when interest rates fall, sometime after a recession bottom. To buy them and hold them for income through the fever cycle merely guarantees that your assets will be destroyed by both inflation and market losses.

The basic strategy for *losing* money during the fever is to buy a fixed-principal, fixed-return debt instrument that guarantees the return of your principal and pays you a near-money-market rate of interest. Perhaps this could be best expressed by saying that, during the fever, lenders are losers, and borrowers tend to win, because they pay back their loans with cheaper and cheaper dollars, while paying interest with tax-deductible dollars. Borrowers win, especially if the money they borrow is invested in things that benefit from the fever, such as income-producing real estate.

The fact is that interest rates tend to lag behind inflation rates on the way up during the fever cycle, and the only way to get a positive return is to be in a zero tax bracket and/or to receive interest well above the rates paid on prudent investments. The search for higher yields often leads people into shaky investment situations and makes them most susceptible to scams promising high yields.

LOSING STOCKS

Another way to lose money in the fever is to buy interest-rate-sensitive stocks such as bank stocks, utility stocks, and savings and loan stocks. During high-interest-rate periods, savings and loans have to pay so much for deposits that the returns they're getting on their old mortgage loans fall short of what they must have to pay for new deposits to support those loans. During 1979–81, savings and loan losses added up to almost half of their total capital, and the stocks took a terrible beating.

Utility stocks are interest-rate-sensitive because they are highly leveraged. By that I mean that their capital structure is top-heavy with debt (bonds), as opposed to equity (stock owned by stockholders).

Utility companies are both short-term and long-term borrowers, continually coming to the capital markets either for new financing or to replace old maturing debt. Interest is their biggest single expense, and as that rises during the fever cycle, their earnings are depressed and their stocks are adversely affected.

Conversely, utility stocks tend to go up during periods of falling interest rates (the chills), but they are a terrific, creative way for conservative investors to lose money during the fever.

LOSING MONEY DURING THE CHILLS

There are even more spectacular ways to lose money during the chills than there are during the fever.

Greed is one of the most difficult of all human emotions to control, right up there with sex. During the 1980–82 recession fortunes were lost by people who had made huge profits in gold and silver during the big run-up of the late 70s and into 1980, but who had refused to take their profits, expecting to make more and more money. Gold, which had soared to $850 an ounce, eventually plummeted to $296. Silver, which had gone from $2 to $50, plummeted back to $4.90.

Another class of investors, similarly motivated by greed, finally began to believe in gold and silver when it hit the cover of *Time* magazine in early 1980. They leaped in very near the top, and rode it all the way down.

Inflation-hedge investing during periods when inflation is falling is a surefire way to lose from 50 percent to 90 percent of your portfolio in two or three years.

Businessmen who aggressively expand their businesses at the peak of inflation, borrowing at high rates to do so, get squeezed by rising debt-service costs on the one hand and falling sales on the other. That's why the business-bankruptcy rate soars during recessions.

Consumers get caught in the same squeeze. Their jobs are in jeopardy during recessions, while borrowing at high rates squeezes their income. Also, their stock and bond portfolios take a terrible beating.

Only a savvy, cool and courageous minority will make money during the Malarial Cycle. The rest are like millions of lemmings, driven by fear, greed and ignorance, plunging into either a sea of inflation and high interest rates or a sea of recession and unemployment. The courageous minority makes money in the long run, and the lemmings drown, over their heads in debt and/or capital losses.

Losing money in the Malarial Economy must be easy because so many people do it. The inflation losses during the fever actually look like taxable profits, so they are not so spectacular. The dramatic market losses during the chills are visible and easy to understand. So is unemployment, if you happen to get laid off; thus we tend to fear recessions more than we fear inflation. The average American believes that inflation's worst threat to his security is the fact that he has to pay more for a head of lettuce or a set of spark plugs. That he can see and understand. Inflation's real damage, however, is the sneaky, misunderstood and unperceived losses savers and investors suffer during the fever. Their fixed-return investments do terrible damage that they cannot yet see, just as termites do more damage to a house than wind, rain and sun, even though the destruction is not as readily apparent.

5

MAKING MONEY

Perhaps my most frustrating problem in working with 170,000 clients is that although most of them generally accept what I have to say, a discouragingly high percentage of those who believe me don't have the courage to act. Perhaps we're in the same position as Admiral Nimitz just prior to the World War Two battle of Midway.

The U.S. Navy had broken the Japanese naval code and had learned of the Japanese plan to send the cream of their fleet, including their four biggest, most effective aircraft carriers, to assault and overrun Midway.

The Japanese Midway fleet disappeared into the Pacific, but we knew the Japanese had also sent another major fleet toward the Aleutian Islands. The problem Admiral Nimitz faced was whether or not to have confidence in the analysis of Japanese plans.

Had the Japanese learned that we had broken their code, and decided to invade the Aleutians instead, knowing that we would concentrate our fleet near Midway? Had they just changed their minds?

Admiral Nimitz stood virtually alone, and he gambled everything. He had to choose—and act. If he was wrong, Hawaii could be helpless. If he was right, he would probably lose to a vastly superior force. Most of his forces had been crippled or sunk in the battle of the Coral Sea or at Pearl Harbor. He couldn't defend both Midway and the Aleutians.

Nimitz had the courage of his convictions, and he was right. The battle of Midway, one of the greatest stories of heroism, courage and luck in the history of modern warfare, was a smashing American victory, and was the beginning of the end for the Japanese in the Pacific.

The Malarial Economy is a battle for Middle Class financial survival, and your investment strategy is your financial battle of Midway.

Most people will not jump into the appropriate markets until most or all of the profits have been taken and the appropriate investments have been widely publicized. Then it's too late. The majority will become poorer.

But if you agree with my Malarial Economy model, it's time for action. It's guts poker time! Here is how to invest in the Malarial Economy.

• *During the fever of the Malarial Economy you must invest aggressively for capital gains in "cyclical" investments—those which respond to the fever phase of the economy, most commonly referred to as inflation hedges.*

• *During the chills phase of the economy you must forget about capital gains and take a defensive position with high-interest-returning investments bought at the peak of interest rates, later to be sold at higher prices when interest rates have fallen.*

You now know that certain investments are inappropriate for each stage of the Malarial Cycle. During the fever, huge capital gains are possible in the inflation hedges, but during the chills, huge losses are unavoidable in the same hedges. During the chills you make real money in CDs, bonds and money funds, but you will get whipped by inflation and taxes during the fever. If you are totally fever-oriented, or totally chill-oriented, you will make money during one period and lose it in the other. You must be fast on your feet and willing to switch with the cycle. There is no one right way to invest long-term. Long-term used to be thirty years. Now long-term might be six months, at the most three years.

You have to develop two different kinds of investment attitude: a conservative temperament that is happy with money market fund yields during the chills, and an aggressive temperament that can live with fluctuating inflation-hedge equities in search of capital gains during the fever. You have no other choices, except to settle for a guaranteed inflation loss and hope your money outlives you—which could be tricky, since you are probably much healthier than your money.

If I have succeeded in persuading you that the Malarial Economy is a reality, do you now have the courage of your convictions? Do you have the guts to set aside your biases, your old habits, the "way Dad used to do it," and act on the basis of this model?

The simple principles I stated above require some modification from time to time, but not enough to invalidate the concept.

Some modifications, for example, would include the fact that some high-yielding interest-returning investments, such as bonds, also give you some capital gains during the chills, and some high-capital-gains-potential inflation-hedge investments, such as South African gold shares or

Exxon, can give you some pretty high yields during the fever. It's not that the ideas are mutually exclusive, but that the investments you will hold during the chills and those you will hold during the fever are not the same, for the most part.

There are only two investments worth holding during the whole cycle: (1) a core precious-metals investment program, which you hold through both cycles as an insurance hedge against national/international financial accidents; and (2) income-producing real estate, which is a special case and will be discussed later.

Before I move into the specific investments that are appropriate for each cycle, I'd like to take some time to talk about something which may be more important than the investment you select.

STRATEGY, PATIENCE, DISCIPLINE

Many people manage to lose money in bull markets, even with appropriate investments, because they lack certain knowledge and personal qualities.

Why do some people make money and others lose money? Obviously the choice of investments is important, but even more important are three factors which are necessary for a successful investor in any cycle: strategy, patience and discipline.

Strategy

First, you must have an overall battle plan. The tactics for fighting each individual skirmish can change from time to time, but the fighting must be done within the context of a strategy. There are two strategies employed in the Malarial Economy: the Fever Strategy and the Chills Strategy.

Most people's investment portfolio consists of a collection of hot tips or investments bought from the last persuasive salesman they talked to. There was no overall plan, no consideration given to whether or not each investment fits into a strategy. They had no opinion on the direction of the economy. They didn't even consider whether or not there would be more inflation or less in their future, and how this investment would relate to it. Your strategy must take into account the Malarial Economy.

Your tactics in this overall strategic plan must give you the maximum potential return with the lowest potential risk of loss, the best possible risk/reward ratio.

As Baron Rothschild said, you must be willing to "buy when the blood is running in the streets." You buy into sick markets, looking for capital gains. You buy things that are cheap when nobody else wants them, when the consensus is that they are dead. In 1976, at $103 per ounce, gold was declared dead by *Time* magazine, *Forbes,* and Elliot Janeway. At that time, I and several of my colleagues had the courage to say, "Buy gold, and silver, because inflation is coming back. If you don't put a gold standard stake through its heart, inflation, like a vampire, is sure to rise again."

Patience

Patience is crucial, because we are dealing with a complete cycle, which lasts roughly six to seven years. When you buy something cheap, sometimes you must hold it for months, as it goes nowhere. You must be willing to sit and wait.

Most people lose patience. We can see it happen in subscription renewals. Many people have been with us for years and made lots of money. However, if we have three to six months where nothing happens, or where our portfolio, after taking ten steps forward, takes four steps backward, people lose patience and abandon their strategy and their subscription, and often unload their investments. An investor without patience is a loser.

Discipline

Discipline gives you the guts to buy something when nobody else wants it, and patience gives you the guts to stick with your plan when everyone else disagrees, or when it is taking longer than you thought to become profitable.

Discipline helps you to avoid greed, to be willing to say, "That's enough. You can have the first 20 percent of the market and the last 20 percent, I'll take my 60 percent out of the middle and be happy with it." Without a strategy, discipline and patience, you won't have the courage to buy when the blood is running in the streets, nor to sell when you should, nor to stick with winners and sell off losers while losses are still small.

The majority of investors do not make money. The public is usually wrong, and the lion's share of the money is always made by relatively few. They have a strategy, the discipline to buy when an investment is cheap and no one wants it, and the patience to hang on through the long, discouraging sideways movements and inevitable setbacks of any bull market.

MARKETS VS. INFLATION: AN OVERVIEW

The accompanying chart, "Investment Snapshot of the Malarial Economy," deserves close attention.

The shaded vertical areas are recessions. The moving black line is the inflation rate, and at the bottom, the bars labeled "stocks," "gold," etc., extend along those time periods during which these investments were in bull markets. Some pretty dependable patterns have developed.

The stock market, for example, has almost invariably started a rally

CHART #1

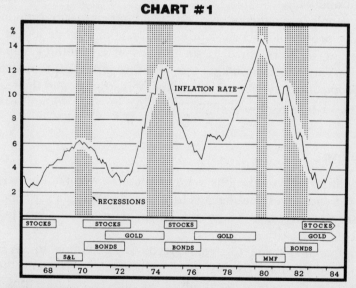

INVESTMENT SNAPSHOT OF THE MALARIAL ECONOMY

This chart is similar to the chart on page 35, except we have shown you along the bottom how various investments have matched the Malarial Cycle.

Stocks and bonds tend to move together. Gold tends to start up near the end of a stock bull market, and all of the investments shown tend to have fairly predictable relationships to inflation and recessions.

sometime after the peak in the inflation rate, but before the recession is over. It continues while inflation is on its way down.

Also, note that bull markets tend to end more or less coincidentally with a clear upturn in the inflation rate, and that there is a long time between bull markets.

In the 50s and 60s, when I was a broker, it was axiomatic that stocks were a good inflation hedge. That may have been true then, but it has obviously not been true since inflation has become a truly serious matter. Inflation is bad for stocks.

Disinflation (a falling inflation rate; not falling prices, which would be "deflation") is good for stocks.

Now take a look at gold. "Gold" is a blanket term which covers gold bullion, gold coins, gold stocks, silver, silver stocks and all other related investments. When one of them is in a bull market, they all are.

Gold began bull markets in 1971 and in 1976. The beginning of the most profitable part of each rally in gold, the explosive third stage, was coincidental with the end of the stock bull market.

As the stock market becomes vulnerable to rising inflation and the beginning of a rise in interest rates, the same forces that are bad for stocks are very good for gold. Money that previously flowed into the stock market and U.S. Treasury securities, because of a strong dollar, now flows into gold.

Bonds tend to move coincidentally with stocks. Bond market rallies also end about the time gold has taken off for the stratosphere.

There are interesting aberrations at both the beginning and the end of the chart. You will notice there was no gold bull market before 1970. That's because gold was a controlled commodity with a fixed international price of $35 an ounce. It was not freed up until the early 70s.

In 1982, there were some interesting differences in the timing of gold relative to the cycle, which, as of this writing (February 1984), are unresolved. The stock market took off as expected near the end of the recession, but gold made a much earlier start this time. Each phase of the Malarial Cycle, although it is very similar to other such phases, also has its own idiosyncrasies, and this one seems to have been characterized by a false start in gold, which looked like a real bull market for almost a year. It fooled me enough that we made some money in it (about 75 percent on our gold-share investments). Gold ran from $296 up to $500 and back down to below $380, and is getting weaker as this is written. Silver ran from $4.90 to $14.50, and back to $8.75. I expect gold to eventually form a strong new base in 1984 at fire-sale prices, before the real bull market begins.

Just as the 1980–82 recession had some strange characteristics, with a double dip unlike previous recessions, so the current economic recovery seems to have its own odd quirk. We could see a real slowdown in the recovery in early 1984 before it resumes in earnest. We might know by the time you read this.

Interest rates generally parallel the inflation rate, which means that during the fever phase, rising interest rates are not harmful for gold. The

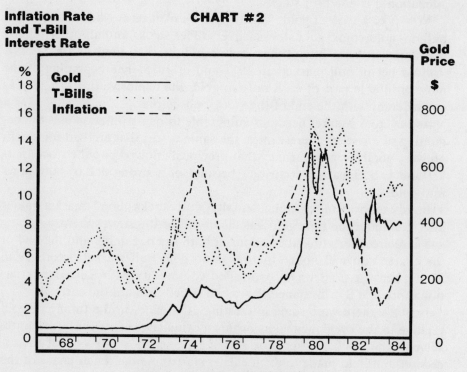

Inflation Rate and T-Bill Interest Rate

CHART #2

Gold Price

Gold —————
T-Bills ·········
Inflation — — — —

GOLD VS INTEREST RATES

The principal purpose of this chart is to explode the myth that high interest rates are bad for gold. There are three points to be made:
   1) Rising inflation (dashed line) drags up interest rates.
   2) Rising inflation also drags up gold prices.
   3) The biggest gold bull market in history (from $103 in 1976 to $850 in 1980) took place during the biggest interest rate rise in U.S. modern history (from 4.4% in December 1976 to 15.5% in March 1980).

biggest gold bull market in our history (1976–1980) took place despite interest rates that rose to unprecedented highs (see chart #2). High interest rates only become bad for gold when the inflation rate starts to fall and interest rates continue to climb, near the end of the fever cycle.

To sum up, the investments on chart #2 behave quite dependably within the cycle. As you can see, money is made by moving from stocks or bonds to gold, into a money market fund, back into bonds, then into gold. Each cycle has been a bit different, so you can't do it exactly the same way you did the previous time, but if you were patient, the cycle would have bailed you out if you were a little too early or a little too late.

When I have a choice between playing the bond market or the stock market, I usually play the bond market because there is only one variable, the direction of interest rates. The stock market has as many variables as there are stocks, and not all stocks rise in bull markets. The individual fortunes of each company are a major factor.

But certain stock groups do move dependably with the cycle, and the movement of the group as a whole will generally compensate for the error of not having picked the strongest stock within the group. Our interest in stocks is not "stocks in general," but industry groups in particular.

The best way to "buy low, sell high" is to look at the end of each cycle for the cyclical-industry groups that have been the most battered by the chills or the fever, where the gloom is thickest. Diversify across a broad cross section of appropriate bargain-basement stocks and commodities and wait patiently for your profits.

LOSERS INTO WINNERS

The Malarial Economy, with its wildly fluctuating interest rates, has created an upside-down cake of a financial world. Ironically, the "safest" traditional investments, like bonds, have become good only for capital gains speculation, and a rank speculation like gold or silver is a far safer long-run bet to gain in value, despite its tendency toward wild fluctuations.

Even recessions and high interest rates aren't bad for everybody. They are good for savers earning interest. Every economic change, up or down, is good for some people and bad for others. *It depends on where your money is.*

Because at least three years of malarial fever lie ahead, we will now concentrate on appropriate fever investments.

The most dependable inflation hedges are:

1. Silver
2. Gold
3. Gold stocks
4. Silver stocks
5. Platinum
6. Rare coins
7. Rare stamps
8. Antiques
9. Real estate
10. Diamonds
11. Colored stones
12. Other collectibles, such as dolls, baseball cards, comic books, oriental rugs, etc.

Let's now examine them one by one.

THE GOLD AND SILVER LINING

Precious metals are deeply embedded in human consciousness as permanent symbols of wealth. The very word "gold" excites emotion. Gold has been eagerly sought through several millennia as both a symbol of wealth and its realization.

When you handle a Krugerrand for the first time, you'll understand why people killed for gold.

Gold has unique qualities. It is among the most stable of the chemical elements. It does not corrode, rust or disintegrate. All of the gold ever mined in the history of the world is still yellow, wherever it may be, whether in a vault in the basement of a New York bank or lying on the bottom of the Caribbean in the wreckage of a Spanish galleon. If it were gathered together in one place, it would make a cube 90 feet square.

It's rare. Most of the cheap gold has been found. It's very expensive to mine. In South Africa, they're going after it 12,000 feet under the ground. One mine I visited there is a huge enterprise where 10,000 people work every day. Their entire daily production is three 70-pound bars. It's ironic that people would expend such prodigious efforts to get something out of the ground and, after converting it into 200 pounds of bars, put it back underground in some vault.

Paper currencies come and go. Ultimately they all go, but gold goes on, generation after generation, century after century, universally acknowledged as real wealth.

In the 1920s, in New York City, you could buy the best suit of clothes, with two pairs of pants, from the best tailor in town, with one $20 American gold piece.

In 1983, you can still get the best suit of clothes from the best tailor in New York for one $20 American gold piece, now worth more than $800.

Gold has been called "the Golden Constant." Even though the value of gold fluctuates dramatically, the fluctuations have been ever upward as it reaches new plateaus of value. That upward movement is a simple reflection of gold's ultimate stability, relative to the declining worth of paper, the supply of which can be expanded at the whim of human governments. Remember, paper money was originally a receipt for gold held in storage in a warehouse. When it became more convenient to pass the receipts around, rather than going to the warehouse to get the gold, the beginnings of confidence in paper were established. Eventually we evolved to the point where the paper itself was considered to be money, and the original intent of the paper was forgotten.

The problem with paper is that as long as there are trees there's an almost infinite supply, and its multiplication in the form of money is at the mercy of political vote-buying decisions.

Ludwig von Mises, the great proponent of the Austrian school of economics, said, "Government is the only institution that can take something valuable like paper and make it worthless merely by applying ink."

You can't do that with gold. That is why inflation is bullish for gold. Inflation is monetary depreciation, and the fear of monetary depreciation drives people out of paper money and into gold, which is still perceived as real money.

Because the masses have been brainwashed into believing that paper is real money, they are the last to discover the value of gold, and they are the ones who will "buy high, sell low."

Ultimately our paper money will disappear, just like all of its predecessors, and only the precious metals will remain until a new gold-backed currency is established. But in the meantime you and I will buy and sell gold during the precious-metals bull and bear markets until such time as we believe that the currency is nearing its ultimate destruction. Then we will convert everything to gold, silver and real estate. That inevitable day is still in the distant future, so for now, unlike our core metals, we look upon gold merely as an investment opportunity. Someday, it will mean far more to us than that.

I have projected the inflation rate based on the previous cycles and examined the relationship between inflation and gold and silver prices. My projection, which is not written in stone and may be modified as we go along, is an inflation-rate peak somewhere around 25 percent in the coming fever cycle, probably before 1987. Twenty-five percent is pretty close to my hypothetical hyperinflation breakout point.

Twenty-five percent inflation means gold as high as $2,000 to $3,000, and silver as high as $100. Gold prices go up much faster as inflation increases, precisely because there isn't a lot of gold around. A relatively small amount of buying, compared to that in other markets, can make the price go crazy.

HOW TO BUY GOLD AND SILVER

There are several ways to buy gold and silver, depending on your objectives.

First, everybody should have some gold and silver coins, kept in a safe-deposit box or concealed at home. This is where you start. It is not an "investment," in the sense that you are buying low and selling high. It is a calamity hedge, to be bought immediately, regardless of price, and kept throughout the whole cycle, both chills and fever, until the cycle is about to end. These are your "core" or "survival" holdings.

First buy some "junk silver" coins, one "bag" for every two or three members of the family, if you can afford it. You're obviously limited by your finances, but do the best you can. Junk silver consists of those circulated 90 percent silver quarters, dimes and half dollars minted prior to 1965. A bag is $1,000 at face value. It weighs about fifty-five pounds, and is about the size of a bowling ball. The market value is usually very close to the value of the silver bullion in the coins—the "melt" value. With silver at $9, a bag of junk coins is worth about $6,500. A bag of junk silver was as high as $35,000 in 1980. If you can't afford a bag, buy a half or quarter bag, or even a roll of silver dimes.

In addition to your junk silver, your core survival holdings should include some bullion gold coins, such as Krugerrands, Maple Leafs, U.S. gold medallions and so forth.

The current advantage of Krugerrands and Maple Leafs over U.S. gold medallions is the greater liquidity. Every coin dealer in America, including every little corner coin shop, makes a market in the Krugerrands. The market for U.S. gold is not yet as broad, so liquidity is not as good, but eventually the liquidity should be just as good as for the Krugerrand. In the long run, it doesn't make a lot of difference whether you buy Kruger-rands, Maple Leafs, Mexican pesos or U.S. gold. You can pretty much let your political philosophy dictate which one. If because of South African racial policy you don't want to buy Krugerrands, buy Maple Leafs or U.S. gold medallions.

Buy through our "Recommended" vendors (see Appendix II), closely following these rules:

(1) Pay cash at the time of delivery. Put down your money, pick up your coins or bullion and walk out.

(2) If you are ordering by mail or telephone, use a "sight draft" through your bank. Let's say your coins cost $3,000. You purchase a $3,000 "sight draft," which is held at the bank. The coins or bullion are then shipped to the bank, where, under the supervision of the banker, you inspect them to make certain everything is in order. The banker then simultaneously releases the coins to you, and the money to the broker.

You should use the above precautions no matter how sound and reputable your dealer may be. Even good guys can get into trouble and go broke, as we will demonstrate in a later chapter. If your money is in transit, you are then subject to their business problems.

You should never store your core survival coins with any dealer. They should be kept either in a safe-deposit box at a nearby bank or at home. After all, the reason you're buying junk silver is as a hedge against sudden calamity—financial, nuclear or natural. Any one of those calamities could prevent you from getting to your coins if they are in somebody else's possession. The above rules for buying also apply to all coins and bullion over and above your basic core holdings.

Junk silver and gold bullion coins are your "worst case calamity" defensive position, the commodity equivalent of life insurance. They are also there in case of limited nuclear war, sudden hyperinflation, banking system collapse and so on.

Those things aren't necessarily going to happen, but the possibility is high enough so that you should insure yourself against them. Even if no such calamity occurs, you'll be glad you did, as you also have an appropriate fever investment.

After you have prepared against calamity, forget about it. Live your life positively, looking for the opportunities. Don't dwell on "survival." That's not healthy.

History is littered with dead paper currencies, and ours has no divine guarantees (despite "In God We Trust"), but gold and silver go on forever. You can still buy a lot of goods and services with a Spanish gold doubloon. I'm sure the Roman Empire thought its currency was immune to collapse, but it obviously wasn't. Nor is ours.

People often ask me, "If you buy those coins, and the currency collapses, who would want them? Who would you sell them to for cash?" In the worst case, you wouldn't sell them to anybody. You would buy something with them. If no "worst case" materializes, you sell them to a coin dealer, probably at a profit. There is a huge worldwide liquid market.

We've seen recent examples of people wanting silver coins in return for their goods and services. At the peak of the inflation in 1980, when we had gas shortages, many service stations advertised gas for ten cents a gallon . . . one pre-1965 silver dime, worth about $2.

After World War II, when the Chinese currency collapsed into a hyperinflation, it only took about a month for everyone in that huge, primitive country to know exactly what an American silver dime was worth in food and other goods. That was a "worst case."

Is there a possibility of limited nuclear war? I believe so. In that case, paper money would probably be worthless for the survivors, as there might be no government to redeem it.

If you really value your privacy, you might want to leave your survival metals off your balance sheet and not even let your banker know you have them. Someday, if all else has failed, and Uncle Sam decides in desperation to seize all the gold, you might want to keep your options open. I'm not advocating breaking the law. Each person must find his own solution.

As for me, they know I've got gold. I couldn't get away with it, even if I wanted to.

BEYOND SURVIVAL

After you have established your core survival position, if we are in a fever cycle, buy more bullion coins, bullion, precious-metals certificates and gold stocks.

The various certificate or accumulation programs offered by big legitimate brokers, such as Merrill Lynch's Sharebuilder Account, or Deak's certificate program, or Mocatta Delivery Orders, are perfectly acceptable. They are paper equivalents of gold and silver. Once you get past your survival position, there are real advantages in dealing with paper equivalents, rather than the physical metals.

At the peak of the last gold bull market frenzy in 1980, it was not very convenient to liquidate gold and silver. Dealers were buying junk silver for discounts as great as 20 percent below the spot price, because the price fluctuations were so wild that the dealer had to protect himself from a market where gold made a $120 round trip in one day and silver moved $8 the same day. After he bought silver coins from you, he had to sell them off to the refinery at a discount. Everybody was hedging and protecting himself. The investor had to absorb the discounts.

Also, when you went to the coin dealer, long frantic lines started forming about 4:00 A.M. People changed their minds about whether they were buying or selling several times before they got to the counter. When the markets closed, the dealers stopped buying, because an overnight position could wipe them out if the market fell. Liquidity (conversion to cash) of the physical metals at the peak of the markets can be poor. That portion of your metals portfolio that you expect to unload at the peak of markets, as opposed to your core survival position, should probably be in the form of certificates. You just call your broker, he quotes you the spot price, you say "sell," and he moves it on the international markets.

If, however, your emotional security depends on having the metal physically in your possession, and if you are aware of those liquidity problems, then whatever helps you sleep well is fine with me.

If you're going to take physical possession, then I strongly urge you to buy bullion coins rather than bullion. The acceptable bullion coins include Krugerrands, Mexican gold pesos, Austrian coronas, Canadian Maple Leafs and the U.S. gold medallions (one ounce and one-half ounce).

You pay a slight premium over and above the price of the metal, which generally runs about 3 percent, but the premium goes with the coin when you sell it. In addition to the premium, there are broker's commissions.

The chief advantage of bullion coins over bullion is that sometimes when you sell, a buyer will require an assay of the bullion. At the very least, you would want to be sure that the bars would bear the stamp of recognized fabricators such as Mocatta or Johnson Matthey.

If you decide to buy bullion instead of bullion coins, gold can be bought in 1-ounce, 5-ounce, 10-ounce, kilo (32.15 ounce) and 100-ounce bars; silver in 1-ounce, 10-ounce, 100-ounce and 1,000-ounce bars; and platinum in 1-ounce and 10-ounce bars.

You might want to consider a dealer-storage program, but the following rules apply here:

(1) Use a large company like Merrill Lynch, with their Sharebuilder program, or our recommended dealers, such as Deak Perera, or Investment Rarities (see Appendix II).

(2) Use a totally "non-fungible" storage program, which means "not lumped with other people's assets." Your coins and bullion are delivered to a bank or independent depository, where it is separated from all other corporate or investor assets and labeled with your name. You have legal title to it, so it is not an asset of the coin dealer, which could be tied up by creditors in case he went broke.

This is the only kind of storage that protects you completely. Even then, you should still use precautions when you buy. Your funds should not be released to the dealer until a certificate of delivery and title on your bullion or coins has been delivered to your banker or to you from the independent storage facility, or verified by an independent trustee.

Anyone who had used these precautions with IGBE or Bullion Reserve of North America would not have lost a penny. If the dealer won't do it, find another dealer who will.

GOLD SHARES

In a gold bull market, you will make more money with a good gold-mining stock than you will with the bullion, in effect leaving your gold in the ground and earning money on the mining operations. The stock should rise 50 percent to 100 percent farther than the bullion. From a strictly investment point of view, you're better off with the shares.

The South African gold mines have long histories of performance and management for you to evaluate, and their policies are well established and controlled to some degree by the South African government.

There are some dangers to be considered before investing in a South African business enterprise, but these are already reflected in the price. That's why yields are so high, and the price/earnings ratios are so low. I believe South African business enterprises are safe for at least three years. After that, my crystal ball gets fuzzy.

South Africa has serious racial problems. There is an overwhelming black majority who are denied any kind of national political power or representation and are subject to official discrimination much like we had in the U.S. two decades ago.

There is also a campaign of anti-South African propaganda and legislation in the U.S. that should be considered before you buy South African gold stocks.

Many liberal American Congressmen, especially those with large black constituencies, have discovered there are a lot of votes to be gained by grandstand plays aimed at crippling South Africa. Their rationale is that American business activity and investment in South Africa, and American purchases of South African mining shares and Krugerrands, are beneficial to the South African government. They say that because the South African government is racist, we should not do business with them.

Consequently, legislation has been introduced by Congressman Stephen Solarz of New York prohibiting American corporate investment in South Africa, or the importation of Krugerrands into America. Also there are bills in committee to eliminate the capital-gains treatment of "hard assets," including gold, taxing profits at the much higher ordinary income tax rate.

I have a few observations:

1. American companies have been the greatest single force for racial equality in South Africa. Most of them do not discriminate by color in pay scales or job assignments. Forcing them to pull out would be a terrible blow to blacks.

2. No one has been able to explain to me how throwing a black South African gold miner out of work will further the cause of racial equality in South Africa.

3. Unlike the situation in all the East European Communist countries such as East Germany and Poland, as well as Red China, Vietnam and Cambodia, no black people are trying to break out of South Africa. They are breaking in by the thousands from all over Africa to get jobs in the mines.

Many black African governments, despite their posturing in the United Nations about doing business with South Africa, have deals with the South African government and the mine operators to provide laborers who stay no more than a year and then are required to come home, bringing their hard-currency earnings with them.

4. The black African has no civil rights. He can't vote and is still subject to discrimination in many humiliating ways. For that, the stubborn Dutchmen who run South Africa will someday have to account to a wrathful God. But South Africa is changing. It's slow, painful and reluctant, but it's changing.

I've been to South Africa three times. Much of the "petty apartheid" is a thing of the past, and the attitude changes are really noticeable each time I go back. In Johannesburg, which is a beautiful, modern metropolis that looks like a cross between Denver and Minneapolis, whites and blacks shop in the same stores, eat at the same coffee shops, stay in the same hotels and often hold the same jobs (I have seen blacks and whites working together as waitresses, store clerks, gold miners, cab drivers and so on).

5. Despite the racial laws, the black South African is by far the healthiest and most prosperous black man in Africa. Some of black Africa's hatred for South Africa may be pure jealousy.

6. To get things back in perspective, very few black African countries allow anyone to vote—black, white or brown. They are more brutal dictatorships than anything in this hemisphere except possibly Haiti. The history of African "liberation" from colonialism is "one man, one vote, one election, one dictator," with intertribal slaughters so common they are hardly noted in the Western press. South Africa is an island of stability in a sea of human chaos.

I would be more excited about legislative punishment of South Africa if: (a) I thought it would do any good; and (b) if those concerned liberals were just as militant about sanctions against the Soviet Union for their slave labor and lack of civil rights; against Vietnam and Cambodia for the massacre of millions of people; against India for their hundred million "untouchables" whose lives of squalor are far worse than that of South African blacks and whose rights are, if possible, even less. I would be favorably impressed if those same Congressmen would also propose sanctions against the half-insane black leaders of Zaire, Uganda, Tanzania, Mozambique, Angola, Ghana and Zimbabwe. Ethiopia has executed 30,000 people. The government of Burundi has killed a quarter of a million. I guess, to the American liberal Congressmen, it's okay if blacks brutalize blacks. And how about Saudi Arabia's suppression of women? All these countries are in good standing with the U.S. and the IMF.

At the moment, South Africa is the most stable country on the African continent. It is a gleaming outpost of Western civilization. It sits astride the critical sea lanes through which much of the world's oil must pass. It is greatly coveted by the Soviet Union, which is behind the "Black Liberation" movements harassing South Africa from surrounding Marxist states that provide bases for guerrilla terrorist attacks.

The reasons are simple. The Soviets would love to have control of the sea lanes, control of Southern Africa's huge stores of strategic and critical metals, many of which are found no place else. They would love to put the South African gold and diamond mines out of commission because the Soviets are the second largest producer of both diamonds and gold, which are the largest source of Russia's foreign exchange. If they were to cripple South African mine production, the prices of these previous commodities would soar, to the benefit of the Soviet Union.

I have struck up a friendship with David Thebehali, the former mayor of Soweto, the largest all-black community anywhere in the world, on the outskirts of Johannesburg.

Thebehali has nothing but scathing words for the American liberals whose actions would only make things far more difficult for the African black man.

Thebehali is controversial among South African blacks. Some refer to him as an Uncle Tom, but he was twice elected to the Soweto city council and elected Mayor by that group, so there must be large numbers of black South Africans who share his views.

For now, I'm not afraid to invest in a South African mine. Despite Marxist-inspired and -financed agitation, occasional strikes or acts of terrorism, and dumbheaded U.S. Congressmen, the basic peace and civil order in South Africa has not changed. South Africa is also infinitely more powerful militarily than its neighbors and probably has nuclear weapons. I also believe it is only a decade away from official equality. All the South African businessmen and government officials I spoke to told me they expect major racial change, and none of them fear it.

You can buy a Krugerrand without a pang of conscience, knowing that it helped pay for dinner for some black family. As this is written, you can safely buy the shares of South African gold mines, as South Africa seems to be no closer to social chaos than it was a decade ago.

South African mines are grouped for all practical purposes into "marginals" and "heavyweights."

Heavyweights have lower costs of production and a fairly long life and pay consistently large dividends. Marginal mines have higher costs of production and tend to rise more dramatically during bull markets and fall further during bear markets. They are not dependable sources of dividends. They are called "marginal" because the price of gold can slip, and does, below the cost of production, and profits can disappear. Conversely, when the price of gold does rise above the price of production, "no profits" can turn into "lots of profits," and the stock prices reflect these swings.

The best strategy is to buy the heavyweights early in a bull market and then switch to the marginals later on, after the price of gold has risen well above the production cost. The following table illustrates the kinds of profit made in these shares in the swings of the Malarial Economy.

	1976 Low	1980 High	% Gain	1982 Low	Close 1/3/83	% Gain From 1982 Low
Heavyweights						
Vaal Reefs	9	109½	1117	36¾	112¾	207
Hartebeestfontein	6⅞	113	1544	25½	70	175
President Steyn	5⅜	72¼	1244	16¼	52	220
Randfontein Estates	14	112½	704	33	126	281
Doornfontein	1½	30½	1933	8¼	24¼	194
Marginals						
Loraine	½	11⅜	2175	1⅛	6⅞	511
Bracken	⅝	6½	940	⅞	3½	300
Durban Deep	1¾	53¼	2942	8¾	37¼	326
Venterspost	⅝	27	4220	3	18	500
ERPM	2¼	46	1944	4	22¾	469

If you want a hassle-free cross-section of South African shares, buy ASA, an investment trust on the New York Stock Exchange that invests in South African shares.

If South Africa's politics still worry you, and if you still want to invest in mining shares, then buy Campbell Red Lake, Homestake or Dome Mining on the NYSE, or Giant Yellowknife on the Amex. You generally get a higher multiple of earnings in the North American mining shares than in the South Africans, but earnings and dividends aren't so good. Moral judgments are a personal matter, and if you don't agree with my philosophy, you can still do okay.

PENNY MINING SHARES

If you have some mad money you can really swing with, buy some American and Canadian penny mining shares. You can get out your trusty dart board, put the list on page 97 on the wall, throw ten or fifteen darts and buy a whole bunch of cheap shares of these companies. Five thousand dollars can buy you a little personal mutual fund.

When the wind blows, even the turkeys fly, and some of them are real turkeys. A lot of them are just holes in the ground surrounded by liars; nevertheless, these stocks go crazy when gold does. In the penny mining shares, you might make twenty or thirty times your money invested.

Before you bet the grocery money and take a flying leap at these little companies, however, there are a few things you ought to understand.

1. A recent survey indicated that the management and promoters of more than half of the new companies issuing penny shares (shares initially issued for under $1, which could be selling for anything under $5 today) have been kicked out of the securities industry for violation of securities laws, have been convicted of various crimes and, in a few instances, were actually imprisoned. Anyone who took the trouble to read the prospectus would have dropped it and run in the opposite direction. (None of these companies is on our list, as far as we have been able to discover.)

2. Many of these companies have mining properties but don't yet know whether there is metal of sufficient quantity and quality to be economically mined. There are usually no "proven reserves."

3. Most of them are grossly undercapitalized and won't be successful until they can raise a lot more money, which will dilute the outstanding stock.

4. Some of them are totally inactive, but the shares trade on.

5. Some of these companies are so thinly capitalized that there is very little stock available and you couldn't take a large position in it if you wanted to. If, however, it is a promising company, thin capitalization is an advantage to the first investors who got in cheap. However, more often than not, thin capitalization precludes large brokerage firms from becoming interested enough to put their clients into the stock.

6. Gold and silver mining is even more difficult than exploring for oil and gas. The odds of finding and developing a producing mine are roughly 10 percent as good.

7. It can take three to ten years to develop a mine after it's found.

8. There are environmental and safety constraints now required by law which did not affect the miners of 1849 who struck it rich. Many mines that would have been feasible then are impossible now.

9. Penny stocks are very volatile and not for those who are faint of

heart or light of wallet. They are long shots with no proven earnings and no track records.

10. Many brokers who specialize in penny stocks go broke, leaving no one to make a market in that stock, so there will be no "bid" or "ask" price, and no buying or selling. For that reason, you should never leave your stock certificates with a small regional penny-stock broker.

Now that I have you thoroughly on guard, let's look at the good side of penny stocks.

1. Between 1960 and 1968, the average stock on the Spokane Stock Exchange, which is where most of these stocks are traded, went up in price over 155 times; $1,000 invested in Coeur d'Alène Mines in 1960 was worth $1 million in 1968.

In the last gold bull market, from 1978 to 1980, gains of 3,000 percent to 5,000 percent were commonplace.

Just since the gold lows in June, 1982, Bull Run, a gold-exploration company whose stocks sold for 27 cents a share in June 1982, has traded as high as $8. That means that $1,000 invested in Bull Run less than a year ago would be worth $29,000.

Not all stocks have shown that much appreciation—but where else is there even a chance for anything like that?

2. The very cheapness of these stocks gives them good leverage. It is far more likely that a stock selling for 10 cents or 50 cents can double, triple or quadruple than a stock selling for $10 or $50.

3. If gold goes to $2,000 an ounce, as I expect, which is roughly five times the market price as this is written, the major gold-mining shares will probably go up ten times, and the penny mining shares, as a group, will probably average an increase of twenty to fifty times their present value.

PICKING PENNY WINNERS

There are two main approaches to picking penny stocks: the random "dart thrower" approach I described earlier, and selection by studying the fundamentals.

With the random approach, you're betting on the assumption that as inflation reappears and the price of gold and everything related to it goes up, all the stocks will move.

Doug Casey, maverick author of *Crisis Investing* (see Appendix II), feels that the fundamentals are impossible to determine, that brokers will probably try to cheat you and that "research" just means "promotion." He even goes so far as to suggest that you "choose 20 stocks whose first initials correspond to those of your mother's maiden name." Doug's method probably will make you a lot of money.

Even Jerry Pogue, the penny-stock broker we recommend (see Appendix II), who takes the fundamental approach, says that method will probably work.

The fundamental approach simply can't be done by amateurs. Expert brokers like Jerry Pogue look for the companies with strong management—people who are honest, experienced and professional—with a promising gold property and sufficient cash or resources to see them through to "proven reserves," which will either enable them to come back to the capital markets and raise the money to get into production or attract a large, established mining company as a joint-venture partner.

I think you ought to divide your penny mining stock money, using both approaches. About half of it can be invested via your dart board, and the other half by following the recommendations of a good broker.

There are two ways to come up with a list of fundamentally sound companies with good prospects.

One is to have a broker do the work for you, but you must choose your broker very carefully. Many brokers are waiting for new clients so they can unload their inventory on you.

Denver, Colorado, and Spokane, Washington, are the centers of the penny-stock industry. Denver specializes in penny oil-exploration companies, which should also do well during the next three or four years, and Spokane is the center of the penny-stock mining industry. You should pick a broker in or near these centers, depending on your interest in either group. Two good ones are listed in Appendix II.

Second, you can subscribe to publications that routinely analyze the capital structure, the history, the management and the prospects for these companies, so you can weed out the obvious crooks, charlatans and incompetents.

Target Publishers, which publishes my *Financial Success Report,* is a joint venturer with Jerry Pogue, a fine Seattle-based penny-stock broker, and Bob Bishop, a former member of my editorial staff, in publishing a monthly newsletter entitled "Penny Mining Stock Report" (see Appendix II). This letter specializes in gold and silver mining shares. Jerry is my personal penny-stock broker.

One other fine publication is "The Bushnell Penny Stock Advisory," by Donna Bushnell, one of the more successful Denver penny-stock brokers. Donna specializes (but not exclusively) in oil and gas exploration companies (see Appendix II).

Other publications are also listed in Appendix II.

After you buy, put your stocks away and wait patiently. As the market rises, you weed out the obvious nonperformers, and then, perhaps when the stocks have doubled, sell part of them, put your money back in your pocket, and sit back to enjoy a free ride.

Penny mining stocks are not for trading. That's the way to get killed. Also, this is not the right market in which to bet the mortgage money. The only way to successfully beat the penny-stock game is to have a broad enough portfolio to spread the risk, and hang on to it all the way through a gold bull market. When it tops out, and you're prepared to sell all your hard asset investments, then you sell your penny mining shares.

Here, in alphabetical order, is a list of some of the better penny stocks to put on your dart board.

1. Alaska Apollo Gold
2. Anglo Gold Mines, Ltd.
3. Aquarius
4. Arizako Mines
5. Pemberton
6. Big Turtle
7. Bitterroot
8. Bonanza Gold
9. Breakwater Resources
10. Bull Run Gold Mines
11. Cal-Denver Resources, Ltd.
12. Consolidated Cinola
13. Consolidated Professor
14. Cyrano
15. D'or Val Mines
16. Flowery Gold
17. Galactic Resources, Ltd.
18. Gallant Gold Mines
19. Gold Concord
20. Golden Triangle
21. Gold Reserve
22. Gold Standard
23. Great Pacific Resources
24. Inca Resources
25. Jenex
26. Kettle River
27. Little Squaw
28. Lockwood Petroleum
29. Lucky Custer
30. Marathon Gold
31. Mines Management
32. Montoro Gold
33. Nevada Resources
34. Northair Mines
35. Outland Resources
36. Pan-American Energy
37. Queenstate Resources
38. Roddy Resources
39. Scottie Gold
40. Sierra Resources
41. Sundance Gold, Ltd.
42. Thunder Mountain

43. Tournigan
44. TRV Minerals
45. Unicorn Resources, Ltd.
46. United Hearne Resources
47. Vanderbilt Gold
48. Volcanic Gold
49. Weaco
50. Wharf Resources

SILVER LINING

Silver bullion, junk silver coins, or the equivalent in paper through some major broker's certificate program is a close second choice to the gold shares. Silver will outperform gold and will give the gold shares a run for their money. The ratio between silver and gold right now (February 1984) is about 41 to 1, meaning one ounce of gold is worth about 41 ounces of silver. That ratio should eventually drop below 20 to 1, which means that silver should move almost twice as far in relation to gold bullion. At the last peak in 1980, the ratio fell to 17 to 1.

Silver is the poor man's gold. When the public really rushes in near the top, they'll say, "I can't afford a $2,000 Krugerrand, but I can afford a few ounces of silver or a roll of silver dimes." And silver will go crazy toward the end of the cycle.

Junk silver, identical to what you have in your core survival program, will probably be more profitable than bullion or paper certificates.

During the excesses of the silver market in 1980, which were wildly exaggerated by the attempt of the Hunt brothers to corner the market, a rare, one-time phenomenon occurred which was to have far-reaching consequences for silver.

The American public did something right, all at the right time!

The price of silver became so attractive that attics and cupboard doors were thrown open as Americans scrounged for whatever silver they could find to sell to bullion dealers.

Not only was Grandma's sterling eventually reduced to silver bars at the refinery, but untold thousands of bags of junk silver were sold and melted.

The meltdown of silver coins has for years been one of the major sources of industrial silver. It has filled "the gap," the highly publicized shortfall between the amount of silver needed for industrial purposes and the amount that was being mined worldwide. The gap has existed for years and has been the basis for the more spectacular forecasts of high silver prices, most notably that of Jerome Smith, author of the book *The Coming Currency Collapse.*

In 1980, that gap was filled with a vengeance by the meltdown of huge amounts of sterling and junk silver coins.

We don't know how many bags are left, but there are a lot less than there were, and the gap has reappeared. Junk silver coins used to sell for just about the melt value of the bullion. In 1981, however, they began to sell at a substantial premium over the silver spot price, reflecting the new scarcity.

As the fever heats up in the mid-80s, hoarding demand for silver should drive the price of silver bags to a substantial premium above that of silver bullion. They will then acquire "semi-numismatic" value. Semi-numismatic means that the coins aren't rare enough to be always graded individually like rare coins, but that they are rare enough to sell for a substantial premium above the value of the silver bullion.

The biggest problem with junk silver bags is their sheer bulk and weight. Remember that 55-pound bowling ball. That makes storage a problem. Even if you get the biggest safe-deposit box at the bank, you can only keep three or four of them there. That means concealment at home or the purchase of a home vault, which can be expensive. You used to be able to buy bags on the futures market, but there are no longer futures contracts for bags, so you're stuck with getting them from your local coin dealer or a national firm, and hauling them home for concealment.

For purposes of your core survival program, the inconvenience is worth it. But for the purpose of investing larger sums of money, you're probably better off buying "paper silver."

The same people who have gold-certificate programs also have silver-accumulation programs, including Merrill Lynch, Deak-Perera, Investment Rarities, and brokers who sell Mocatta delivery orders or Johnson-Matthey certificates.

Why do I believe silver will outperform gold? Silver has several things going for it that gold does not. When people start hoarding gold, they will also start hoarding silver, so it has the same inflation-hedge fundamentals.

It is far cheaper than gold. One ounce of gold will now buy approximately 44 ounces of silver (although as I indicated earlier, I expect that ratio to narrow substantially in favor of silver). Silver will be the public's choice when it decides to buy precious metals, simply because of its cheapness. When my kids start off on a precious-metals investment program, I don't start them out on a Krugerrand. They can't afford it. I start them with a roll of silver dimes. That they can handle.

Silver is also a critical strategic and industrial metal. It is the best reflector of light, and as a conductor of electricity it's superior even to copper. A small amount of silver is used in every home computer, and if there's any lead-pipe cinch you can bet on, it is that the home- and personal-computer markets will expand dramatically over the next several years.

We're also engaged in a military buildup that should continue for several years. Almost one million ounces are used in each new missile submarine. The Defense Department's consumption of silver is so great that we even maintain a strategic silver stockpile, although there have been efforts in recent years to unload it. The efforts were successfully blocked by Senators and Congressmen from silver-mining states.

When inflation is accelerating during the fever, the economy generally expands in a feverish artificial boom. The industrial demand for silver expands, right along with the economy. That, coupled with the hoarding demand, is why silver tends to rise further than gold, and the silver/gold ratio tends to narrow during bull markets.

SILVER-MINING SHARES

There are several fine silver producers providing you with a good way to invest in silver in the ground. I don't like silver shares as well as I do gold shares, because the silver producers rarely pay decent dividends, and they tend to get into deep trouble during bear markets, whereas a good gold mine continues operating and makes money even during bear markets.

The best silver stocks, in alphabetical order, are:

    *1. Anaconda Co.
    *2. ASARCO, Inc.
     3. Callahan Mining Corp.
     4. Gulf Resources & Chemical Corp.
     5. Hecla
   **6. Homestake Mining Co.
    *7. Kennecott Corp.
    *8. Phelps-Dodge Corp.
     9. Silver King
    10. Sunshine Mining

 * Primarily a copper-mining operation, with silver as a byproduct.
** Mainly a gold producer, with silver as a byproduct.

Most silver is a byproduct of the mining of other minerals, most notably copper. Phelps-Dodge and Asarco, although they are copper producers, are copper-silver investments, as silver contributes substantially to their profits.

One reason silver does well early in a bull market is that during recessions copper generally becomes uneconomical to mine because of low prices and shut-down copper mines. This cuts silver production. During the 1980–82 recession, most American copper mines, if they did not shut down completely, cut way back on production. The only worldwide production was in countries like Chile and Zaire, where they had to continue producing, even at a loss, because they desperately needed the foreign exchange. Also they feared that the laid-off miners might revolt.

Silver-mining stocks belong in a fairly large, diversified metals portfolio, but on my scale of investment values they are subordinate to the gold-mining shares, and to gold and silver bullion.

SUNSHINE MINING BONDS

There is one unique way to buy silver, get income and get some downside market protection at the same time so your silver can be profitably held through both phases of the Malarial Economy.

Sunshine Mining Company, which is one of America's largest silver producers, has raised capital by issuing bonds that are indexed to the price of silver.

One bond with a par value of $1,000 is backed by fifty ounces of silver. At the maturity date of the bond, the company has the option of either receiving $1,000 cash, or fifty ounces of silver. If silver has risen above $20 an ounce, you will receive more than the face value of the bond. If silver reaches $100 an ounce, which is possible, your bond would be worth $5,000.

Conversely, when the price of silver falls, interest rates are also generally falling. All bonds tend to rise during periods of falling interest rates, making the Sunshine Mining Company bond more resistant to declines during falling precious metals markets than silver might be.

That doesn't mean that the bond cannot fall in price. It can, and sometimes does. But it is far less susceptible to the kind of washout that we saw in U.S. Treasuries, municipals and corporates in 1981 and 1982.

The Sunshine Mining Company bond will let you have it both ways.

The coupon isn't super, at around 8 or 8½ percent, but it ain't bad either—not when you consider the inflation-hedge potential.

LARGE PURCHASES

The least expensive way to buy large quantities of gold and silver is on the futures exchanges.

The futures exchanges were not originally conceived as a place for speculators to make highly leveraged profits, but as a place for producers of basic commodities to sell their commodities on a future delivery date at a currently fixed price. This locked in their profits and provided stability for their industries. Gold and silver producers use those markets for that purpose.

You can buy a 5,000-ounce silver futures contract, or a 100-ounce gold contract on the New York Commodity Exchange (COMEX) and take "delivery" or take "possession" of the silver. The commission is nominal.

You purchase the "nearest month" contract (explained further in Chapter 9), pay the required margin and, on the settlement date, pay off the balance of the contract and take delivery.

"Delivery" means that the silver is "delivered" to you at the COMEX warehouse in New York and held there in your name with a nominal storage fee. It is the cheapest, safest storage program. If you choose to sell the silver, there is no need for an assay or certification as long as it has not left the system and is still sitting in the warehouse.

If you wish to take physical "possession," you simply order the COMEX warehouse to ship it to you and you'll end up with 5,000 troy ounces of silver buried in your backyard. That's a little over 350 pounds.

If I were buying a large amount of silver, I would either take delivery, and keep it in the COMEX warehouse, or forget the whole idea and buy paper silver, as I have already explained.

Theoretically, a silver-accumulation program such as Merrill Lynch's Sharebuilder program is not as safe as a totally non-fungible storage program where your bullion is segregated and held for you to pick up, or merely to visit and admire anytime you want.

With the Sharebuilder program, you own "an undivided part of the whole," which means that on a daily basis Merrill Lynch simply adjusts the amount of silver necessary to meet its obligations to all of the investors in Sharebuilder, by buying or selling the appropriate amount. You are simply betting on the size, financial strength and stability of Merrill Lynch, and that's a pretty good bet. They are probably the safest, strongest financial institution in America.

If you are dealing with anyone smaller than a major brokerage firm (and I include Deak-Perera and Investment Rarities among the major firms), insist on non-fungible storage, or physical delivery.

MOCATTA DELIVERY ORDERS

Mocatta Metals of New York is the biggest wholesale supplier of metals to industry and to brokerage firms.

They have developed an interesting method of acquiring metals, which is also the only remaining legal way to move large sums of money in or out of the United States without any government-reporting requirements.

You purchase a Mocatta delivery order through a metals dealer or brokerage house and specify delivery either in Delaware (which, along with Oregon and Utah, has no sales or use tax requirement for purchases of gold and silver bullion kept in the state) or in Switzerland.

The metal is delivered to the warehouse in Delaware, or to a secure area at the airport in Zurich, where it is held for you with a nominal storage charge until you pick it up or sell it. Foreigners could purchase Mocatta delivery orders and specify delivery in Delaware. Americans can specify delivery in Switzerland.

Treasury Department regulations require you to report when you take $5,000 in cash or "bearer certificates," such as traveler's checks, out of the country. Because a Mocatta delivery order is not a "bearer certificate," where any "bearer" could claim the metal, but is specifically made out in your name, it is exempt under present regulations. You can pick up your metals in Switzerland by simply presenting the certificates and properly identifying yourself. It's perfectly legal.

AVOIDING SALES AND USE TAX

If you buy Mocatta delivery orders, there is neither sales nor use tax due in Delaware, where the metal is stored, or in the storage area at the Zurich airport. If you take your silver and gold out of the Delaware depository and walk fifty feet one direction you might be liable for the use tax in your home state, but until then, there is no tax. In most states, sales and use taxes are added to your purchase cost, except as noted above. There is also no sales tax on Merrill Lynch's Sharebuilder account.

GOOD NEWS AND BAD NEWS

First the good news. The following factors are good for precious metals.

1. Rising inflation. This is fundamental to precious-metals investments. No precious-metals bull market can exist without prospects for an imminent rise in the inflation rate. If the market turns out to be wrong on timing, as it was in 1982–83, higher prices cannot be sustained.

2. War or revolution. When a country where there is a significant amount of cash denominated in the local currency is in danger of revolution, collapse or takeover, such as the oil sheikdoms of the Middle East, its money will flow into gold for security. That only happens, however, if gold is already in an inflation-caused bull market. If the precious metals are in a bear market, the security-seeking investor will invest in something else, such as the U.S. stock market, U.S. Treasury securities or dollar-denominated CDs.

An international crisis, such as the American/Iranian hostage crisis, or the Soviet invasion of Afghanistan, is good for a big rise in gold and silver only if a fundamental bull market is already in motion. If the market is bearish or flat, the hostilities in Lebanon and the invasion of Grenada will do absolutely nothing for the metal.

3. Increase in the money supply. These are good for gold because they are ultimately inflationary. When the market is flat, as it was through much of 1983, almost all metals trading is by short-term-oriented "day traders" on the floor of the futures exchanges. A Friday afternoon announcement of an increase in the money supply can actually have a negative effect on the gold price for a day or two, since the traders assume that the Fed will react to the increase by tightening the money supply, which is deflationary.

In the long run, that's foolish. Money is like any other commodity; if you create too much of it, you diminish its value. Supply and demand rule here, too. That's the essence of inflation. In the long run, increases in the money supply will do good things for the price of gold and silver.

4. Rising interest rates when inflation is also rising. Rising rates are only bad for gold during a falling inflation period. During the fever, rising interest rates don't hurt gold at all. The biggest gold bull market in history took place when interest rates were rising dramatically from 1979 through late 1980.

5. A falling dollar. When the U.S. dollar is falling in relation to other currencies, it is good for gold in the long run. Currency prices relative to each other are determined by their respective national inflation rates. A falling dollar relative to the yen means our inflation rate is higher than the Japanese. When we sneeze, the world catches pneumonia. Because our currency is the world's dominant currency, gold reacts positively to a falling dollar.

6. Unrest in South Africa, which paralyzes the gold mines. This would be bad for the stocks of South African mining companies, but very good for gold, as it would have a depressing effect on the supply while doing nothing to hurt demand. South Africa is by far the world's greatest supplier of newly mined gold, so much less gold would hit the market. It would also have a positive impact on the stock of North American gold producers, and as the world's second largest gold producer, the Russians would love it.

The following events are generally bad news for gold.

1. Interest rates rising while the inflation rate is falling. This generally means that the Fed has tightened up on the money supply to "break the back" of inflation, and a recession and falling inflation are clearly in the future. It happened in 1980–83, and is always very bad news for gold and generally means the end of that bull market.

2. Short-term interest rates rising above long-term interest rates. This is an extension of point #1, one of the final signals that the bull market is over.

3. Rising interest rates when a gold market is flat or declining. This happens just at the peak of the fever, or afterward during the chills. Rising interest rates can put a damper on gold only when there is very little bullion changing hands and when it has very little natural buoyancy anyway. Then the influence on the market of the futures market "day traders" is paramount.

4. U.S. government actions. When Uncle Sam considers rising gold to be an insult to the falling dollar, he usually tries to depress the gold market by auctioning gold from his substantial holdings. This can temporarily depress gold, but, in a true bull market, gold will be inconvenienced

only temporarily. Such auctions tend to increase public interest in gold, and more buyers seem to come out of the woodwork. The bull market in gold of 1977 through 1980 took place in the face of both regular and unannounced U.S. Treasury auctions.

5. Changes in the tax laws. As this is written, there is a bill in the Senate that would eliminate the capital gains treatment of gold, silver, diamonds and other collectibles. This viciously unfair, anti-free-market legislation is based on the assumption that investments in precious metals are "non-productive" as compared to buying CDs or stocks. I'm sure the workers in the gold mines would dispute that contention, as would the manufacturers of mining equipment and the tens of thousands of people who work for coin and bullion dealers and computer manufacturers. Of course, such "productive" investments as casino stocks and racehorses would still qualify for capital gains treatment.

There is no question that a change in the capital gains treatment of the metals would have a depressing effect on them. It would not be enough, however, to stop a true bull market, but it would limit its profit potential. Although a lot of money would be made, it wouldn't be as much as if investors knew they would receive the more favorable capital gains treatment at the date of sale.

This would be a big boon for gold-mining stocks, however, as most precious-metals-oriented investors would buy the stock instead of the metal because the stock would still qualify for capital gains treatment. Free the Eagle is working on this one.

6. A gold standard. A true gold standard with real teeth in it, which would restore confidence in the stability of the currency, would be a disaster for gold as an investment. After all, who needs an inflation hedge if you're sure there won't be any more inflation? I know I wouldn't.

PLATINUM

Platinum, like silver, is both a precious metal and an industrial metal. It is much rarer than silver, and its price usually fluctuates around the price of gold. At the bottom of bear markets it usually sells for less than gold. During bull markets it rises above the price of gold. Consequently, during the fever, it can be expected to outperform gold rather dramatically.

The situation is similar to that of silver. Platinum is an important industrial metal, primarily used as an essential component of catalytic converters in automobiles. When the economy is booming and car sales are up, platinum demand is high. There is also a very strong inflation-hedge hoarding demand for the white metal during bull markets.

Platinum 1-ounce and 10-ounce bars are available through coin dealers, just like gold or silver. Platinum has the double whammy of both hoarding and industrial demand going for it, as does silver.

Platinum doesn't belong in your core holdings, but it does belong in your investment portfolio. The principal producers of platinum, Impala Mines and Rustenberg, both located in South Africa, are excellent platinum plays, as is Oregon Metallurgical in the U.S. (OTC). Just as gold- and silver-mining shares will outperform the metals, the platinum-mining shares should outperform platinum.

COLLECTIBLES

Over the last five years, rare stamps have outperformed every investment except Chinese ceramics, and coins have done almost as well. I won't recommend Chinese ceramics because that market isn't big enough to be of interest to most investors, but during the fever, rare coins and stamps can be terrifically profitable as investor demand is added to collector demand. They have several advantages.

1. They're fun. The history of coins and stamps is absolutely fascinating.

2. They have great esthetic value. Many of them are truly beautiful.

3. They tend to be more resistant to declines during the chills, as collector demand sustains the market, giving it more stability than other inflation hedges in down markets. They rise further and faster than the metals during the fever, as the good merchandise is scarce. Even though coins and stamps did decline during the 1980–83 chills period, they did not decline as far or as fast as gold and silver bullion or mining shares.

Stick with the highest-quality merchandise. The principal pitfall with stamps and coins is that there is much subjective judgment in grading and appraising. A relatively minor error in grading can mean huge differences in market value, so you must develop a good eye for grading, or you must have a knowledgeable hobbyist or stamp or coin dealer to guide you.

If your kids are inclined in this direction, they can become very good at it. My foster son, David, is terrific at that sort of thing, and I rely on him almost entirely.

You should avoid coin and stamp collecting, immensely profitable though they are, if you are not willing to become knowledgeable. That means making your investment a hobby, or at least hooking up with a smart, honest dealer who will find you good deals and not just unload his inventory on you. We have found the dealers listed in Appendix II to be very trustworthy.

There are several good books and periodicals on the subject, including *A Guidebook of U.S. Coins* (*The Red Book*), by R. S. Yeoman (yearly release); *Coin World* (a magazine published weekly, $18 a year), P.O. Box 150, Sidney, OH 45367; *High Profits from Rare Coin Investment,* by Q. David Bowers, $14.95 (available from Target, Inc., P.O. Box 25, Pleasanton, CA 94566); *World Coin News,* $16.50 a year, Krause Publications, 700 East State St., Iola, WI 54990; *Stamps and Stories,* a guide prepared by the U.S. Postal Service, $3.50 at local post offices; *Linn's Stamp News* (weekly newspaper), Box 29, Sydney, OH 45367.

Myron Kaller (our recommended stamp vendor) 333 N. Broadway #30003, Jericho, NY 11753 will send you a bibliography critique of the above-mentioned U.S. Postal Service guide.

DIAMONDS AND COLORED STONES

Diamonds and colored stones are excellent inflation hedges. Diamonds are more dependable because stringent grading standards and identification through "gem prints" (X-ray identification) have created a market where evaluation and pricing are much less subjective than they used to be.

These markets, however, fluctuate dramatically with the cycle. As of January 1984, stones are very cheap and represent a good buy. Their liquidity falls somewhere between gold (very liquid) and real estate (often very illiquid).

If you're going to invest in diamonds, refer to the chapter on diamonds in *How to Prosper During the Coming Bad Years,* Warner Books, New York, 1980.

ANTIQUES

Antiques as a Malarial Cycle hedge investment are generally winners, as is almost anything "they ain't makin' no more of" if there is an active collector's market. Antique collecting requires an eye for esthetics and an enthusiasm for collecting that I'm afraid I simply don't have. I have a "tin eye," so to speak. When friends show me their antiques and rhapsodize over their beauty, try as I may, I can't see what all the fuss is about. However, I don't for a minute wish to minimize the value of antiques as investments.

My brief consultations with experts have produced a recurring theme: with antiques, just as with rare stamps and coins, you should stick with the highest-quality merchandise of proven value. Antiques are most often found at auctions conducted by auction houses such as Sotheby's. You will rarely find a really valuable piece stashed away in a corner of a secondhand furniture store.

A store in Modesto, California, where I used to live, stated the case for buyer caution perfectly in a sign outside the shop: "We buy junk, we sell antiques."

Antique collecting is a hobby. You have to love it, care about it and be willing to frequent auctions and develop an eye for values that can only come with experience. If you're not prepared to do that, stay away from antiques.

THE INCOME TRAP—AND HOW TO ESCAPE IT

Millions of Americans, especially retirees and widows, depend on their investments for income. The need for income has cost investors more inflation losses than any other factor.

During the chills cycle, the solutions to the income dilemma are much easier than during the fever. All of our preferred "chills" investments are good income producers, such as:

1. Money market funds, because of their superior liquidity and high return during periods of rising interest rates and falling inflation, even after inflation and taxes. You must constantly reassess the earned interest against the shifting inflation rate and your tax bracket. Whether a money fund is a good deal is a simple mathematical calculation. If you're at the break-even point or losing money because of rising inflation, falling interest rates or a change in your tax status, look elsewhere. During a recession, a money fund is a sound defensive position and a fine source of income.

2. U.S. Treasury bonds, bought at the peak of interest rates. In 1980–82, they were great income producers and dirt cheap. A long-term Treasury bond with a face value of $1,000 was going for around $540. (If you have forgotten how that works, please go back to page 70, Chapter 4, *Losing Money.*) It was also yielding around 17 percent. Prices rose spectacularly as interest rates came down. That same bond became worth about $800. Bonds are the surest aggressive capital gains opportunity to be

found during the chills cycle, and you can also lock in very high yields for excellent income. As soon as the real interest rate, after inflation and taxes, shrinks below 2 percent, sell out. Take your nice capital gain and put it in a money market fund until the time is right to get back into inflation hedges.

Stay away from municipal bonds. Their tax-free yields are very tempting as a recession bottoms out, but municipal financial troubles tend to multiply during recessions, increasing the risk of default. A sound AAA rating can suddenly become an A or a B overnight, causing prices to fall abruptly. That's also true of corporate bonds to a lesser degree. In 1983, WPPS (a huge bond issue funding nuclear power plants in the Northwest) defaulted on $2.5 billion in bonds. The investors were mostly widows and retirees, for whom the losses were a disaster. U.S. Treasury bonds carry no such risk. Only one variable affects their prices—interest rates. Corporate bonds are better than munis, but less safe than U.S. Treasury bonds, which have equally good capital gains potential. Stick with the T-bonds, or spread the risk by buying into a good no-load bond mutual fund.

INVESTING FOR INCOME: THE FEVER

During the fever you might need income, don't necessarily need investment profits, but can't afford to lose money. Unfortunately, in a fever cycle, I know of no investment that will simply maintain your purchasing power. It's "grow or die!" An investment portfolio that isn't growing is shrinking. In a zero-inflation world you could buy a 4 percent CD, cash value insurance, or an annuity, sock it away and forget about it while still increasing your purchasing power. But inflation in the Malarial Economy has made that impossible. You must be aggressive during the fever, and defensive during the chills, even if all you want is income.

During the fever stage of the cycle, one way to get income and keep your purchasing power is to buy income-producing investments that also have a high probability of capital gains, such as some high-yielding South African gold stocks, oil stocks and income-producing real estate. Of course, that also raises the possibility of capital losses, but the odds are on your side over the long haul. These investments inevitably prosper from rising inflation and produce satisfactory income.

Oil companies and gold mines are a case in point. You can go for very high income and modest capital gains by buying the stock of South African mines that are nearing the end of their useful life. The South African Government requires mines with a long life to mine their lower-quality ores when gold prices are rising. The older mines, however, as they near the end of their useful life, are mining their highest-grade ores, and they pay out 80 percent of their profits in dividends. As inflation drives up the price of gold, the dividends will rise to keep up with inflation.

There are other "heavyweight" mines that pay smaller but still pretty good dividends, but that have enough life ahead of them to give you good capital gains potential and rising income. Heavyweights are mines with a low cost of production that generate high dividends and stable earnings despite market fluctuations. The best heavyweight mines, in order of dividend yield, are as follows:

GOLD-MINING HEAVYWEIGHTS

NAME	PRICE (11/8/83)	YIELD *BEFORE S.A. 15% WITHHOLDING TAX
Western Holdings	43	11.65
Harmony	17	11.30
Buffels	43½	10.97
St. Helena	33	10.72
Randfontein	112	10.27
Vaal Reefs	92½	9.65
Pres. Steyn	40½	9.59
Hartebeest	60	9.06
West. Deep Levels	44½	8.21
Drief Cons	28¾	7.43
Kloof	42½	6.17
Southvaal	50½	5.84

* South Africa withholds 15% of all dividends. You recover them by claiming a tax credit on your 1040 next April 15.

All of these investments will make you money, and they have a fine capital gains track record. As the price of gold rises with inflation, their dividends will grow enough to keep you even with inflation. If my inflation and gold price objectives are met, the dividends could rise until they are as high as today's stock prices.

The oil companies also offer some excellent choices. For dividend income, with a high probability of good capital gains, I like Texaco, Standard of Ohio and Exxon (the biggest cash cow of the bunch). The oil shares should be winners at least through 1984.

INCOME INTO CAPITAL GAINS

There is a way to generate income from gold coins.

One of the arguments used by the anti-gold crowd is, "gold generates no income." That does not need to be true at all.

Way back in 1976 I suggested that my subscribers who need income would obviously be better off if they paid taxes at capital gains rates on their income, rather than at ordinary income tax rates, because the capital gains rate was about half the ordinary rates.

The strategy is simple. If you believe gold is in a bull market, you buy a number of Krugerrands, or any other gold coins, including some of the smaller coins. As the price of the coins goes up, after one year you simply sell off from 8 percent to 15 percent of your coins each year, depending on your income needs. If the Malarial Cycle functions as anticipated, the value of the remaining coins will increase sufficiently to keep your capital intact. The proceeds generated from the sale of the coins will be partly "return of principal," which is nontaxable, and partly a long-term capital gain (provided you held the coins for one year), which is taxable, but at about half the ordinary income-tax rate. (The long-term holding period may have been reduced to six months by the time you read this. Check with your tax adviser.) Your purchasing power will increase, despite the sale of the assets, and you will have the income you need.

This strategy, which in a sane world would be "consuming your capital"—usually an investment no-no for people who need income—is now a form of "living on your income." But in this crazy upside-down financial world, buying bonds or CDs and "living on your income" during the fever cycle—which should make sense—really becomes "consuming your capital" for all the reasons we've described in earlier chapters.

I can't think of a more explicit example of the perverse effect of this monetary insanity, or a better example of why it is so difficult to help people understand the financial world in which we live. It's pure craziness, and maybe you have to act a little crazy to get along in a crazy world—just like the truck driver with his load of chickens.

INCOME FOR THE ELDERLY

Unfortunately, investments act the same whether they're owned by young people or old people. There is no investment which is better for old people than young people, or vice versa. The only question is, "Do you need income, or don't you?" The income suggestions in this chapter apply to young and old alike.

I do have one very serious suggestion for people who are approaching retirement.

The best advice I can give you is, "Don't retire!" The need for income almost always means sacrificing some capital gains potential.

When you retire, however, and your income stream is cut off, unless you have huge sums of investment capital, you are forced to reach for higher yields and sacrifice some capital gains. The South African shares that will give you the best capital gains are not the same ones that will pay the biggest dividends.

Most retired people depend heavily on their Social Security and their company pension fund to supplement their investment income.

If there is any one thing that is likely to let you down, it is Social Security, followed closely by private, corporate and state pension funds.

Social Security is facing an incredible crisis. I've already referred to the $7.5 trillion unfunded deficit. One of two things will happen. Either Uncle Sam will fund it with the printing press, and that printing-press money will unleash a flood of inflation that will make the income relatively worthless, or the next generation will revolt when they find that as much as 40 percent of their income will have to be taken from their paychecks to support the elderly. There are no guarantees that the next generation will decide to stand still for this.

The future of Social Security is uncertain at best, and if you are depending on it, you are leaning on a thin reed indeed.

Many corporate, public and private pension funds are also terribly underfunded. During the last recession, many companies fell behind in making their required payments to those funds. Also, most of the funds have been invested unwisely. Many big pension funds own, as a significant percentage of their portfolio, New York City debt securities. That's not exactly a prudent investment.

Most pension funds are almost entirely invested in all the things I've been warning you against, such as bank stocks, utility stocks, bonds and CDs. As far as I know, only Alaska has a substantial precious-metals component in the portfolios of its state pension funds, and it may abandon that policy soon because it took a big beating between 1980 and 1983. Alaskan officials did not understand that they had to shift out of inflation hedges during the chills.

Because pension funds are very chancy in the very uncertain years ahead, you will need more income from your personal savings and investments. The longer you can remain employed and maintain an income, the longer you will be able to reinvest your investment income and profits and build your assets for a safer future.

Unless you are very wealthy, you should lower your expectations about your "golden years." Most long-term retirement plans are based on the assumption that the money is stable, which, as we have amply demonstrated, it is not.

Postpone your retirement as long as possible. In fact, if you are facing mandatory retirement, develop a second career or consider starting a small business.

Better still, invest in the next generation.

THE PACT BETWEEN THE GENERATIONS

I can't think of a better inflation hedge, in terms of keeping one's income ahead of inflation, than to find a bright young entrepreneur with energy, talent and a sound idea, and provide him with your capital, your experience and your maturity. A fifty-fifty partnership could be just what you need to take care of you in your "golden years."

More than 50 percent of America's new small businesses fail, but that's because they lack capital, experience, financial controls and/or good marketing. This "pact between the generations" can combine all the missing elements and reduce the risk of failure to an acceptable level.

Contact your local college business school and tell the placement counselor you are looking for a partner. You'll have all the candidates you can handle.

I don't intend to stop writing and editing my newsletter, or writing books like this. I chose my ancestors very wisely, and they are a long-lived crew, so I expect to be around for thirty or forty years more. I will not retire at the age of sixty-five.

Stay active and productive as long as you can. Don't just rot away in a "retirement community" with nothing to do but watch TV, play pool and watch the hearses carry away your friends and neighbors when they die of boredom and inactivity. The sheer fact of continuing to be actively involved in a profession or business will extend your useful, happy years and contribute vastly to the financial success of your retirement program.

CHAPTER
8

REAL ESTATE

I'm not going to pretend to tell you all there is to know about real estate in one chapter. Most of what I have to say on the subject is scattered throughout several chapters in this book, including Chapters 5, 7, 9 and 12. There are many great books on the subject, such as Bob Allen's *Nothing Down* and *Creating Wealth,* and Al Lowry's *How You Can Become Financially Successful by Investing in Real Estate.* I will limit myself to teaching you how real estate relates to the Malarial Economy, and I will be brief.

Let's look first at the home you live in.

Doug Casey, the maverick author of *Crisis Investing,* and I have been debating whether or not real estate is a good investment. He believes that certain fundamentals in the real estate marketplace, including high interest rates, have turned real estate into a very poor investment. His advice is to rent. He may be right—*and* wrong.

I was recently in Washington, D.C. in the men's room of a public building, not far from Doug's home. Someone had written "Jesus Saves" on the wall. Under that someone had scrawled "But Moses Invests." Under that, the final word was, "But Doug Casey Rents."

I guess whether you agree with Doug will depend on whether or not you believe in the Malarial Economy.

History doesn't show a single example of an inflationary spiral in which real estate did not increase in value at a rate faster than the inflation rate. But the peculiarities of the American mortgage market may create some unprecedented splits in the real estate market along several lines.

Generalizations about whether real estate is a good or bad investment that do not clearly define "what kind" and "where" will probably turn out to be at least partly wrong.

Some kinds of property could become less valuable, and others more valuable, at least for a while.

One split could occur between properties that are equal in amenities, appearance and utility. However, one may have a fully amortized, assumable, fixed-rate mortgage that the average person can afford, while the other one requires new financing at ruinous interest rates, which most buyers could not afford.

Only 22 percent of Americans can afford to buy a house at 13 percent mortgage rates. They cannot qualify for a typical standard new loan on the basis of their income, even though there are a lot of new and innovative mortgage concepts such as the "shared equity mortgage" (more about that in a moment), which should enable some people to buy homes who otherwise could not. Most Americans, however, are unaware of these innovations.

Another split could occur along regional lines.

Real estate could remain in trouble in areas the middle class is leaving, such as suburban Chicago, and boom where they are going, such as Tucson.

In a marketplace where very few people can qualify for a mortgage, single-family, owner-occupied homes in some regions could become a drag on the market until the market is finally overtaken by the creation of new households with enough money and credit to buy a new home. More and more people, especially young couples, will be forced to rent until they have saved a lot more money. This prolonged period of renting could create upward pressures on the rental market, and the "owner-occupied" single-family home could lag behind the rest of the market.

Also, for almost three years (1980–1983) there was a huge shortfall in construction of new rental units. New rental units were not being built at a rate anywhere approaching the increase in new households. That means that residential rental property will probably be one of the outstanding investment opportunities of the 80s. In fact, I'm betting on it.

Income-producing real estate is an interesting special case because it works in both the chills and the fever cycles.

There are three reasons to buy rental properties: (a) capital gains; (b) income; and (c) tax shelter. During the fever cycle you get all three. Values go up, and negative yields turn into positive cash flow, because inflation allows you to raise rents, and leverage enables you to beat the whey out of inflation. During the chills, you still get income and tax shelter.

This coming round of fever should benefit single-family dwellings in the lower price ranges (the bulk of the single-family rental market), as well as apartments in all price ranges.

OWN OR RENT?

Should you own your own home? If you think of your home simply as the place where you live, a moderately good inflation hedge with some tax-shelter benefits, and not as your surefire way to riches through a rapidly increasing equity due to inflation, home ownership still makes sense.

A home provides the following benefits for the owner/occupant:

1. A home base for you and your family where you have pride of ownership. This totally intangible benefit justifies owning a home, even if there were no profits to be made.

2. Tax deductions. The mortgage payments are tax deductible, which substantially reduces the real cost of home ownership.

3. Equity buildup. Part of the mortgage payment goes toward building up your equity. Although it is very small in the beginning, after a few years your equity buildup can become substantial. My mother lamented to me a thousand times that after thirty years of renting, all she had to show for it were shoeboxes full of rent receipts.

4. Some inflation protection. The overall value of your home should increase at a rate at least equal to the inflation rate. If you are properly leveraged (have a large enough mortgage), the rate of return on your invested money should be several times the rate of inflation.

If you are buying the house as a rental unit, you obviously don't derive the psychological benefits that you do from your own residence, but you substitute another valuable and tangible benefit: there are additional tax-shelter benefits that you can't get with your own residence—depreciation and other expense deductions.

You can deduct the cost of garbage collection, repairs and maintenance, the money you pay your kids to mow the lawn and trim the hedges, and your travel costs to and from the property, among other expenses, as well as depreciation (discussed at some length in Chapter 12, "Taxflation"). And, with each inflationary fever higher than the last one, you have been paying off your mortgage in increasingly worthless, inflated dollars.

During the chills of recession, home values do tend to fall somewhat, as high interest rates dampen demand for homes, but most of the net growth realized during the inflationary fevers still remains intact, especially compared to other inflation hedges. In the 1980–82 recession, gold fell 65 percent and silver fell 90 percent, but home values dropped only about 10 percent.

Even though the owner-occupied home may not do as well in the future in relation to inflation as it has done in the past, it should still be a sound investment. I recommend home ownership.

HOW TO BUY A HOUSE

After doing a little research, I found that all the books that have been written on real estate investment assumed that you knew how to buy the house that you live in. Unfortunately, based on my experience with many subscribers, most people do not know how to buy a home, even if they have bought several. In particular, they do not know how to buy a house in today's financing environment. Today's home buyer needs to know new tactics and strategies.

Let's discuss how to buy a personal residence and a rental house.

GOVERNMENT FINANCING

The Veterans Administration (VA) and the Federal Housing Administration (FHA) are the two principal sources of lower cost, government-guaranteed and insured loans. They do not actually lend you the money, but they stand behind you and the bank while the bank makes the loan.

FHA and VA loans are fixed-rate mortgages, which means you can lock in a specified interest rate for thirty years—even during the worst fevers of inflation. They are also assumable by a buyer, which makes them immensely valuable and adds value to your home. After 1984, I expect you will not see fixed-rate loans again in your lifetime. This is the last train out.

In most circumstances, FHA and VA mortgages are available only for owner-occupied homes, not for investor-owned properties.

Typically, these loans will cover from 90 percent to 100 percent of the basic purchase price, up to the maximum loan amounts. There is, however, also the usual amount of government red tape to wade through. Some lenders are reluctant to work with government loans because of the restrictions placed on interest rates and other charges.

CONVENTIONAL FINANCING

Conventional financing is more common, with savings and loans handling the lion's share of the market.

The term "conventional" means that the government is not involved, so terms and conditions are a lot more flexible, but the interest rates are higher.

The fixed-rate mortgage is the most preferable and, not surprisingly, the most difficult to get.

Next best is a variable-rate mortgage with a cap. This means the interest rate is tied to some market rate like the prime rate or the long-term government securities rate, but there's a ceiling on how high it can go. You can never be charged more than the cap or ceiling rate.

The most undesirable type of financing is the straight variable-rate mortgage. If interest rates go to 25 percent, then that's what you pay. Avoid these like the plague, as they will seriously erode your inflation-hedge advantage in owning a home and will make your home more difficult to sell.

Variable mortgages have lower rates on the front end, but our inflation scenario says interest rates will rise, perhaps to as high as 25 percent by 1987. Therefore, an unlimited variable-rate mortgage is totally unacceptable compared to a fixed-rate mortgage, even if the fixed-rate is one or two points higher to start with.

Mortgages can also include several types of payment plans. For young couples starting out, one worth noting is the graduated payment mortgage (GPM). It starts with relatively low monthly payments, which gradually increase over several years, hopefully to match increases in your income.

CREATIVE FINANCING

Creative financing usually results in the seller's "carrying back" part of the financing—accepting a note secured by the property as part of the down payment. This may be ideal if it helps you to buy your first home, or if you are strapped for cash.

There are two pitfalls to watch for. First, make sure you are strong enough financially to pay the interest and pay off the seller when your note comes due. This may simply mean being able to find and qualify for a new loan.

Second, be sure you know exactly what will happen if the seller dies or assigns the note. The laws differ from one state to the next, so I can't cover this situation here, but investigate this possibility thoroughly.

SHARED EQUITY MORTGAGES

The shared-equity mortgage is a beautiful innovation which may help keep housing strong and may make it possible for you to buy a home you could not otherwise afford.

Let's say you found a house you like for $100,000, requiring $25,000 down and monthly payments of $1,070, but you could only afford $15,000 down and $640 per month. You could find an investor to put up $10,000 and make up the monthly deficit of $430. You live in the home as the owner-occupant, and, under the current tax laws, your partner can take depreciation, interest and other expense deductions to the extent of his ownership, just as if he owned it and had a renter.

Because you are a part owner, not a tenant, you are more likely to care for the house, and less likely to walk away from your equity. That's good for your partner. You have a house you could not otherwise have afforded, and that's good for you. When the house is sold, the profits are divided. That's good for both of you.

The pitfalls are obvious and avoidable. Be sure your partner is financially capable of holding up his end of the deal, or you could be stuck with the whole burden, although in that case, you could end up with his equity.

A really smart realtor will expend as much effort sniffing out potential investors as he will seeking listings and buyers.

CREATIVE NUTS AND BOLTS

Al Lowry's newsletter, *Winning with Real Estate,* of September 1983 (Impact Publishing, monthly, $195 per year, tel. 415-861-1655), provides an excellent example of using creative financing to purchase a single-family home. (I have taken the liberty of editing and adapting the article for our purposes.) The assumption is that you are buying the house for investment purposes as a rental, although the same strategies work fine when you are trying to buy your own residence.

How do you buy a house if you are just starting a real estate investment program and you have very little money?

You are looking through the newspaper and you see an ad:

Seller Anxious. Leaving State. Must Sell. 463-4357.

You call up and get some details. The house is in a nice area, and it is clean and well kept (according to the owners), has three bedrooms, two baths and 1,600 square feet. The asking price is $68,000, and there is a first loan of $43,000 at 9 percent, with payments of $348 a month. The seller has $25,000 equity if he sells it for full price. This gives him a lot of flexibility. Don't even worry about asking him what terms he wants. Just go look at the house. If you like it, make an offer and make up your own terms.

For example, start off by offering the seller $60,000, with no cash down payment. You will take over (assume) the existing $43,000 loan and give the seller a note for $17,000, also at 9 percent. But there is one catch. Since you figure that taxes and insurance will add at least another $100 a month to your payment, making total payments of about $450, and the house will only rent for $500, you can't afford to pay much on the $17,000 note. The normal payment of $127.50, interest only will give you $77.50 a month negative cash flow, and that is no good.

Therefore, you ask the seller to carry that $17,000 note for ten years with no payments. At the end of the ten years, the principal and accrued interest will be due in one lump sum. It is not likely your offer will be accepted, but it is a good starting place, and you never know. If the seller is anxious enough, he just might say yes. But let's assume that he doesn't. He objects to getting no cash for his equity, and he objects to getting no payments for ten years.

Don't just take no for an answer. Ask him to make a counteroffer.

The chances are good that he will want three things: more money, some sort of cash down payment and monthly payments on the balance. His counteroffer would probably look something like this:

Counteroffer

1. Purchase price to be $65,000, not $60,000.
2. Buyer to make cash down payment of $10,000.
3. Seller to carry a note, secured by a second deed of trust, in the amount of $12,000, with interest-only payments of $120 a month.

All other terms and conditions to remain the same.

This is what the seller says he will accept. You have to start negotiating from there. Basically your position is this: If necessary, you can afford to make payments of up to $50 a month. This will give you a break-even cash flow. Anything more than that gives you a negative cash flow.

Therefore, your main concern is to get those payments on the seller's note down to $50 a month or less. If you can do this and still give the seller what he wants, then so much the better. But how do you do it? That is what true creative financing is all about.

[If you are buying the home for your own residence, of course it's all negative cash flow, but if your funds are limited, it still pays to think in the same terms. You negotiate the payments downward until you can afford them. HJR]

You are not going to give the seller everything he wants. He is going to have to compromise, too, if he wants to make the deal. If he wants $65,000 and a cash down payment, then he is not going to get monthly payments on the balance. He is not going to get $10,000 down either.

Since you have no money to put down, you must borrow it. Assuming that the interest rate will be 15 percent, and the loan will be amortized over fifteen years (the standard term for a second mortgage from an institutional lender), $50 a month will pay off a $4,000 loan. This means you can put up a $4,000 down payment and the seller will have to carry the balance of $18,000 with no payments. Since you know the seller doesn't like this idea, you can compromise by offering to pay it off in seven years instead of ten years.

Or you can offer the seller another alternative. He can carry the entire loan for you at 12 percent interest. You will pay him $50 a month, and the other $170 a month will be added to the principal and be due and payable at the same time.

Thus, $170 a month times seven years (84 months) equals $14,280. That is how much it will cost you to defer $170 a month of your interest-only payment. So the question becomes, "Is it worth it?" Will the property go up in value by at least $15,000 over the next seven years? Whichever choice the seller makes, $4,000 down or $50 a month, it is just about the same to you. The chances are that the seller will prefer the $4,000 cash, so let's write up the contract that way. It would look something like this.

Purchase Agreement And Receipt For Deposit

Received from John Smith, or nominee(s), hereafter referred to as buyer, the sum of ten dollars ($10) as deposit on the purchase price of $65,000 for the real property known as One Creative Court, Anytown, USA, under the following terms and conditions:

1. Buyer to make cash down payment of four thousand dollars ($4,000).
2. Buyer to asume first loan in the approximate amount of forty-three thousand dollars ($43,000).
3. Seller to carry back a note, secured by a second deed of trust in the amount of eighteen thousand dollars ($18,000) to be all due and payable in one lump sum seven years from close of escrow with simple interest of 12 percent per annum.
4. Seller to provide a pest-control clearance from a licensed pest-control contractor.
5. Contingent upon buyer's approval of a complete structural-inspection report to be done at buyer's expense within ten working days of acceptance.
6. Buyer reserves the first right of refusal to buy the second deed of trust if seller should decide to sell or otherwise dispose of it.
7. Any variation in the true amount of the first loan shall be handled as follows: If the true balance of the first loan is more than forty-three thousand dollars ($43,000), the buyer's down payment should be lowered accordingly. If the true amount of the first loan is less than forty-three thousand dollars ($43,000), then the purchase price shall be lowered accordingly.
8. Seller to deliver the property in clean, safe, habitable con-

dition, with no broken windows and with electrical, plumbing, roof, etc., in good working condition.

9. Buyer reserves the right to a final walk-through inspection.

10. One thousand dollars ($1,000) to be left in escrow to cover the cost of any possible repairs once buyer takes possession. Buyer will have ten days to submit and/or approve all bills for labor and materials. At the end of the ten days, any excess will be refunded to seller.

What are the fundamental principles learned from Lowry's discussion?

1. Almost any terms or conditions might be acceptable. Don't be afraid to propose anything. You must have a clear idea in mind of your wants and needs and ask for them. If the deal isn't right for you, be prepared to walk away from it.

2. The most money is made by buying into a distressed situation. They need a deal, you can offer it. They are free to refuse or accept your offer. You are not responsible for their profit or loss. In a negotiated transaction, freely arrived at by consenting adults, there is no such thing as "fair" or "unfair" unless you are taking advantage of someone who is mentally or emotionally incapacitated or senile. You aren't trying to hurt anyone, but be sure that the deal fits into your parameters. If it doesn't, there's another deal around the corner.

3. The above-described transaction is to the buyer's advantage. If it were written from the seller's point of view, we might have arrived at totally different terms and conditions. Don't use it as your model for selling a house.

4. Give the seller more than one choice. If he wants more money down, you want better terms. If he wants better terms, you want to pay less money down. In this case, we let the seller choose.

5. You might have to look at twenty-five or thirty properties before you find a deal you like.

6. Even if you have some cash you could throw into the deal, try to hold it back and get more favorable terms—you might need cash reserves in case of vacancies. Don't allow yourself to become so strapped financially that everything has to go perfectly to keep you out of trouble.

7. Try it, you'll like it. Negotiating and purchasing real estate is exhilarating, and the tax advantages, cash flow and inflation-beating benefits are real. You don't have to own a 100-unit apartment building to be a real estate investor. We all have to start somewhere.

In 1981 and 1982, when the multiple-listing books were roughly four times thicker than usual, anyone with a good grasp of the Malarial Cycle who had the guts to assume some obligations and to speculate on future lower interest rates made out like a bandit. The best time to get a positive yield is to buy when there are depressed prices and the prospect of a future refinance opportunity at lower rates, but real estate can be bought and sold profitably at any time, if you know what you are doing.

I like the Lowry approach. Buy well-located but distressed properties that are run down and badly managed, often owned by a dentist or a doctor or a lawyer, the worst landlords of all, because they are so busy. Buy cheap, fix it up, improve the property, raise the rents, cut the expenses, manage it well, refinance and create a positive yield. The period near the bottom of recessions is real-estate-bargain time.

Hang on to your properties until you believe that the Malarial Cycle is about to break permanently. Then you sell, or trade off all of your equities for fully-paid-for buildings, using a tax-deferred exchange under Section 1031 of the IRS Code. When you believe that the cycle is just about over for good, then 100 percent-owned real estate is the only kind to own. Until then you should be highly leveraged. Leveraged real estate is advantageous only as long as the Malarial Cycle, which is essentially inflationary, even with its intermittent chills, is intact.

There is one important real estate "don't."

Don't buy rental properties in a community where a large tenant population has political clout. That's where you're likely to get local rent controls when inflation gets bad again, especially in places, to use Robert Ringer's term, like "The People's Republic of Santa Monica." Generally speaking, that leads you to look in smaller communities of 500,000 and less, and the Sunbelt and the intermountain West. In those areas the middle-class population is growing.

If we get nationwide rent controls, such control laws have historically exempted buildings of four units or less. With that in mind I recently bought a sixteen-unit complex consisting of four 4-unit buildings, with separate deeds on each building.

SYNDICATIONS

You can either buy your own buildings and manage them or you can buy a limited-partnership share of a real estate syndication. When people ask me if I like real estate syndications, I usually respond as I did as a young man at BYU when asked if I liked girls. "It all depends on the girl. Some I do, and some I don't."

Real estate syndications depend on the syndicator—the general partner. Does he have a track record of making money for his clients, being fair and not skimming off all the profits in fees and commissions before they get to the limited partners? Talk to some of his former limited partners. Have similar deals survived an IRS audit? Has he made all the proper disclosures? Both public and private syndications can work fine. "Know your syndicator" is the first rule. Check his track record. Don't just jump in and buy any old real estate syndication. This subject is discussed further in Chapter 12, "Taxflation," and Chapter 10, "How Not to Get Ripped Off."

Newcastle Financial Group (see Appendix II), our recommended financial-planning firm, handles both public and private syndications, and they have an excellent track record. One real estate syndicator they checked out said he'd never been put through the mill like that. It took six months for Newcastle to complete their "due diligence" research before they approved it for their clients. They don't do syndications themselves, but they do screen the available deals.

ACREAGE

What about acreage? For most people, it's a poor investment compared to income property. Not that it won't go up. Maybe it will and maybe it won't. I wouldn't touch lots sold by a developer in some desert community. Absolutely no-no's! He has bought wholesale and sold to you retail. You can't make money in real estate buying retail.

Undeveloped land has carrying costs. You have to service your debt, pay property taxes and keep the weeds cleaned off if local law requires it. It produces no income to service those costs, and it provides no tax shelter. Remember the three objectives of buying real estate: capital gains, tax shelter and income. Acreage can provide only one of them—potential capital gains. After you subtract expenses from your gains, deduct the capital gains tax and divide the net profits by the number of years you've held the property, generally the capital gains potential turns out to be less than with rental property. But rental property would have given you income to service the debt, with a break-even or positive cash flow, plus tax advantages, which are real cash benefits on April 15.

The only people who ought to invest in acreage are those who know how to buy it wholesale, develop it, rezone; put in streets, sewers, and so on; and sell lots. That is more of a business enterprise than an investment.

COMMERCIAL AND INDUSTRIAL

I prefer residential property to commercial and industrial property because, in this up-and-down cycle, you have intermittent periods of rising business bankruptcies, each time to higher peaks. That means your business tenant might go broke or he might close down the branch office. You say, "You can't do that, I've got a lease." And he says, "Sue me!" You find the property was expensively remodeled just for him. Now you must find somebody who fits that custom design.

One apartment, however, looks pretty much like another. You might have to paint, or replace an old refrigerator. But people accept standardization in rental units.

Another reason I like rental units is the fact that we underbuilt rental units from 1980 through 1982 and created a real shortage, so that now young couples, because of inflation and high interest rates, are having to postpone buying a home for a longer time, and will rent longer. The population of renters will increase at a rate faster than the general population, while the supply of rental units is shrinking relative to that demand.

The amateur investor can make more mistakes in rental properties and be bailed out by inflation than he can in raw land or commercial or industrial properties.

Money is made in commercial and industrial real estate and raw land, but the average guy is better off buying a small apartment building.

Anything can be either a good or a bad investment, depending on what you pay for it. I'll buy anything, anywhere, if it's cheap enough, with a few exceptions. That's the strategy recommended by Baron Rothschild who said that the way to get rich was to "buy when the blood is running in the streets."

Even so, you must exercise some care. I'm sure there were wonderful bargains in Saigon real estate the week before Vietnam fell. You need a favorable long-term trend to bail you out of your mistakes. Our trend is the Malarial Economy.

CHAPTER
9

GOING FOR BROKE

"We have nothing to fear but fear itself."
FRANKLIN D. ROOSEVELT

People who follow our basic investment strategy will win out over the Malarial Economy, but there will be a few venturesome spirits with more courage and savvy who will actually get rich by investing. They will do so by applying the principle taught in this chapter.

This is not light reading. If you are not willing to reach for the stars, to assume more risk in pursuit of spectacular profits, skip it.

If you understand and have the courage to apply this principle you can turn a little money into a great deal of money. I know of no one who ever got rich by investing without it. But first, you have one major hurdle to cross.

FEAR OF FAILURE

If you read my Introduction, you know that I consider the seeds of my success to have been planted during my failure in 1968.

Fear of failure is, in my opinion, the greatest single impediment to success and intelligent, profitable risk-taking, so I would like to spend a few moments on the subject of "failure management."

Most people conduct their lives as if failure were the worst possible thing that could happen to them. When a failure occurs, they are so traumatized that they become like the cat who sat on a hot stove—he will never do it again, but he won't sit on a cold stove either.

From then on they tend to try to eliminate all risk and avoid all failures, small or large.

People who conduct their lives with the primary objective of eliminating *all* risk will live bland, homogenized lives and become living examples of the angel's words to Saint John as recorded in Revelations: "I would that thou wert cold or hot, but because thou art lukewarm I will spew thee out of my mouth." They probably won't fail, but they won't enjoy much success, either.

You could follow all of the advice in this book except this chapter and meet with a degree of investment success. It would keep you from dropping out of the middle class, but your success would be modest, defensive in nature and would never lead to real wealth.

We hear a lot of pitiful stories in the War Room from people who have been forced into bankruptcy or who have been defrauded of large sums of money by a friend, a family member or a partner, or who were caught up in the IGBE or Bullion Reserve scams. They are devastated. Their self-image is shattered, their morale is destroyed and they feel scarred for life.

This can happen even to nations. Our inflation results partly from the fact that we have people in control in Washington who have vivid memories of the Great Depression. Consequently, much of our policy is unconsciously geared toward avoiding depression, no matter how much inflation we have to create to do it.

The generals are always fighting the last war.

The failure lessons of history can be positive, but they also can lead to cowardice and a willingness to settle for modest success or a small loss when a smashing success is possible. That is negative and destructive.

Let me tell you what I really learned from my 1968 failure.

I learned that failure is not only not the end of the world, but that, properly managed, the recovery and rehabilitation can become an exhilarating, even euphoric, experience. There is nothing more exciting than picking yourself up and proving that your failure was merely a freak happenstance, one of those things that doesn't need to be explained or excused.

I'm on the Utah State Board of Directors for the Special Olympics, as well as on the Organizing Committee for the 1985 International Games. I'm in that position because I went to the Special Olympics Summer Games at BYU last summer at the urging of Jeff Carneal, my talented young personal assistant, who devotes a lot of time and effort to this worthy cause. I have remained deeply affected by something I saw that day, which I will never forget.

I watched a young woman in her early teens, profoundly retarded and probably 75 pounds overweight, who had entered the 60-yard dash. No more than two steps out of the starting blocks she fell flat on her face. She got to her hands and knees and stared at the retreating backs of her opponents as one by one they crossed the finish line with fists in the air and faces lighted with joy.

The crowd became silent, feeling terribly embarrassed and hurt for her.

One of the "huggers," the young folks whose job it is to see that every contestant gets emotional rewards for participating, ran out, knelt down beside her and put her arm around the girl on hands and knees on the track. She whispered words of encouragement. She didn't pick her up, but she stood up and watched and waited, urging and pleading for her to get up and finish. It seemed an eternity, but was probably about two minutes.

A look of determination came over that girl's face. She pulled herself to her feet and began to run with all the strength she had. She wasn't very good at it, because of the lack of coordination that often characterizes Down's syndrome, but she ran and ran, and as she lumbered across the finish line she threw her head back and both fists in the air in triumph. She then proceeded to hug everyone in sight while the crowd roared its approval, and we all wept rivers. I was an emotional basket case. We had seen a profoundly handicapped human being, whose I.Q. was probably in the 50s or 60s, who had turned a failure into the greatest moment of triumph I have seen in my fifty-three years.

The girl had lost the race. In fact, she was two minutes late. She had fallen on her face in front of thousands of people. She had failed temporarily, but even though she had fallen down, she was not a failure, because she hadn't given up.

I'm sure that girl will run in the next Special Olympics. She's clumsy, awkward and overweight. She probably knows she may even fall down again. But she doesn't care. She will run again. She doesn't fear failure.

When someone comes to me with a tale of woe, blaming failures on others, or even accepting the blame for having failed and labeling himself "a failure," he receives no sympathy or reinforcement of his self-destructive behavior from me. You can call it "lack of compassion" if you wish, but I think I'm doing him a favor.

The investor who took his first shot at a highly leveraged investment opportunity with good odds to make big money and suffered a loss is not a failure. He has learned very important things, if his attitude is right.

I believe so deeply in this principle that one of my company's basic values, which has been formalized and presented to every worker and which is continually pounded into my vice-presidents and managers, is that we will reward "useful failures." We will encourage our people to venture, to take chances, to try out wild ideas. A useful failure is one from which something is learned that can lead to some new or different success.

Sometimes what might be called failure is just narrowing the possibilities as you move inexorably and inevitably to success. Thomas Edison tried thousands of substances on his road to creating the filament which would make his electric light work. He did not add up the failures—he merely thought of each one as a step closer to success.

The strategies in this chapter carry with them a much higher probability of "failure" than anything we've recommended in this book. But inherent in the possibility of failure is the only chance of hitting the investment jackpot. If you adopt these leverage strategies, you should understand that you may fail temporarily and have to pick yourself up and start again. Big deal! That's part of the price you will ultimately pay for genuine wealth.

I've known many people who have a terrific idea for starting a business, but they won't go ahead until they think there's no chance of failure—which means they will never start. No great enterprise will ever begin if all objections must first be overcome.

I wish I could pound into them the attitude that says, "There's a chance I will fail, but so what? At least I will have tried and learned more from my big failure than I would have from a small success. I am not a failure until I have quit trying, I don't care how many failures there are along the way, I'm going to make it big."

Fortunes have been made by shrewd commodity traders, but they will tell you that even the best lose money on at least two out of every three trades. The key to success is not to be afraid to fail. Failures are inevitable on the way to great success.

Simply accept at the start that you will experience failures on the way to success. *The trick is to manage your money so that no one failure will knock you completely out of the game.*

Perhaps the greatest skill you can acquire in failure management is knowing when to accept a failure, write it off and move ahead without labeling yourself "a failure," so you are emotionally able to give it an even better try next time.

Perhaps the most common fault among investors is an unwillingness to accept losses when they are small and to cut them off, so their money can live again to fight another day. They are so afraid of failure they won't admit small failures, which then grow into large ones. Accepting losses is a routine part of the most successful investment program. If you're not failing, you're not succeeding, because you're not trying.

I hope this idea will catch fire. I hope I have inspired you to give that terrific idea a try, to cut the job ties with "Giant Widgets Consolidated," to throw off the golden handcuffs and launch off on your own with the attitude that even if you fail, it will have been worth it. Then *my* efforts will have been worth it.

In this chapter I'm going to show you some of the tactics and strategies that can lead to real wealth. They are risky. Mistakes in timing or unexpected events early in the game can upset the plan and discourage you. I urge all of you to take 10 percent or 20 percent of your money, prepare yourself emotionally to write it off if you hit a bad streak and give some of these tactics a whirl.

Accept in advance that some of your first efforts may result in failure, but that with proper money management and with proper emotional management of fear and greed, terrific things can happen.

I have bought and read almost every "self-help" inspirational book ever written, ranging from Psychocybernetics to Think and Grow Rich. Their authors were on to something. Success or failure is not determined by talent, good looks, capital, good luck or any other circumstance beyond your control. I know salesmen with poor personalities, modest talent and physically unattractive features who outsell their more talented, slick and personable counterparts.

I know businessmen and women who have made fortunes who, by every conceivable measurement, are nowhere near as smart as the failures around them. Failure, in the long run, is rarely a matter of luck, and you cannot blame others. Too often when we succeed we say, "Here I stand, a self-made man," and when we fail we say, "Here I stand, as God made me."

In 1968, when I was rooting through the ruins of my reading school, I knew I had to face the facts about why it had happened. I knew that the precipitating event was a cancellation of my franchise by other people. There was also a newspaper strike. But I also had to face the fact that the real reason was my stupid management of my affairs. I had made myself vulnerable. The responsibility was mine and mine alone. There was nobody to blame but the man in the mirror.

You must decide that no matter what happens, no matter how much "bad luck" you experience or how many unsuccessful tries, you're going to be a success. You're going to pounce on the rare opportunities that come your way. You're going to follow your instincts and take intelligent risks. You're going to accept the certainty of "useful" failures along the way, experiences from which you learned something important enough to increase the odds of success the next time around.

Learn to live with risk and failure. It is the other side of the success coin. Failure is a precondition for success.

THE STRENGTH OF TEN

Archimedes the Greek discovered the principle of the lever. He said, "Give me a lever and a place to stand and I can move the earth."

The term "leverage" is kicked around a lot by people who think they understand it but don't. Through leverage, fortunes are made—and fortunes are also lost. Whether the two-edged sword of leverage helps or hurts you depends on your understanding and mastery of the principle of the lever. Like fire, leverage is a wonderful servant but a fearful master.

Leverage is the principle of multiplying one's strength beyond one's natural capabilities. In the financial sense, this means using a small amount of your own money to control a much larger investment. The lever that multiplies your financial strength is usually borrowed money. By using leverage to take advantage of the Malarial Economy, the benefits of betting with the trend are multiplied five, ten or even twenty times. Understanding the Malarial Economy can reduce the risk of loss incurred by guessing wrong on the direction of an investment.

Unfortunately, many people who use leverage ignorantly put at risk money they never intended to risk, and end up going broke. The risks of leverage vary greatly depending on the investment, as we shall see, but all forms of leverage are volatile and should be considered only if you have risk capital and the ability to sleep at night despite having invested your money at substantial risk.

Opportunities abound for the speculator in both the chills and the fever stages of the Malarial Cycle, but timing is crucial for the leveraged investor, as the market environment can change quickly. Volatility works for the leveraged speculator, but it also works against him if he doesn't know how to protect himself and finds himself on the wrong side of a fast-moving market.

LEVERAGED REAL ESTATE

Perhaps the soundest, safest use of leverage to beat inflation is in real estate.

If inflation is 15 percent and real estate is only going up 10 percent per year, without leverage you're going to lose money, as measured in after-inflation and after-tax dollars. But if you borrow 75 percent of the money needed to buy a $100,000 home, only putting down 25 percent, or $25,000, you now have four-to-one leverage. If the value of the home or property goes up 10 percent, or $10,000, that's really a 40 percent before-inflation return on your $25,000 down payment, and that does a dandy job of beating 15 percent inflation.

For example:

$100,000 PROPERTY WITHOUT LEVERAGE

	$100,000	Cash invested
	10,000	10% annual appreciation
	110,000	Equity after one year
less	15,000	Inflation *loss* on invested money at 15%
	$95,000	Real value of equity after inflation
less	100,000	Investment
	($5,000)	Net real (loss) on cash invested, after inflation

$100,000 PROPERTY WITH LEVERAGE ($25,000 DOWN)

	$ 25,000	Cash invested
	10,000	10% annual appreciation on $100,000 property
	35,000	Equity after one year
less	3,750	Inflation loss on invested money at 15%
	$ 31,250	Real value of equity after inflation
less	25,000	Investment
	$ 6,250	
	or 25%	Net real gain on cash invested, after inflation

The key point to remember is that with leverage you can own more properties, giving you more mileage for your money, more tax shelter, more income, and you turn a modest inflation winner, or even a loser, into a big inflation beater.

I have excluded interest payments from the above example for simplicity, and it does reduce the return somewhat, but the interest is tax deductible, which softens the blow. I have also excluded rental income, which should more than offset interest.

Fortunes have been made by real estate investors who have patiently, over the years, utilized this leverage principle.

Real estate leverage is the safest application of the financial lever because you are not operating under the shadow of the risk of a margin call, and short-term fluctuations in the value of your investment are totally irrelevant or nonexistent. All you have to do is make the mortgage payments and your investment is completely safe.

There are very few emotional risks attached to leveraged real estate, because the price of your home or apartment building isn't quoted every morning in *The Wall Street Journal* to ruin your breakfast. All you need to know is that the basic trend is up, and short-term fluctuations mean nothing. You simply buy a piece of property, rent it out and allow the mortgage payments to be made by the tenants. Your risk is minimal, and patient investing over ten or twenty years can truly create millionaires. If you do make some mistakes, inflation will bail you out. You have paid tax-deductible interest and paid off your loans with ever-shrinking dollars. Then, when you have met your wealth objectives, or it looks like the Malarial Cycle is about to end, you liquidate your debt by selling enough property to pay off all your mortgages, or trade your equities for fully paid-for properties.

The only real estate investments in which using leverage might hurt you are those that generate no income to service the debt, such as raw land—which I don't like.

THE MARGIN CALL

Using leverage in markets more volatile than real estate is much more dangerous, but potentially much more profitable. Most leveraged public markets are very volatile. Prices are quoted daily in financial publications. Brokers generally attach conditions to the money they are lending you, which can create big losses if the market goes against you in the short term.

These conditions almost always include the right to impose a "margin call" if the investment declines enough to wipe out more than half of your "margin" (your equity in the investment, the money you contributed to the deal). This is the right of a broker to require you to put up more cash margin, or he will sell you out to pay off your loan in order to protect himself.

During the Malarial Economy, we will use leverage in inflation hedges such as gold, silver, selected stocks and, of course, real estate.

BUYING STOCKS ON MARGIN

After real estate, perhaps the simplest and mildest form of leveraged investing is buying stocks on margin.

The basic concept behind leverage is to use other people's money (OPM) for your own benefit. This works quite well as long as you pick investments that go up, which means that in the fever of the Malarial Economy, you have to be "long" (betting it will go up) on inflation-hedge investments. A basic rule is never to "go short," against the primary trend, especially on margin, because the risks are twice as great.

If your credit is good, stockbrokers will allow you to open a margin account. They will automatically lend you up to 50 percent of the money necessary to buy stock.

Although 50 percent is the present standard, the Federal Reserve has the power to alter the margin requirements if it wants to control the amount of speculation. Brokerage houses charge margin buyers interest a couple of points above the "broker loan rate" for the use of their money. To stay ahead of the game, the value of your stock has to increase fast enough to cover the loan costs, as well as the brokerage commissions.

BUYING WITH THE TREND

Bonds and utility stocks typically rise in value during the chills of a recession, whereas gold stocks or energy issues are likely to appreciate during the fevers of inflation. I prefer to stay with those cyclical investments.

With a typical 50 percent-leverage margin account, you can make roughly twice as much money as if you had simply paid 100 percent of the cost for the stock or bonds.

The two-edged sword of leverage, however, means that if your stock goes down, you will lose twice as much. The multiples of gain or loss are determined by the amount of money you are able to borrow. In the stock market, 50 percent leverage is the best you can get.

If the market moves against you and the value of the securities declines, your broker will give you his only unqualified piece of advice—a margin call. If your equity in the stock (the total market value of the securities, minus the amount of the loan) falls below 25 percent of the total market value, your broker will call you to put up extra money. If you don't meet the margin call, the broker will sell out your position in order to protect his loan, and you will absorb the losses.

ASA, the closed-end investment trust investing in South African mining stocks which we discussed earlier, is a good example of an inflation-hedge investment that can be purchased on margin.

You could buy one hundred shares of ASA, trading at $50 a share, for $5,000. You would put up $2,500 and the broker would put up the other $2,500. The broker's interest charge will vary according to the amount borrowed. Buying on margin not only gives you double the percentage of return if the stock moves in your direction, but it will allow you to buy twice as much stock with the same amount of money.

Remember, however, the interest on the $2,500 loan must be paid, regardless of whether or not ASA goes up or down.

Let's see how an actual transaction works.

If you had bought 100 shares of ASA on 50 percent margin in October 1982 when it was trading at $50 a share, and sold it early in 1983 at 79⅞, the value of your shares would have risen to $7,987.50 for a gain of $2,987.50. Had you not bought on margin, you would only have bought half as many shares and made half as much money, just under $1,500.

ASA later dropped back down to $50 a share, and if you didn't sell, your paper profits would have evaporated. In fact, if you consider the broker's commission and the interest on the loan, you would have a net loss on the transaction, despite the fact that the price is precisely the same as you paid for it.

If the value of the hundred shares of stock had fallen below $3,750, you would have received a margin call.

The margin buyer has to be prepared to move more quickly than the fully vested stock buyer, and must be much more willing to cut his losses. The decision to ride out a temporary decline is not completely yours. If it drops far enough, the broker will certainly make that decision, unless you put more money at risk.

Margin stock investing should be done only when you are betting in the same direction as the basic trend. If we're in a bull market for precious metals, I never take a short position contrary to the Big Picture, even if I think we're facing a substantial reversal against the long-term trend.

THE FUTURES MARKET

Futures contracts are the riskiest kind of leverage. I really want to scare you off, as there are better forms of leverage with less risk.

A futures contract is a firm legal commitment between two parties in which the buyer agrees to accept delivery of a specified amount of a commodity at a specified price from the seller of that commodity, in a specified month in the future. A futures contract is not an option, where you can choose whether or not you will buy or sell. It is a specific obligation to buy the contract on the expiration date.

Each contract calls for a definite amount and grade of product. For example, a person buying a March silver contract at $10 is making a legal commitment to pay for and accept delivery of 5,000 ounces of silver of a specified quality during the month of March. He will pay $10 per ounce, unless he sells the contract before the delivery date to someone else, who must then assume the obligation. The required margin on this $50,000 contract is $3,000. (Margin requirements are set by the exchanges, and can change, so check with your broker.)

The original intent of the futures market was for producers of farm commodities to sell their crops in advance at a specified price so that their risk and profit would be clearly defined. The farmer could make plans based on a locked-in sale price for his wheat, and General Mills could make specific marketing and pricing plans, knowing what it would be paying for its wheat.

In today's futures market there are essentially two types of traders: the hedger and the speculator. A hedger buys or sells a futures contract to reduce the risk of loss, as our farmer did in the above example. General Mills in the above example was also a hedger, protecting itself against price increases.

A speculator, on the other hand, is a trader who buys or sells futures contracts on margin (usually 2 percent to 5 percent of a contract's value), with the idea of making big leveraged profits on the advance or decline of prices. He doesn't have the slightest desire to actually own 5,000 ounces of silver, so he always sells his contracts before the delivery date. He just wants to make money from the price movement.

The speculators provide the liquidity and volume of transactions so there is a free and active market with enough transactions to provide the hedgers with a quick buy or sell. The hedger has lowered his risk by buying or selling a futures contract, but in the real world, risk doesn't just disappear. It is merely transferred—to the speculator. He is willing to accept the risk in return for the possibility of gigantic profits.

Because you only have to put up from 2 percent to 5 percent of the value of a futures contract, giving you leverage of anywhere from 20 to 1 to 50 to 1, you can make or lose a whole lot of money in a very short time in the futures market.

The good news is that if your investment goes up 2 percent to 5 percent, you double your money. The bad news is that if it goes down 2 percent to 5 percent, your margin is wiped out—you get a margin call. If you won't or can't meet it, the broker sells you out and you've lost everything you've invested.

Actually, it can even be worse than that. If the market should suddenly drop "down the limit," which means that it has fallen below the amount which the exchange regulations permit in a given day, trading stops and nobody can get in or out unless transactions can be conducted at a price higher than the "limit down" price.

If the market opens "down the limit" again the next day, both you and your broker are sweating. You sweat because you may be losing money you didn't even put up. You are liable for all losses incurred on the contract. The broker sweats because he may not only have to sell out your position to prevent more losses, but he may have to bill you for losses over and above the margin money you put up, and he worries about whether or not you are willing or able to meet the additional margin requirement.

If you believe that we're in the fever cycle, you might "go long," or "buy" a 100-ounce gold contract or a 5,000-ounce silver contract to take leveraged advantage of a bullish trend. If, on the other hand, you believe we are in the chills phase of the cycle, you would probably "short" silver and gold, betting on lower metal prices by selling a contract that you don't own to someone who has the opposite opinion. You later "cover" your contract by "buying" a futures contract, offsetting your short position. If you guessed right about the market, you are able to buy at a lower price than you sold. This isn't "buy low, sell high." It's "sell high, buy low." The result is the same.

Most people classify futures speculation in the same category as gambling. However, for the knowledgeable speculator, there is a substantial difference, and he does serve a useful purpose, providing the liquidity which makes the hedgers' market possible.

Futures contracts combine the best and worst aspects of leverage. If you guess right, you make more money than with any other leveraged investment. If you guess wrong, you lose more. Your potential profit is unlimited, and your potential loss is awesome.

The prudent use of "stop-loss orders" can help you to limit your risk, but that's a bit like saying you won't have an accident because you're wearing a seat belt. The futures market has a nasty habit of opening above or below your predetermined "stop order" and you have suddenly lost more than you previously decided was acceptable.

The problem with the futures market and its margin-call risk is that it is far easier to forecast a long-term trend than an unexpected event. You could be right about the long-term trend and get killed in the short term, either "stopped out" of the market or sold out of the market by your broker to meet his margin requirements. Even in powerful bull markets, dramatic declines can and do happen.

Most of you should not trade futures. There are far safer ways to get similar leverage. Leave the trading to the "locals," the guys who trade right on the floor of the exchange. Only they can act fast enough to protect themselves in this volatile market.

The main principle to remember when using leverage is that the smaller the percentage of the investment you put down in cash, the more volatile your profits or losses will be, and the futures market is the classic example.

STOCK INDEX FUTURES

We should not leave the futures market without examining an interesting new development.

1982 and 1983 provided an incredible opportunity for speculators who perceived that the economy was coming out of the chills and entering a recovery period. The Dow Jones Industrial Average had collapsed below 700, and the growth potential was incredible for those who perceived that situation. Those who invested in individual stocks made money for the most part; but even in bull markets a substantial number of stocks will go the wrong way. For a while, the dart-board technique of choosing stocks was quite successful, because the majority of stocks were going up.

However, by far the most successful participants in the bull market of 1982 and 1983 were those who speculated in a new type of financial futures contract—stock index futures.

Until 1982, the only way to bet on the stock market in general was to buy shares of a mutual fund which owned a cross section of the key stocks in the Dow Jones Industrial Average. With the advent of stock market futures, however, it became possible to make a leveraged bet on the direction of the stock market without having to pick a specific stock, by buying a commodity futures contract on a stock index such as the Dow Jones or the Standard and Poor's 500. The line between securities and commodities is now permanently blurred as this new hybrid combines the characteristics of stocks and commodities.

In the case of the stock index futures there is no underlying commodity such as pork bellies or platinum—just an index—so you're in no danger of having a truckload of stocks dumped on your doorstep. But apart from the required cash settlement of contracts that mature at each quarter's end (March, June, September and December), stock index futures act just like other commodities.

Like commodity futures contracts, they're not just a leveraged speculator's bet on the direction of the market. The stock market hedging equivalent of the wheat farmer and General Mills is the portfolio manager who uses stock index futures as a "risk management" tool, a means of hedging his stock portfolios with only a 10 percent margin deposit.

If you or an institutional-portfolio manager own a broadly diversified stock portfolio, and you believe that a market decline is imminent but you still believe in the long-term prospects for your stocks, you may "go short" on some stock index future contracts by selling. This may be preferable to selling the stock and incurring tax liabilities. If the market goes down, the loss in your portfolio's value will be offset by the profits in your futures contracts.

You can buy futures on the Value Line index on the Kansas City Board of Trade, an S & P 500 contract on the Chicago Mercantile Exchange, and a New York Stock Exchange Index contract on the New York Futures Exchange. The Comex also offers a contract based on the S & P 500, and the Chicago Board of Trade has a contract based on the Dow Jones Index.

Like all futures contracts, they are highly leveraged, speculative, volatile and high-risk, and inappropriate for most of you, but they offer great potential profits (or losses) for people with money, guts and a correct view of the direction of the market.

STOCK OPTIONS

At some time you may be convinced that gold will go up and want to make a leveraged bet on it. Still, you prefer to avoid the margin-call risks of the futures market.

One much safer alternative is to take options on listed gold stocks. You can make a fortune on these if you bet correctly on the direction of gold prices.

Stock options differ from futures in several crucial ways. First, they deal in specific stocks, rather than commodities. However, stock options can be a "commodity play" if you buy options on stocks that move with the commodities. Gold shares are ideal for that purpose. When the price of gold goes up, so does the value of gold shares, only gold shares rise farther.

Second, and most important, stock options, unlike futures, are not a contractual obligation to buy or sell, so there is absolutely no way you can get nailed for a margin call. When you buy a stock option, you have the right, but not the obligation, to buy (a "call") or sell (a "put") a given number of shares at a given price, before a given date. After that date the option expires worthless. The maximum you can lose is the price you paid for the option, and that is determined by the free market, just like stock prices, and quoted in the newspaper every day. That means you can get leverage the same as in futures contracts, but at a clearly limited risk. It sounds a little ironic when you find out that the risk is "limited" to 100 percent of what you pay for the option, but remember, in a futures contract "worst case," you could lose 100 percent, 200 percent or even 500 percent of the money you put up.

Like futures, leverage is gained by "controlling" a large block of stock with a relatively small investment. Small movements in the price of the stock can net you large profits.

The leverage isn't quite as good as in futures contracts, but it can still be 10 or 15 to 1 and just as exciting, because you have the same volatility in gold stock options that you would have in a gold futures contract. The biggest advantage is the comfort of knowing that if you guess wrong short-term, but still have confidence in your judgment, you can wait it out. Remember, no margin calls!

I believe it bears repeating: a stock option is simply the right (but not the obligation) to buy or sell 100 shares of a given stock at a given price before the option expires on a given date.

Options are listed in the financial section of most major papers as well as in *The Wall Street Journal,* which carries the option listings for the American, the Chicago Board and the Philadelphia option exchanges.

Let's look at an actual option listing for Homestake Mining on November 18, 1981.

OTION & NY CLOSE	STRIKE PRICE	CALLS — LAST			PUTS — LAST		
		JAN	APR	JUL	JAN	APR	JUL
Homstk	40	2½	4¾	6	3¼	4¼	4⅝
38⅞	45	1⅛	2¾	4¼	6⅝	7¼	7¼
38⅞	50	⁷⁄₁₆	1⅝	2¾	11⅛	12	11
38⅞	55	¼	⅞	2⅛	16⅛	15¾	17
38⅞	60	³⁄₁₆	³⁄₁₆	s	21¼	22	s
38⅞	70	⅛	s	s	32¼	s	s

(r = not traded, s = no option offered)

Now let's untangle that complicated batch of figures. Under the name of the stock in the far left-hand column, you see 38⅞. That is simply the closing price of the stock on the previous day.

The next column lists the "strike price" of the options, ranging from $40 a share to $70 a share. That is the price at which you have bought the right to buy 100 shares of the stock (in the case of a call), or sell 100 shares of the stock (in the case of a put).

If you bought a Homestake April 40 "call" option at 4¾, that means you paid $475 for the right to buy 100 shares of Homestake at $40 any time on or before the third Friday in April, gambling that the price would go above $44¾ by then (the $40 strike price, plus $4.75 per share you paid for the option), giving you a profit.

The third, fourth and fifth columns headed "January," "April" and "July" are for call options. A call option is a bet that the stock will go up.

To make sure you understand, let's recapitulate.

When you buy a call, you have bought the right to purchase 100 shares of the underlying stock before the expiration date at the strike price. If you own an April 40 call, you have the right to buy stock at $40 per share, no matter how high the stock goes, at any time on or before the third Friday in April.

A put option (the last three columns of the table) is just the opposite of a call. It is a bet that the stock will go down. Everything works in reverse. When you buy a put, you have bought the right to sell 100 shares of the underlying stock at the strike price. If you own an April 40 put, you have the right to sell the stock at 40, no matter how low it goes, any time on or before the third Friday in April.

If you have a call on 100 shares of stock (the standard size of each option contract) at $50 a share on or before the third Friday of April (all stock options expire on the third Saturday of the expiration month), there are some interesting possibilities. When you buy an "April Homestake 50" call option (the right to purchase the stock at $50 before it expires in April), you are betting that the stock will rise above $50 by then, and you are willing to pay a small premium for the leverage and the time. As you can see, the option is trading at 1⅝. That means that whenever the price of the stock rises above 51⅝ (which is the striking price of the option, plus what you paid for the option), you continue to generate handsome profits. Every time the stock goes up another $1.63, you will add another 100 percent return on your investment. As a practical matter, if the stock rises close to the option striking price well in advance of the expiration date, your option will rise in anticipation that the stock will continue rising.

Conversely, if the stock should go down, unlike a futures contract, your option can't be worth less than zero. Your loss is limited to the money you put up for the option. You can lose 100 percent of the money you put up if the stock never rises above the level at which the option would be profitable and if you held it until it expired.

Also, you probably wouldn't exercise the option by buying the underlying stock. You would just sell the option at a profit.

The closer the option expiration date, the cheaper the option, because you are now in a race with the calendar. As you can see, the July Homestake 50 call option is 2¾, but the January 50 call is only ⁷⁄₁₆, because of the increased safety factor of time. If you got a move in the stock that ran it up quickly, you'd have better leverage in the January call. If it didn't move quickly you'd also have a surer loss.

Any call option striking price which is higher than the current price of the stock is referred to as "out of the money." Conversely, any call option striking price which is lower than the current price of the stock is referred to as "in the money."

There are many different levels of risk and leverage. These are the basic risk-evaluation facts:

1. Options are safer than futures contracts because you won't have a margin call. You can't lose more than you paid for the option, plus commissions.

2. You get the best leverage with the closer expiration months and/or the farthest out of the money because they are cheaper, having the lowest premiums.

3. You risk the least by buying the farther-out option months, and/or the farthest "in the money" option because that gives you more leeway to be wrong on your timetable, and the option has some intrinsic (real) value. However, you pay more for that farther-out, in-the-money option as the price of safety, so the leverage isn't as good.

A reasonably aggressive compromise is the first or second option out of the money, and perhaps the second or third available month, such as the Homestake April 45, at 1¾. It's not the cheapest, nor the most expensive. It's not the riskiest, nor the least risky. Because of the better odds that Homestake will go to 45 than to 55, you'll pay more for the 45 option.

The most conservative way to play the options is to buy in-the-money options, or the first option out of the money, and the farthest-out month. When an uptrend is so clearly established that you feel you can safely bet on it, then you get more "bang for the buck" leverage with the highest risk by taking the farthest-out-of-the-money option, in this case, the Homestake 70, and buying the nearest month, January. This assumes, of course, that you are not susceptible to cold sweats and nightmares, and groove on risk. It is a pretty exhilarating game.

4. The leverage of options lies in the fact that once the price has risen above your striking price, the stock does not have to double in order for you to double your money. It merely has to move ahead an amount equal to what you paid for your option. If you paid 1½ for your option, every $1.50 move above the strike price adds another 100 percent to your investment.

5. You have a floor because you can't lose more than you put up, but you have no ceiling on your profit potential. Obviously, success or failure depends on whether or not you catch the direction of the stock. If you do, there is no better way to make a whole lot of bucks.

The price of an option is determined by the free market of investors and speculators, which collectively evaluates the prospects for Homestake and determines what that option is worth.

The best investment hit I ever made in all the years I've been in the investment business was in May 1980, when I jumped into ASA options, on the basis that gold was going to rise sharply. ASA was trading around $39 a share, and I jumped on the ASA 45 option. ASA eventually went to $90.

At the time we went into the market, gold was at approximately $480 an ounce. I thought it would go to $850 by the end of the summer. Well, it only went to $700, and it took until September. On the way down, at about $650 gold, ASA was at $75, and I got out. Starting with a $20,000 investment, I paid for a huge indoor swimming pool, complete with men's and women's locker room, and a king-size whirlpool, a racquetball court, a guest apartment, a brick-and-wrought-iron security fence, a three-stall stable and a lighted tennis court. If I'd been 100 percent wrong about the direction of gold, I would have lost only about $20,000—a not inconsiderable sum, but one I could handle. The risk/reward ratio was incomparable. I did about as well as I would have in futures, but in futures, if I'd been temporarily wrong, my loss would not have been limited to my original margin, and I could have been knocked out of the game.

If you are going to trade options, you should become very familiar with Camera Angles 10, 11 and 12 in Appendix I.

OPTIONS TO REDUCE RISK

For the smart investor, options can also perform conservative functions 180° away from speculation. Anyone who buys stocks would be crazy not to understand option strategies to reduce and limit risk and increase income.

You can actually use options to create income from a nondividend-paying stock.

To most people, buying put and call options sounds like dressing up a crapshoot, but there is an insurance justification for options, just as there is for futures. Simply speculating with puts or calls is like owning a Swiss army knife and only using one of the ten blades. Let's look at some of the other blades.

The options page of *The Wall Street Journal* has thousands of options to choose from, on hundreds of stocks. But where did these options come from? Who created them? Who is on the other side of the deals? If you exercise a call option on ASA, who has to sell you the stock? Somebody like you, that's who.

For every buyer of a new call option, there must be a seller who grants this option. Those who sell options on stocks they own are known as the writers of options, and anyone can do it on any of the stocks for which options have been approved. They create the option on the stock in their portfolio by writing (selling) a call option through their broker to a speculator who expects the stock to rise in price. The price paid for this option is called the "premium," as shown in the table we just looked at. Your broker can give you up-to-the minute quotes for any listed options.

You can be the one who sells (writes) calls to speculators who expect a stock to go up, if you own the underlying stock and want to get additional income, or want to protect paper profits in declining markets without selling the stock. If the price of the stock goes up you can still enjoy the profits on your stock, although you will limit your profits somewhat. If the stock price rises above the exercise price by more than the premium, the calls you have written will most likely be exercised by the buyer, but that's the price you pay for having protected yourself against loss.

Here's an example:

Let's say you own 100 shares of XYZ Consolidated. You originally paid $40 a share and it's currently selling at $50 per share. You are concerned that it may go down short term, wiping out your $10 profit, but you don't want to sell it because you like its long-term potential, or you haven't held it long enough for long-term capital gains treatment, or whatever. Let's also assume that the price of a six-month XYZ 60 call option is $4 per share. Each contract is 100 shares. Four dollars times 100 shares is $400. You "write" (sell) a call option by calling your broker, who phones your sell order to the Option Clearing Corporation in Chicago. They route it to the exchange where that option is traded. The floor specialist who makes the market in that option offers it on the floor, and a buyer is found who pays you the $400 premium, which is rerouted to your account through the same process.

Now, three things can happen: the stock price can go up, go down or stay the same. Let's see what then happens in each case.

IF THE STOCK GOES UP

XYZ has risen to $56 as the option expires, still less than the $60 strike price. You have a $600 paper profit on your stock since writing the option ($56 minus $50, times 100 shares), plus the $400 premium paid by the option buyer. He loses his bet that the price will rise well above $60, and his option expires.

Your total return (profit on the stock, plus the option premium) would be $1,000 ($400 premium, plus $600 stock profit). Had you not written the call option, you would have made only the $600 profit on your stock.

If XYZ rose above $64 (the strike price of $60, plus the $4 the buyer paid for the option), he probably would exercise his option, and you now must deliver him your 100 shares, and he pays you $60 per share, or $6,000. He won his bet that the stock would go above $64. You made $10 per share in additional profits on the stock (remember, the stock was $40 when you bought it and $50 when you sold the option), plus that $400 he paid you for the premium, for a total of $1,400.

Had you *not* written a call option against your stock, and sold out at $60, you would have only made $1,000 in the same period. You gained an additional $400 by pocketing the premium. But you could not have made any more than that, even if the stock went to $100. The guy to whom you sold the option makes everything over the strike price, minus, of course, the $400 he paid you.

In a hot bull market, the risks are high that your stock could get "called away," thereby limiting your profits.

IF THE STOCK GOES DOWN

Now let's see what happens in the same transaction if XYZ drops from $50 to $46. You lose $400 of your stock profit—but you were paid $400 for the option. You break even. Only below $46 do you begin to lose more profits. Now you could make a real mistake. Should the price go below $46, and you fear more losses, you might be tempted to sell your stock. If you do, you don't own the underlying stock, and are said to be "naked." If a quick price reversal drives the stock back up above $64, the option owner now has incentive to exercise his call. This would force you to buy back the stock at a higher price to deliver to the option buyer. Or, you could buy back his call option at a higher price to get off the hook.

IF THE STOCK GOES SIDEWAYS

If the stock price remains unchanged, you simply pocket the $400 premium. That's 10 percent on your original investment, and every bit as good ,as a dividend. You created income, even from a nondividend-paying stock.

Actually, the best hedge against a drop in the price of your XYZ stock would not be to sell a call, but to buy a put option.

Let's say you bought XYZ at $40, and it went to $60, giving you a paper profit of $20 per share. You believe a correction is possible and want to protect your profits, but you don't want to sell. You buy a November 60 put option for $4 per share, or $400. You now have the right (but not the obligation) to sell your stock ("exercise" your put) at $60 a share at any time before the option expires, even if the price falls below $60. Your $20 profit has been reduced to $16, because of the $4 you paid for the put. That's the cost of your insurance. Should the stock fall sharply to $50 by November, you can, through your broker, force the option seller to buy your stock for $60.

If the stock dropped to $55, your put would have gone up in value by $5, because every $1 decline in the stock's price adds $1 to the value of the put. You can sell your put for a profit about equal to the drop in the price of the stock, and still own the stock.

These strategies are simple compared to some of the really exotic uses of options. Unless you really grasp these techniques you shouldn't try them, but the benefits can be worth the effort it takes to learn.

TRANSLATIONS

To refresh your memory, here is a glossary of the terms we have used.

Stock Option: A contract granting the right to buy from or sell to another person 100 shares of a stock at a specified price, before a certain date. That's a "right," not an "obligation."

Call: An option giving the holder the right to purchase stock at a specified price before a certain date. It's a bet that the stock will go up.

Put: An option giving the holder the right to sell stock at a specified price before a certain date. It's a bet that the stock will go down.

Buyer: The person acquiring the option.

Writer: The person who sells or creates the option.

Striking Price or *Exercise Price:* The price per share at which the option buyer may buy (in the case of a call) or sell (in the case of a put) 100 shares of the underlying stock.

Expiration Date: The day after the last day an option can be exercised—the Friday after the third Thursday of the expiration month.

Premium: The price the buyer pays and the writer receives for the option.

Covered Writer: An option writer who owns the underlying stock.

Uncovered Call Writer (naked): The writer of a call option who does not own the underlying stock.

There are several in-depth books on stock options detailing far more sophisticated strategies than the ones outlined in this discussion. They are listed in Appendix II.

MOCATTA OPTIONS

Eventually someone was bound to see the value of using option-like contracts to buy commodities. The motivation, of course, was to eliminate the margin call risk.

Mocatta Metals Corporation is the undisputed leader in the field. They are affiliates of Mocatta, Goldsmid Ltd. of London, one of the five companies that sets the London gold "fix" price twice daily. Mocatta's U.S. sales exceed $25 billion a year.

Their commodity-option contracts are "off exchange," that is, not a formal part of any commodities or stock exchange. They "make the market," providing both bids and offers. But my close relationship with their management has shown me that their absolutely impeccable reputation is completely justified, and their close working relationships with the SEC and the CFTC, coupled with their conservative legal stance and their association with the best attorneys specializing in regulation, make it unlikely that they will not perform as agreed.

As the market maker, Mocatta does not legally guarantee a two-way buy-sell market, but has always been willing to repurchase every option it has ever sold. If you have bought a Mocatta option and wish to sell out, they provide you a firm buy-back quote. The fairness of these quotes and Mocatta's rock-solid integrity and sheer size have allowed them to actually create and maintain a viable marketplace for their products.

Basically, a Mocatta option acts just like a stock option. It grants the right (but not the obligation) to buy or sell a stated amount of a specific commodity (like gold or silver) for a specific price before a specific date.

Mocatta prices its options by simply offering a striking price and date for the commodity in question. For example, the "March 1981 650 gold call" had a striking price for $650 per ounce on 100 troy ounces of gold and expires on March 2, 1981. The option provides an excellent method for leveraging your investment in gold during well-established bull markets. A put option serves the opposite purpose and gives you a chance for leveraged profits when gold is in a bear market.

Mocatta doesn't care whether gold and silver go up or down, as their options give their customers a chance to profit in either case, and Mocatta, of course, includes their markup in the price of the option. They protect themselves by hedging in the futures market.

Mocatta options are available from Prudential-Bache and E. F. Hutton, and from sales companies that have been set up specifically for the purpose of selling them. You should shop around, because sales-commission markups can vary dramatically, ranging from the 5 percent markup at Prudential-Bache to the approximately 40 percent at International Trading Group (ITG).

Obviously your potential profit is determined by what you pay for the option. The more you pay, the farther the underlying commodity has to move before you can make a profit. When buying Mocatta options, the price is strictly a "buyer beware" situation.

The table on pages 154–155 illustrates the fascinating variety of options available through Mocatta.

COMMODITY OPTIONS

Another kind of commodity option is also offered by the Chicago Board Options Exchange (CBOE).

A CBOE commodity option gives you the right (but not the obligation) to buy or sell a specific futures contract at a stated price within a defined period of time. The difference between a CBOE commodity option and a stock option or a Mocatta option is that the underlying asset is not a stock, or the commodity itself, but a standard commodity futures contract. It's the equivalent of trading futures with no margin call risk.

Whereas one stock option conveys a right to buy a "round lot" of 100 shares, and a Mocatta option conveys the right to buy 100 ounces of gold, a Comex gold call entitles (but does not obligate) the purchaser to buy a

Commodity	Options Available	Grantor	Quantity	Equivalence	Striking Prices in Increments of:*	Expiration Dates up to 10 months forward on the first business day of:*
Gold	Puts & Calls	Mocatta Metals Corporation	100 troy ozs. of .995 fine gold (plus or minus 5%)	One IMM or Comex gold futures contract	$25 per oz.	January, March, April, June, July, September, October, December
Gold Krugerrands	Calls	Mocatta Metals Corporation	50 South African gold Krugerrands	50 troy ozs. of gold	$25 per oz.	January, February, April, May, July, August, October, November
Gold Maple Leafs	Calls	Mocatta Metals Corporation	10 Canadian Maple Leafs	10 troy ozs. of gold	$25 per oz.	February, March, May, June, August, September, November, December
Silver	Puts & Calls	Mocatta Metals Corporation	1,000 troy ozs. of .999 fine silver (plus or minus 5%)	1/5 of one CBT or Comex silver contract	$1.00 per oz.	February, March, May, June, August, September, November, December

154

					Increment*	Months
U.S. Silver Dollars	Calls	Mocatta Metals Corporation	1 bag containing $1,000 face value of U.S. 90% silver dollars minted between 1837 & 1935	760 troy ozs. of silver	$1,000 per bag	January, February, April, May, July, August, October, November
Copper	Calls & Puts	The Mocatta Corporation, a member of the Mocatta Group	25,000 pounds (plus or minus 2%)	One Comex copper futures contract	4¢ per pound	February, March, May, June, August, September, November, December
Platinum	Calls & Puts	The Mocatta Corporation, a member of the Mocatta Group	50 troy ozs. (plus or minus 10%) of .998 fine platinum or platinum metals containing at least .995 pure platinum	One N.Y. Mercantile Exchange platinum futures contract	$25 per oz. up to $700; $50 per oz. over $700	January, February, April, May, July, August, October, November

* Increments may vary depending upon the volatility of the markets.

100-ounce gold futures contract at a predetermined price before a predetermined date.

For instance, on Monday, November 29, 1982, the April gold futures contract closed at $447.50 per ounce. Also on that day, you could have bought a commodity option on the same futures contract for $5,600 (listed as 56.00 on the futures page of *The Wall Street Journal*—see the table below), giving you the right to buy 100 ounces of gold at $400 an ounce (an April 400 call).

If you exercise that option before it expires (you probably won't, as I'll explain later), the total price you will have paid is $456 per ounce (the $400 exercise or strike price, plus the $56 per ounce cost of the option).

That means you have paid an $8.50 per ounce premium ($456 less the current futures contract price of $447.50) for the privilege of having a fixed price, time to wait for the price to rise and no liability other than what you paid for the option—no margin calls.

That premium is a free market reflection of investor opinion. It reflects the current price of the commodity, volatility, interest rates, investor supply and demand, the length of time before the option expires and the momentum of the market.

The above example was an in-the-money option, which means the strike price of $400 per ounce is less than the current futures contract price of $447.50.

An out-of-the-money option would be one in which the exercise or strike price is higher than the present futures contract price—for example,

MONDAY, NOVEMBER 29

STRIKE PRICE	FEB	CALLS-LAST APR	AUG
360	. . . .	88.00	. . . .
380	62.00	71.00	88.50
400	44.00	56.00	75.50
420	30.00	43.50	63.50
440	17.50	31.50	54.00
460	10.50	24.00	44.00
480	5.50	15.50	34.50
500	. . . .	12.00	28.00
530	. . . .	6.50	20.50

an April $460 call option. The out-of-the-money option is cheaper, giving you better leverage, as there is no intrinsic value.

Choosing an option is analogous to betting on Secretariat at 3-to-2 odds or going with a talented but unproven 2-year-old at 50-to-1. The more distant the strike price, the cheaper the option; the more distant the expiration month, the more expensive the option will be.

In either case, the call option price (and the premium) should grow in a rising market and shrink in a falling market. A put option will do the opposite.

In the case of the in-the-money option cited above, theoretically the market price of gold would have to move $8.50 for you to break even, assuming you were going to exercise your option. In practice, however, as the price of gold rose, the premium would increase, and the market value of your option would go up. You wouldn't exercise your option. You would just sell it for a higher price. The market price of gold wouldn't have to move $8.50 to give you a profit, as the market would assume further increases, and the premium would grow in anticipation.

The most conservative (and expensive) way to play it is to stay as deep in-the-money as possible with the farthest-out month. According to our table, this would be the August 380 call. The most speculative (and the cheapest) way to play it is to go as far out of the money as possible with the closest month (in this case, either the February 480 or the April 530 call). Just as in stock options, the biggest profit potential and the highest risk is in the nearest month (giving you the least time for the market to work in your favor) and the highest strike price (requiring the biggest move to show a profit).

Commodity option leverage is just about the same as a futures contract, dollar for dollar, and the risk is less.

One real advantage of the new options is the availability of distant out-of-the-money options. In stocks, especially in a rising market, the highest available option strike price will usually be close to the current market price of the stock, and relatively expensive. The highest branches sometimes bear incredible fruit, as that's where the best leverage is.

Although option prices certainly will fluctuate along with the underlying commodity, owners of options have bought themselves more staying power and peace of mind than they might have if they were in futures. The option premium makes the break-even price a little more distant, but that's the price paid for taking out the unlimited risk. "Gold for the not so bold" is the Comex's apt phraseology.

In a neat piece of overkill on the part of the CFTC, client-suitability standards are higher in commodity options than in futures. Be prepared to bare your financial soul to prove you can afford the risk. That's ironic, because the risks in options are less than the risks in futures.

Like stock options, a commodity option is also a "wasting asset" that will see the premium erode as the expiration date approaches. This erosion accelerates in the last four to six weeks of an option's life, so you must sell before it fades away. If the option is in the money, the intrinsic value will not erode unless you foolishly allow it to expire worthless, but the premium will. Hopefully, if you have caught the right trend, the out-of-the-money option you bought a few months back will be in the money by then, and increasing intrinsic value will more than offset the shrinking premium, which it should in the case of gold.

TAKING PROFITS

There are two ways to take profits on a commodity option: sell it or exercise it.

If you exercise your option, you assume a position in the futures market at the strike price. For example, if you had bought the April 400 call option, you would assume a futures position at $400. Original margin, currently $3,500, must be posted with your broker, but any option profits would be credited to your account.

As a practical matter, such options are rarely exercised. They are simply sold to take profits or cut losses.

The expiration date of a Comex commodity option is the second Friday of the month prior to expiration of the futures contract. The futures expire the third-to-last business day of the delivery month, six weeks later. The month listed on the option chart in *The Wall Street Journal* is the expiration month of the underlying futures contract. The April 400 call option expires the second Friday in March.

Futures contracts, commodity options and leverage contracts all have their merits. They span the spectrum from the unlimited risk of futures to the precisely defined risks of commodity options.

If you can accept the financial risks and the emotional wear and tear, futures offer the best liquidity and leverage at the lowest cost, combined with the highest risk.

Options limit your risk—a big advantage—but you pay a premium for that, so the market has to move further to give you a profit. Leverage, while still good, is slightly less than with futures.

This chapter has been lengthy and complex, and it requires more study than any other section of the book—but where there is great potential for profit, greater knowledge is required. When you strap on your two-edged sword of leverage, you must protect yourself from getting hurt by carrying it in the scabbard of knowledge.

I rarely, if ever, buy futures when there is an equivalent in some form of option. I never make a leveraged investment until (1) all of my short-term indicators are lined up (described in Appendix I, Camera Angles 10, 11 and 12), making it a high-odds bet; (2) I have a clear long-term trend (the fundamental direction of the Malarial Economy; and (3) I'm sure that I don't have a lot of things weighing on my mind and influencing my emotions that will distort my ability to cope objectively with volatility.

If the situation meets all of the above criteria, then I grasp my two-edged sword firmly by the handle and start flailing away.

There are many unscrupulous boiler-room brokers selling commodity options and futures contracts. Never buy from a fast-talking telephone salesman who will try to get a verbal (yet binding) agreement during a telephone conversation, which is usually recorded. It is best to deal only with CFTC registered brokers, preferably those listed in Appendix II, and to ask for a financial statement from the firm.

The following questions should all be answered (preferably in writing) before doing business with any option or futures telephone salesman.

1. Where did they get your name?
2. What is the total cost of the contract, and the commission structure?
3. How much could you lose, and in what ways?
4. When and how often must you make payments?
5. What are the margin or storage costs (and may excess margin be kept in Treasury bills so you can earn interest?)
6. What is the current market price for the commodity, and how may this price be verified?
7. What is the basis for the recommendation?
8. *Exactly how much must the market move before you get your investment back and start making a profit?*

Of course, the most important question should be addressed to yourself: Can you afford to lose all of the money you're putting in, and possibly more?

GETTING YOUR FEET WET

This has not been easy going. Even if you have read this chapter several times and think you understand it, you won't master the techniques until you actually have some money on the line. The best way to learn about a market is to buy a little bit of it.

If you get a buy signal from a financial newsletter, or by making your own charts, get your feet wet by buying one option contract. You will learn more in the next week about options than you would learn from many hours of study. When your money is on the line, everything you learn gets internalized, even if it's just a very few bucks.

Your broker may not want to handle an order for one contract, but he will if he values your account. Then watch it just as closely as if you had a thousand contracts.

I've used this tactic over the years to get a grasp of markets that I didn't understand. Ignorance is usually expensive. If you want market savvy, there is no substitute for an inexpensive experience.

If you do well, a new hazard arises. If you make a few bucks, perhaps several times the money you threw on the table, the big temptation is to get greedy, throw caution to the winds, and plunge, just because you think you've got this game figured out.

I have several friends among my subscribers who made a lot of money in the past on an option trade from one of our buy signals.

The next time around, thinking they had found a sure thing, they threw in all the profits of the previous trade, plus a lot more money, on the next trade, and lost it.

Even if you are a very successful option trader, you will realize a profit only about half of the time. The key is to cut your losses short and let your profits run. If you're right half of the time, you can make a fortune, but not if you have more money on the line when you lose on a trade than you did when you won.

There are several failure-management strategies to help you hang on to some of your winnings, such as raking off half of the profits of each trade and setting that aside for real estate investment. That way, if the next trade is a failure (a limited loss), you have not been knocked out of the game, and like the girl at the Special Olympics, you can get to your feet and continue the race.

You don't really know whether you have the temperament to make leveraged investments until you've tried it. Getting a start with a minimum purchase will tell you a lot about yourself. The danger signals to watch out for are:

1. The inability to sleep for thinking about your investment (fear and greed).

2. An overwhelming urge to throw caution to the winds once you've made a big profit on one trade (greed).

3. A feeling of huge relief once you have liquidated your position (relief from fear).

4. An overwhelming temptation to bet the grocery money (greed).

5. Depression lasting more than 24 hours if you take a loss (greed).

6. A tendency to build dream castles in the sky if your option is going up, coupled with an unwillingness to sell, regardless of what the market says, because you haven't "made enough money yet," or "paid off the mortgage" or whatever. The market doesn't care about your objectives. When the market says get out, get out. You can't set some artificial profit objective that blinds you to the danger signals of a market giving off bad technical vibes.

Financially speaking, people who should try leveraged investments are those who are (1) young enough, and with good enough future income prospects, to shake off a loss and recover; and (2) older folks who have enough investment funds so that losing some speculative money would not reduce their standard of living.

Generally speaking, I would avoid the futures market unless you are dead set on investing in a commodity for which there is neither an option nor a stock that moves with the price of that commodity, such as pork bellies or soybeans. However, that's outside the Malarial Economy strategy. I can't help you on that.

As I said at the beginning, only through the use of leverage can you get rich through investing. A 100 percent-owned investment is just too slow. If you don't have the capital and the temperament for leverage, you can still remain a member in good standing of the shrinking middle class by following the other Malarial Economy strategies, and there's nothing wrong with that. But a select few of you will take 10 percent or 20 percent of your investment capital and go for broke—and with proper failure-management strategies, you can succeed beyond your wildest dreams.

Nothing ventured, nothing gained.

HOW NOT TO GET RIPPED OFF

There are two types of calls our phone consultants in the Financial War Room have learned to dread.

The first is from someone who has just bought into a really malicious investment scam and wants to know if his new investment is okay. You would be amazed how deaf people can become when their greed has been aroused, even when their life savings are on the line.

I've watched our consultants come close to tears in their frustrated attempts to convince these people that they are about to make a grave mistake. They obviously called only to get our approval and don't have the slightest interest in our real opinion, if it collides with their greed.

The second type of call is generally from the very same people, weeks or months later, wanting us to "save" their money for them after the scam has been exposed in the press or in my Financial Success Report. They wouldn't listen in the beginning, when we could have helped, and now they're begging for help when the only help we can give them is the address of the bankruptcy court or the Attorney General.

MANAGING RISK

I'd like to teach you some simple principles that will keep you from falling prey to the vultures who would rip you off. A few simple rules will help you overcome the potential victim's three worst enemies: greed, fear of missing the boat and ignorance. These are the real reasons why people lose millions every year to hucksters.

Greed is so blinding that some otherwise sophisticated people who really should know better often get sucked into these deals and end up with their names on the victim list in the newspaper. The desire to get rich quick, or to get something for nothing, totally smothers their critical faculties.

Next comes the fear of missing the boat. People are often pressured into making a decision before they've had a chance to cool off and think it over, just because a salesman has told them "tomorrow will be too late."

Victims are also ignorant of how to manage risk. Every investor should constantly analyze his portfolio for ways to reduce the risk and increase the possibility of reward. It is possible to eliminate from your portfolio all risks *except* market risk—the possibility that the market will move in a different direction from the one you thought it would. Market risk is quite enough risk to accept. Unfortunately, however, people who lose money to scams have exposed themselves to nonmarket risks, making serious risk-management errors. They may do business with a firm in such a way that they are either ripe for plucking by crooks or, if the company goes broke, they are reduced to picking through the ashes, trying to get back some small portion of their investment.

Sorting out the scams and warning our clients is the toughest, most frustrating thing we do in the Financial War Room, but it does have one reward.

Because of the sheer number of our subscribers, and the fact that they all have the privilege of phoning us at any hour of the day or night free of charge, we have become a central clearinghouse of information on investment scams. Routinely we get information that even the law-enforcement agencies don't yet have.

The happy result is that when we expose a deliberate scam like International Gold Bullion Exchange, or simply a sloppy business operation that has evolved into a scam and is on the verge of going down the tubes, like Bullion Reserve of North America, we can exert tremendous economic pressure so that our subscribers can liquidate their accounts before the general public discovers the risks and brings down the company.

Our investigative staff also routinely provides valuable evidence to state and federal authorities as part of our consumer-protection program.

Along the way we've gained a unique perspective on investment scams that will help you see and avoid the hucksters, the con artists and, equally dangerous, the starry-eyed promoter-visionaries who don't know what they are doing.

Because we have had so much to say about gold and silver, you may be particularly susceptible to precious-metals scams unless you get an education.

Learning to avoid scams by reading about them in the newspaper is like trying to learn about traffic safety by examining wrecked cars. The damage is already done. Instead, you should know how scams operate—how they fool people to begin with.

IGBE AND BRNA

There are two fascinating case histories that epitomize the most dangerous scams. First, let's look at an out-and-out precious-metals scam. International Gold Bullion Exchange (IGBE) is a prime example.

According to their ads, you could buy gold at below "spot" prices if you were willing to delay delivery for ninety days. They offered to send you monthly "rebate" checks during that ninety days, which they claimed were tax free. At the end of ninety days, if you requested your bullion, they would seduce you into giving them further time by pointing out the terrific advantages of getting that monthly tax-free check.

It was pretty attractive. They offered you the lowest price around, which was actually below wholesale, and then gave you free money to boot. It was irresistible, and many people were seduced. As a result, naive and ignorant investors lost between $60 million and $80 million.

A few minutes' thought would have revealed that it is economically and rationally impossible for a company to survive indefinitely by doing business that way. The only way they can stay in business is by using money from new investors to pay their obligations to old investors—the classic Ponzi scam.

In reality, IGBE's owners, the Alderdice brothers, were using customer funds to start other businesses and to speculate in the futures market.

We exposed them in the July 30, 1982, issue of my newsletter, long before they went down the drain. After explaining the dangers, I said:

> Companies we have thus far identified who are using this technique (the buy below spot, delayed delivery pitch) or something close to it, are as follows: United Precious Metals, Inc., International

Gold Bullion Exchange, and Premex. We are still checking out others and we'll list them later.

The safest way, of course, to avoid getting into trouble, is to take immediate delivery of your gold and silver. If you want the company to store the metal, do business with firms where actual title is transferred to you, like Deak-Perera or Investment Rarities.

In January 1983, a trickle of complaint calls started coming into the Financial War Room. In a month, it was a flood. By March 1983 we were running more stories on IGBE, warning people away. In May the company folded, and later that summer the Alderdices had gone from riches to jailhouse rags. Many people had lost their life savings.

In effect, investors were making IGBE an uncollateralized, no-interest loan. They had literally given an unsecured loan to a perfect stranger (who later turned out to be not so perfect), and they didn't even have a binding promissory note to show for it.

The second type of scam, typified by Bullion Reserve of North America, is the "straightforward scam."

Greed plays a role here, but usually takes a back seat to the customer's ignorance of the inherent business risks of the bullion industry. The key here is not what the company tells the buyer, but what it does with the customer's money without his knowledge.

Our initial investigation of Bullion Reserve revealed that its "ironclad" storage program was a sham. I actually visited Perpetual Storage, a perfectly reputable independent storage facility inside a mountain in Utah. I saw that Bullion Reserve's assets were not segregated from company inventory, as their literature claimed, nor identified properly, and the legal protections for the customer, as evidenced by the documentation, left much to be desired.

Also, there was no way of knowing whether or not the amount of metal in storage was actually equal to the obligation of the company to storage customers.

Alan Saxon, Bullion Reserve's president and owner, was interviewed by the able editor of *Silver and Gold Report,* Dan Rosenthal, who confronted him with the information that we had acquired through my inspection of Bullion Reserve's holdings at Perpetual Storage. Saxon admitted to some "oversights" and, much more disturbingly, was very vague and uncooperative about providing proof that he had enough metal to cover customers' storage accounts.

The "oversights" were, at best, a blithe disregard for customer protection and a calculated policy of exposing customers to risk without their knowledge or consent.

What we did *not* know, and what only Saxon knew, was far worse. Most of the customers' money earmarked for storage had never even been used to buy bullion at all, but had gone into Bullion Reserve's accounts and had been loaned out in huge quantities to Saxon and his ex-wife. The money had disappeared from sight. The amount of bullion in storage was only about 5 percent of what should have been there. He even had a special computer program, called the "120" program, in which, if someone wanted a statement of Saxon's storage obligations, the computer randomly selected one account out of every twenty and added it up.

In the following weeks, in response to pressure from Dan Rosenthal and me, the company fully disclosed its real storage policies, altered its advertising, cleared up its documentation and went through the charade of setting up a fully segregated pile of gold and silver bullion at Perpetual Storage, which they duly showed me on a second visit. We congratulated them for that progress in subsequent issues of my newsletter, but, fortunately, my follow-up articles were still bristling with distrust and additional warnings.

At that time, even we did not know that there had been out-and-out theft. It had appeared to be only a sloppy operation that did not live up to its advertised standards. That was also Dan Rosenthal's position, although he was beginning to suspect there might be something more here than loose business practices.

Our recommendation on August 22, 1983, and that of *Silver and Gold Report,* published at roughly the same time, was that customers immediately liquidate their storage accounts at Bullion Reserve. This caused an immediate $15 million run on the storage program. We were quite disarmed when Bullion Reserve met these liquidation requests without hesitation. It gave further credence to the theory that they were merely sloppy, not out-and-out frauds.

Eventually, however, the run on assets and cash finally convinced Saxon that he could not maintain the farce. Shortly afterward, he took his own life.

In the days that followed, Saxon's shocked and bewildered staff discovered that he had apparently stolen nearly $60 million to cover personal expenses, losses in the futures markets and heaven only knows what else. They are still trying to figure out where the money went. Saxon was the only person aware of the company's real financial condition. Against nearly $60 million of customer storage liabilities, they found only about $2 million in storage inventory. Even Saxon's closest employees and business associates and members of his board of directors apparently didn't know what had been going on.

Newsweek said, "Financial Cassandra Howard Ruff was the first to sound the alarm. After a visit to the vault of Bullion Reserve of North America in Salt Lake City, he advised his subscribers: 'Liquidate your stored assets with Bullion Reserve. We don't know if [the company] is dishonest or just sloppy. . . .' Ruff estimates that his warning alone prompted investors to withdraw $12 million."

What did we learn from the BRNA fiasco?

We learned that they were probably a reputable company in the beginning, but customer naiveté simply made it too easy and tempting for Alan Saxon to begin to tamper with customer funds.

BRNA differed from IGBE in that it probably did not start out to be a scam. IGBE was a scam from the beginning—BRNA evolved into one. Bullion Reserve's problem wasn't an inherently impossible program, like "buying below spot" or "delayed delivery." The risk was the customer's money "in transit." When the money went into the company account, it fell victim to Saxon's lack of integrity. It wasn't used to buy bullion as the customer hoped and expected. It was simply used for other purposes in direct violation of Bullion Reserve's advertising and the customer's expectations. What makes this type of scam so hard to detect is that such companies start out doing a good job for you, then become dishonest when the temptation is great enough.

Investors could have easily avoided both the IGBE and BRNA scams with a little intelligent risk-management thinking. IGBE enticed you to delay delivery so they could speculate with your money. BRNA offered a bogus storage program to allow its owner to do exactly the same thing.

How do you avoid these traps?

You either (1) take delivery at the time of payment; (2) do business with a sight draft through your bank; or (3) use an independently owned storage-facility account. Don't pay until the storage facility has certified that the product has been received. That's good risk management. Neither IGBE nor BRNA nor the devil himself can rip you off, if you follow these simple rules.

The last type of precious metals scam would be downright funny if it didn't cost investors millions per year. I call it the "naive" scam. This one works on fear and ignorance like the rest, but its real strength lies in the fact that the perpetrator of the scam is just as ignorant as the investor, and probably just as sincere. He is often genuinely honest, sincere and decent. In fact, he's a guy like you and me, with a red-hot idea. He's also dumb. He genuinely believes he's offering you a ground-floor opportunity in a skyscraper of success, not understanding himself the kind of risks to which he is exposing you.

If I got shot, it wouldn't matter a lot to me whether it was done by accident or on purpose. It would feel about the same.

The sales pitch is generally very low key and folksy—no boiler-room, high-pressure tactics. Unfortunately, his tenuous grasp on reality is equaled by his fanatical belief in how much of a favor he's doing for you. If you look closely at what he has to offer, however, it's often laughable.

For example, we reported on something called a "Liberty Bond," offered by Great Western Precious Metals in the summer of 1983. It all seemed very patriotic and exciting until you discovered that you were essentially lending money to a bank on Guam for several years. The "Liberty Bond" was the IOU they gave you. The idea was that you could be paid off with a fixed amount of silver, regardless of its price, at the maturity date. The offshore bank was used to escape "repressive U.S. banking laws."

Calling the thing a bond was one of the problems. Jim DeMers, the company's president, maintained he could call it that, based on the dictionary definition of bond. Technically he was right, but the definition was of little use against Nevada's securities laws or the SEC's regulations. Complaining loudly to the end that he was being unfairly persecuted, and genuinely believing it, DeMers signed a consent order and withdrew Liberty Bonds from the market. Since we had alerted Nevada authorities soon after his Liberty Bonds appeared, no investor losses occurred.

I don't know how many people we saved that time. We can't measure our value by the money people did not lose, as that is unknowable, but that's one we are proud of.

Naive scams like Liberty Bonds tend to be characterized by their short lives. Eventually the sincere, naive promoters figure out what they're doing and, hopefully, disappear before they take many people with them. They are moths that die in the flames of their own ignorance. The genuine sincerity of the naive hucksters can melt even the toughest cynic, so be very, very careful.

Although we can't publish a list of companies that we suspect are scams before we are positive (we'd be buried in libel suits), we can point out some common *modi operandi*.

Actually, the outright deliberate scams happen infrequently. The well-intentioned dealer who didn't protect the client is a more common danger. The genuinely lovely people over at Bramble Coins didn't segregate their clients' funds from their own operating funds. One of their suppliers, to whom they had extended themselves financially, went under, driving Bramble Coins under, and a lot of investors lost money.

The most common loss occurs when an investor sends a dealer money and, before he gets delivery, the dealer goes under. The investor's claim against the dealer is the same as the local stationery store's. He's just another creditor. That's what happened with Bramble's customers.

Bramble's misfortune was nothing compared with what happened at North American Coin and Currency, one of the five largest dealers in the U.S., because of poor internal controls. North American had been operating impeccably for years.

When a dealer sells you ten Krugerrands or 1,000 ounces of silver, he usually will not have it in inventory. When he sells you ten Krugerrands, by that very act he has "gone short the market" by ten Krugerrands. Normally he will immediately cover his short position by going long in the futures market or ordering the coins from a wholesaler.

In July and August 1982, North American sold silver short just after the June market low, as the market was starting up. Their sales were booming. They were selling to their customers and not covering. As the market went up and up, they lost and lost when they should have been making money. They soon owed a lot of money to their supplier, who wouldn't extend them more credit, so they had no cover. When they went into receivership the clients got stuck, because North American didn't have sufficient client safeguards. Thousands of investors lost over $10 million in that single bankruptcy.

They lost because of "money in transit." You send your money, they cash the checks, but then go belly up before they can send you the coins.

If you buy and leave your bullion in storage with the dealer, if it's not exactly the right type of storage it may be worthless if the dealer goes under.

Look for non-fungible storage; this is when your bullion or bag of coins is labeled with your name as your specific property and stored separately from company assets. It is yours; you can go in and fondle it, or take delivery. Non-fungible storage is the only type of storage that you can fully trust. The dealer can't be tempted to use your assets as operating capital.

Fungible storage occurs when you own a piece of the dealer's total. You have a partial claim on an "unallocated mass" of silver and gold. Your dealer may have two million ounces of silver in inventory, of which you have, for example, a claim on 127 ounces of the total. In case of bankruptcy, all creditors have an equal claim on fungible assets.

Non-fungible storage is the only perfectly safe storage, although there are relatively safe forms of fungible storage. The greater the separation of your assets from the dealer's, the safer you are.

If you are betting on the soundness of the institution you do business with, go for the biggest one around, the one most likely to be bailed out by the U.S. government. Given the political power of the big bankers, do you really think Uncle Sam would let Merrill Lynch (whose money funds buy CDs and T-bills) go broke? Be sure, however, that your account executive knows metals. I trust some of the large dealers, like Investment Rarities or Deak-Perera, whose personnel are well trained.

The next pitfall is silver and gold in transit. You sell your metal, ship it off to a dealer, and the dealer goes belly up before he pays you. Your metal has become part of the operating funds of the corporation. You can make a lot of paper profits, but if you are a victim of bad timing when the dealer goes under, your profits can be blown away like sand.

BEGGER, BROKER, TINKER, THIEF

Most stockbrokers are hardworking professionals, but even the big companies like Merrill Lynch can have problems with a dishonest or unethical broker. A large brokerage house does not an honest broker make. It's entirely individual.

There are two things you can do to broker-proof your investment account.

First, never give your broker discretionary trading authority. Unethical brokers, or brokers who have a temporary need for cash, can engage in "churning," or making numerous trades for the sole purpose of getting commissions. Your account will then be literally commissioned to death. This churning problem is even more common with commodity brokers because of the high velocity of commodities and the increased justification for frequent trades.

You should also fully understand the charges that your broker levies by very carefully deciphering your monthly statement. Many unethical brokers throw in small, unexplained charges and adjustments to customer accounts.

When shopping for a broker, check out some of his customers. If you are making your own decisions based on the Malarial Economy, you are most interested in good, quick execution and the willingness of the broker to do his homework to understand the kind of investments you're interested in. He should, at the very least, understand the concept of the Malarial Economy, so you don't have to argue with him every time you decide to make a trade.

High-commission brokers prey on the gullible, charging rates way above the market. A little comparison shopping before and after you establish an account can be very enlightening.

"Non-discount" brokers can cost you unnecessary money, because they're not about to volunteer to you that, when pressed, they will give discounts to even modestly substantial investors. My experience has been that even Merrill Lynch and E. F. Hutton will give big enough commission discounts to make their service as reasonable as that of the heavily advertised discount brokers like Schwab.

BOILER ROOMS

It is a reliable rule that where there are great rewards, there will be boiler rooms.

Boiler-room telephone-sales operations have milked the gold, silver, sugar, diamond and strategic-metal markets. A new favorite seems to be the oil and gas lottery conducted by the government. Let's take a look at the lottery before we evaluate the pitch.

Every other month, the Department of the Interior, through the Bureau of Land Management, offers 1,000 to 1,500 parcels of land for oil and gas exploration. Adult U.S. citizens may apply for these parcels in a simultaneous filing procedure that's come to be known as the "Oil and Gas Lottery." To assure that individuals are on the same footing as the oil companies, only one filing per parcel is allowed, and employees of oil companies can't file on their employer's behalf. Individuals as well as energy firms can, however, file for as many properties as they are willing to pay the $75 per parcel filing fee.

The lottery is conducted in eleven regional offices of the Bureau of

Land Management (BLM), and those whose names are pulled from a drum or chosen by computer can lease the land for $1 per acre (the rental goes to $3 per acre after five years). The parcels range from a few acres to several thousand. You choose the parcels you want to apply for, and the amount of company you have got will depend on the likelihood of finding oil or gas. It's not uncommon for highly contested areas of Wyoming to generate 3,000 applications. It should be added that, although some lands have much more promise than others, there are no known oil reserves on any of the offered land. Land with known reserves is required by law to be sold at auction, where oil companies are the usual bidders.

You enter the lottery hoping to win a lease that an oil company will want to purchase from you. If the oil company finds what it is looking for, the royalties exceed the purchase price many times over. If the luck of the draw is with you, the rewards can be substantial. If you should win, many companies will guarantee to purchase your lease, as blocks of land are more valuable than scattered parcels.

The odds, however, are not in your favor. At a recent lottery, there were 4,000,000 entries for 8,000 parcels, or 500 to 1 odds. The odds are much worse for hotly contested parcels, and much better for parcels that don't show much promise.

Some of the boiler-room operators do their best to make the lottery sound more like a sure thing than the crapshoot it really is, and to make their services seem indispensable. Obviously they won't guarantee that you'll win a lease, but they'll certainly do their best to imply you'll be a winner.

The boiler-room filing services have programs that begin at around $5,000, for which you'll probably get ten to fifteen filings. Doing it yourself, you'd get sixty-six filings for $5,000. In other words ten to fifteen filings would cost you $750 to $1,125, if you looked after it yourself. Guess who gets to keep the other $3,875 to $4,250 you send the nice telephone salesman? The filing services also supply you with ample literature on the abundant energy reserves in the Overthrust Belt running down the eastern side of the Rocky Mountains. The brochures are complete with pictures of smiling winners and the dollar amounts they won, and headlines imploring you to "Strike it rich," "Act today so you can be rich tomorrow" and "Turn your tax dollars into liquid gold." They'll also promise to apply your dollars only toward "sleeper" leases that have presumably gone unnoticed by all the other experts in the field.

Do you get the feeling that someone's trying to arouse your greed?

Once a boiler room has someone convinced he's likely to strike it rich, it's often very difficult for anyone else to persuade him otherwise. We find this over and over in the War Room. It's a shame to spoil someone's day with the truth, but that's what often happens when we tell people they'd probably have more fun and better odds in Las Vegas or Atlantic City. Some of them actually get mad at us. Unfortunately, the prospective investor in the lottery would much rather believe the guy talking instant riches than someone else talking sense.

Some services merely take in all the money they can, move on, change names and sometimes even switch products.

If someone phones you with stories of big returns on your money in sleeper leases, don't send money. If you're called by someone pitching the lottery (or anything else, for that matter), you may safely assume that you're dealing with a boiler room.

If you've ever had such a call—or for that matter, if anyone has ever tried to sell you something—you know that the primary goal is to "qualify the prospect." After all, why waste time talking to someone who can't buy what you're selling? The standard line is usually this: "If you found you were interested after hearing more about the lottery, would you be in a position to invest $10,000?" The amount might vary, but your response should always be noncommittal. A yes answer will only expose you to an increasing string of phone calls.

If you've already made the mistake of telling someone how much money you've got to spend, and don't wish to hear from them again, just tell them you've decided to invest in a new kitchen or, better still, lent the money to a relative. Chances are excellent that you'll never spend another minute with them on the phone.

The BLM has a pamphlet that will probably discourage you still further. Their address is: Bureau of Land Management, Washington, D.C. 20240. If you're still interested, there's ample information to pursue the lottery through the regional offices of the BLM.

To paraphrase radio commentator Paul Harvey, good luck! You're going to need it.

THE STRATEGIC METALS SCAM

Strategic metals have also been most attractive to the hucksters, particularly during the fever of 1976 through 1980. I expect this interest to revive in the fever of 1984 through 1987. As inflation hedges, they were the hottest thing going. The irony is that during the inflation, strategic metals *are* a fine investment for well-heeled savvy investors. But "well-heeled" and "savvy" are the operative words.

The strategic-metals hucksters are the same guys who used to sell the oil and gas lottery.

First, let me stipulate that strategic metals are absolutely essential to our industrial activity and defense effort. Usually they are produced in small quantities as byproducts of base metals. The more exotic the metal, the scarcer it is. Prospects for higher prices are excellent. Several are generally unobtainable except from unstable, vulnerable Third World countries that are falling under the Soviet Union's sphere of influence.

The hucksters have been able to make an incredibly seductive pitch for strategic metals. They are "what gold was to the 70s," "what oil was to the 70s," and "a ground floor opportunity to get rich" and patriotically rebuild our national defense and stockpile at the same time.

Don't let a strategic-metals telephone pitchman get between you and your money, even if he quotes *Reader's Digest* to back up his claims. Strategic metals are a perfect vehicle for the unscrupulous. They are a big-ticket investment, and, as this is a long-term investment, your encounter with reality will be a few years off, after the salesman is long gone, working another scam.

If you want to get into strategic metals, buy through a major broker. Prudential-Bache is the first brokerage house to offer strategics, and it has recently scaled down its "minor metals" program to make it more affordable.

The suede-shoe smoothies will probably be correct in the long run about strategic-metals prices, but if you do business through them, they are the only ones who will benefit.

Commissions will eat up most of your investment, and strategic metals will have to move a long way before you break into the black. It is a classic example of a legal but unethical scam that benefits the perpetrators of the scam at the expense of the investor.

PYRAMIDING

There is a method of cheating yourself that a reputable commodities broker will warn you against, but if he is greedy for the commissions, he will cheer you on when you try it.

Pyramiding is a disease that hits greedy investors when they get on the right side of a market and accumulate large paper profits in futures or options. They then use these paper profits to buy more positions. As leveraged as they were on the way up, they own twice as many contracts on the way down, and the margin calls proliferate.

One angry subscriber called to tell us he had lost $175,000 that day in highly leveraged silver futures, and he blamed me because I was bullish on silver. By the time we got him all sorted out, we found he'd been pyramiding. He had grossly ignored my tactical advice. His broker knew he was a novice and should have warned him, but the commissions were too attractive.

I refuse to accept any kind of responsibility—moral, editorial or otherwise—for collapsed pyramids in the futures market, especially when I haven't recommended leveraged futures.

In any bull market you can expect dramatic retreats. Government announcements can temporarily send a bull market into disorder. Markets that go too far too fast have necessary technical corrections. Pyramiding greed can leave investors subject to large margin calls and can give their portfolio unacceptable volatility. Only the broker wins for sure.

LAND EXCHANGE

In terms of money lost, one of the biggest scams to come down the pike in a long time is the exchange of real estate for colored gems, allegedly on a tax-free basis.

The boiler-room operator finds out that you have some real estate you'd like to sell. He will oftentimes use the "for sale" section of the real estate classifieds. He offers you diamonds or colored stones that are supposedly worth much more than the land, in exchange for your land, and informs you that under section 1031 of the IRS code it will be a tax-free exchange.

The fraud is in two parts: (1) the stones are overvalued; and (2) this is not a tax-free exchange. Section 1031 exchanges require "like property," and stones and real estate don't have an awful lot in common.

One transaction that came to our attention involved about a half million dollars' worth of land. We advised our subscriber to have the stones checked. The first stone was junk, worth about $5 per carat, but priced at about $14,000 by the boiler-room operator for purposes of the exchange. There were also carved emeralds and Burma rubies of very poor quality.

The stones were worth a fraction of the land. By the time we got involved, it was too late. The dirty deed had been done, and the boiler room's phone had been disconnected.

Another exchange involved a number of rubies and sapphires. Stones worth $20 per carat were valued at $600 and $800 per carat. The rubies were so heavily flawed and of such poor color that they probably couldn't qualify for the lowest rating of the American Gemological Laboratory's (AGL) chart.

Sometimes the stones will bear some very high appraisals from respected names in the industry. Unfortunately some of these people have also been caught up in greed.

One horror story involved a $60,000 piece of real estate for which the owner had accepted some cash and stones worth, supposedly, $100,000. The appraisals were written by the seller. They were all very official-looking, stating that he was a graduate gemologist from the Gemological Institute of America (GIA). Stones that could be purchased for $20 to $33 a carat were appraised at $500 to $1,000 a carat. The gems were somewhere between commercial quality and junk. The victim of the scam gave up valuable land for trash.

One of these stones had an absolutely fascinating history. It was a sapphire weighing 2.23 carats, appraised at $1,000 a carat. First, an honest wholesaler sold it, and stones like it, to the gem promoter for about $30 a carat, in quantity. Next, the gem promoter wrote an appraisal on the sapphire for $1,000 per carat and sold it to the real estate developer for $150 per carat. The real estate promoter offered it, along with other stones of equally dubious value, in an inflated dollar-for-dollar exchange, to a property owner for $600 per carat, telling the property owner what a fine value he was getting for his money, that is, $1,000 per carat "real" value.

The property owner now thinks he has $100,000 worth of stones for which he paid $60,000, but which are really salable for about $3,000.

The broker now has $60,000 worth of land for which he paid $15,000. He's made four times his money.

The gem promoter has now made $15,000 for an outlay of $3,000, five times his money.

The real estate broker feels he gave the property owner a good deal because he was told the gems were worth that much. He had no business in a field he knew nothing about, and should not have passed on information to one of his customers without checking. If he had tried to sell one of those gems to a reputable dealer, he would have found out the truth.

Because the broker did not do his homework he cost the property owner about $50,000.

Guess who got the short end of the stick?

The FBI has recently arrested six people in Washington, D.C., for interstate fraud in similar transactions.

In theory, land/gem exchanges can work if both parties are entirely honest and if the land owner goes to an outside appraiser before the deal is made to find out what a willing buyer will pay a willing seller in the marketplace.

As a practical matter, however, I have never seen a legitimate gems-for-land deal, because legitimate gem owners have no real incentive to make such a deal.

The one sure thing is that the tax claims are fraudulent. This is not an exchange of "like goods" under section 1031 of the IRS code, and capital gains must be paid, contrary to the promoter's claim that you don't have to pay capital gains until you liquidate the stones.

There's a new variation on the gem scam involving "gems for gems." This scam capitalizes on the presently depressed levels of the diamond market. There are several firms in Florida that phone diamond investors offering to take their "worthless" diamonds off their hands for a diversified parcel of "valuable gems." Of course, you must send your diamonds and some additional money. You will get no AGL certificate with the gemstones, and you will get very small stones. I expect this scam to reach epidemic proportions when diamonds begin recovering their value during the inflationary fever of the next few years.

TAX SHELTER SCAMS

In the past, you probably could get away with a dubious or poorly structured tax shelter due to the IRS's lack of manpower, but major provisions of the 1982 tax legislation were dedicated to the elimination of "unfair" tax loopholes and a crackdown on some high-profile tax shelters. The IRS was given authorization for 5,000 new enforcement personnel who will concentrate on the tax rebellion and tax shelters they don't like. They now have vastly expanded authority to define arbitrarily "abusive tax shelters." They are looking at everything from limited partnerships in jojoba bean farms in Costa Rica to horse-breeding deals to motion picture or television production and distribution tax shelters.

The sales of tax-shelter programs set new records every year as more and more Americans are pushed into higher tax brackets. A lot of people are going to have unpleasant surprises when they get audited.

The guidelines are pretty simple. Purchase tax shelters *only* through a reputable Certified Financial Planner or broker with an unblemished reputation, and follow the guidelines given in Chapter 12.

Brokers love to sell tax-shelter plans, and unfortunately they get the best commissions on the more dubious deals. They receive about eight times the commission on a tax shelter as they do on a stock sale, giving them considerable incentive to persuade themselves of the virtues of a dubious deal.

One thing that works in favor of a tax-shelter scam is the fact that the customer is the last person who wants to expose the fact that he's been defrauded. After all, who wants to hoist the red flag on his own tax return?

In general, the IRS hates all tax shelters, but is forced by law to accept those having the potential for generating honest profits.

Partnerships financing lithographic prints, books, records and movies are examples of those shelters which are not only high-profile in terms of triggering an audit, but they are also high-risk in terms of an investment. They generally aren't crooked, they just have less chance for success, although a good movie deal can hold up.

It used to be that if a tax shelter were disallowed, you were billed for the additional tax and a reasonable interest charge. Now you can be socked with penalties severe enough to take the fun out of playing IRS roulette.

Newcastle Financial Group, the financial planners that I use for my own personal tax-shelter program (see Appendix II), are a great source of information and/or sound tax shelters. There's also a financial newsletter called *The Limited Partners Letter* that regularly deals with shelters. They sell a 15-page, 117-question tax-shelter checklist for $9.50 (P.O. Box 640, Menlo Park, CA 94025). B. Ray Anderson of Newcastle writes an excellent newsletter, which keeps you up-to-date on tax shelters (see Appendix II). Independent evaluations of oil and gas tax shelters are also available for $100 from Investment Search (223 Gloucester St., Annapolis, MD 21401).

The IRS will review a prospectus if it is sent to the Assistant Commissioner, Technical, 111 Constitution Ave. NW, Washington, DC 20224, but you can count on the IRS to give you far more conservative advice in the gray areas than you might get from a good financial planner.

HEARTACHES

One of the great heartaches in the Financial War Room is dealing with someone who has been swindled, when one simple phone call beforehand could have saved the investor from being taken.

My concern for these people is one of the reasons I've written this book. Please do your own legwork before investing. You can often learn if others have had problems with a specific company by calling a local Better Business Bureau, Chamber of Commerce or Consumer Affairs Department of your state, especially if substantial amounts are at risk. You also might want to try the state Corporation Commission, the Attorney General's office, the SEC and the Commodity Future Trading Commission (CFTC) or other governmental agencies; and, of course, our subscribers can call the Financial War Room.

Investing blindly is like diving into a lake head first because you've been told that the average depth of the lake was ten feet. By the time you figure out that it is a hundred feet deep in the middle and six inches deep on the edges, it's too late. You're committed.

At the risk of my sounding like a broken record, just remember that you must not allow yourself to be dominated by fear, greed and ignorance. If you've plowed through this chapter, ignorance is not now the problem that it used to be. Because you can't expect to be an expert on everything, do as I do. Find the best experts available and accept their good advice. Our War Room is one such source, and the experts listed in Appendix II of this book are also excellent references.

A fool and his money are soon parted.

11

HOW TO ANALYZE INVESTMENTS

Whether you realize it or not, you have learned a lot about the economic cycle and how to invest in it. I have given you some blunt instruments to help you approximate the turns in the Malarial Economy. The performance of short-term interest rates versus long-term rates is a good example.

Now let's look at the intriguing world of fine-tuning, the tools most successful investors and advisers use to catch more of the bull-market profits and avoid more of the bear-market losses.

This chapter, along with Appendix I, has five objectives:

1. To give you a peek into the fascinating workshop full of tools that a professional uses to analyze investments.

2. To show you how investments tend to operate in cycles and patterns that reveal themselves in various kinds of charts.

3. To teach you enough of the language and charting techniques of investment analysis that you can understand and effectively use investment advisory services, including mine. We all use charts. These publications will be far more useful if you can decipher the jargon.

4. To inspire some of you to become "chartists," to begin to analyze your own investments so you're not dependent on my judgment or anyone else's.

5. To introduce you to the Eldridge Strategy, an automatic trading method that vastly improves your investment odds in the Malarial Economy.

Parts of this chapter may be tough sledding and may require two or three readings and some careful study. You may not master all of it, but you should stay with it until you at least understand the gist of it, as the odds are heavily against the serious investor who doesn't understand the main principles and techniques of investment analysis.

So, whether it is merely to satisfy your curiosity as to my methodology or to develop a methodology of your own, this chapter and Appendix I (a more detailed discussion of technical analysis methods) may be the most important section of the book. They will certainly have the biggest payoff if you're willing to study them. If you want to understand the Eldridge Strategy, the simplest, highest-odds trading strategy I've ever seen, you must understand the Moving Average discussion that precedes it. There is no other way.

CAMERA ANGLES

You are watching the seventh game of a World Series on TV. In the ninth inning there is a bang-bang play at second base—is the runner out or safe? It's too close for you to tell, but the umpire calls him out and the World Series is over.

Then come the instant replays from several camera angles. Of the six angles, five look like he's out, and one looks like he's safe. The preponderance of the evidence says the umpire was right—he's out!

When I examine an investment to determine whether or not it is in a primary bull market or a bear market, or to determine my buy and sell timing, I use two basic forms of analysis—technical and fundamental. Both of them give me several different camera angles. Unlike the umpire, however, I can examine the preponderance of the evidence before making any decision.

FUNDAMENTAL ANALYSIS

Fundamental analysis means looking at all the known facts about a particular investment.

These can be internal, such as earnings per share, the track record of management, the price/earnings ratio, a new and valuable patent representing a technical breakthrough, a valuable government contract or cost of production.

Then there are external fundamentals, which are most often used to choose the general investment area or industry group to which I'm going to commit my money. The Malarial Economy is an external fundamental.

Among other external factors are: the future course of inflation and interest rates; the movement of oil prices; whether or not this investment is "cyclical" (moving in a fairly well-defined rhythmical pattern of lengthy uptrends and downtrends); interest rates; and, in the case of multinational companies, the political stability of the nations in which they do business, as well as government policies that might affect corporate earnings. An external fundamental for the buggywhip industry was Henry Ford. An external fundamental for the international bankers is the political stability of Argentina and Brazil.

Fundamental analysis is best used to determine whether or not an industry or a commodity complex is a serious candidate for further analysis.

TECHNICAL ANALYSIS

Technical analysis is a different breed of cat. It totally ignores fundamentals. The technician charts the past performance of an investment in various ways and draws conclusions about buying or selling from an analysis of current price movements and chart patterns in relation to past performance. The technician assumes that all investments can be analyzed with the same basic mathematical charting methods, and the past and present can tell you much about the future.

There are various technical tools (charts) which apply equally to all investments, and there are other tools which are best used when adapted only to specific kinds of investments.

Some technical indicators are more sensitive than others and are used to catch short-term moves. Others work best at catching long-term primary trends. Some give dependable buy or sell signals all by themselves, but most technical signals work best in combination with others.

There are investments that tend to run in packs, or complexes, and your technical evidence must fall into place for the majority of the investments in that complex, or you don't touch any of them.

My staff and I use both methods of analysis. We use the fundamentals to tell us whether we're even interested in doing in-depth technical analysis, and we use technical analysis for buy-and-sell timing and detecting primary trends.

For example, the fundamentals of the Malarial Economy tell us that this rhythmic economic cycle is still intact, and the technical charts of the investments that follow the rhythm tell us when that cycle is about to turn.

As my own "external fundamentalist" at Target, I look at government fiscal and monetary policies, as well as the political trends that underlie them (as described in earlier chapters), to determine whether or not these fundamentals are changing. If the fundamentals are intact, we can then assume, with a reasonable degree of accuracy, that the technical analyses produced by my resident technical geniuses will be dependable and that history is likely to repeat itself. We examine the chart history of the cyclical investments and make reasonable assumptions that in the future they will perform approximately the same as they did in past cycles.

Technical analysis can help you not only to determine the turning points for the long-term trend, but can also give you the actual price at which an investment is most likely to be a good "buy," "hold" or "sell."

Whole libraries of mind-numbing books have been written on this subject, and I don't want to add to that pile of insomnia cures. I just want to help you understand a few of the basic analysis techniques that I use in drawing my investment conclusions.

If you are technically inclined, you also might want to do some simple charting of your own. It is a tremendous confidence builder to be able to look at the technical evidence when an investment takes a sharp, temporary setback, know that the preponderance of the technical indicators are still overwhelmingly bullish, and be kept from panicking out of an investment at the wrong time. Charts can also get you out of an investment before a long decline and save you from losing a lot of money or giving a lot of profits back to the markets.

Some simple technical strategies can be used to follow certain cyclical investments so you can automatically and mechanically buy and sell and keep the odds heavily on your side. I'll show you one in a moment. Once you understand the explanations, then, as Tom Lehrer, my favorite comedian, has said, the strategy will be ". . . so simple that only a child can do it."

CAMERA ANGLE #1——FUNDAMENTALS

The fundamental Camera Angle that I follow most closely is the Malarial Cycle. Once you have determined that the cycle exists and is dependable, then you can analyze the fundamentals that cause it and perpetuate it to determine whether it's going to continue. These fundamentals include such things as government deficits, the consumer savings rate, Fed behavior, the political climate and the performance of the short-term interest rates against the long-term interest rates. The latter I have already covered.

CAMERA ANGLE #2——CYCLICAL COMPARISON

Now we look for investments that are "cyclical," that move with, or are heavily influenced by, the basic Malarial Cycle. This is not the only way to make money in the markets, but it is the safest, because when you make a mistake in timing, the basic cycle will eventually bail you out if you are patient.

The investments that move most dependably with the cycle are as follows:

1. Bonds. When interest rates are rising, bonds go down. When they're falling, bonds go up. Long patterns of falling or rising interest rates, lasting one to four years, are characteristic of this cycle, and make bonds a prime candidate for investing at appropriate times.

2. Silver and gold are obvious candidates during the right phase of the cycle. So are the rest of the metals complex, which includes the platinum family, gold-mining shares, silver-mining shares, copper and the nonferrous metals mining stock industry group.

These investments tend to run in a pack, although each has its own personality and may not always run with the others. But when that entire group is "in synch," on the way up, they are all good bets, and technical analysis can help us determine which ones are most likely to outperform the others by showing their relationships to each other. They rarely go far in any direction without each other, but some lead and others follow, and some go farther and faster.

If I'm trying to decide whether gold is in a bull market, I won't look only at gold charts. I will look to see whether or not the other investments in the complex are confirming what my gold charts are telling me. There have been times when we knew that gold was in a bull market but that other investments would outperform it. For example, in the summer of 1982 we decided that the metals bear market was over and it was time to invest in them, but we didn't buy any gold at $300. Instead, we bought silver at $6, and bought gold-mining shares. Silver was selling for approximately 1/50 of the price of an ounce of gold, and we knew that historically it usually sells around 1/30, so silver was cheap relative to gold, making it our number one choice. We made 125 percent in silver, while gold, during the same period, was rising about 60 percent.

Our historical studies told us that gold-mining shares tend to move farther and faster than gold, so most of our remaining funds were put into ASA (a closed-end investment trust, which invests in South African gold shares), and Homestake Mining, both listed on the New York Exchange. Sure enough, they vastly outperformed gold, and we sold ASA when our charts gave us sell signals in most of the metals complex.

Now let's look at one of the most important technical Camera Angles that we use to determine basic trends.

CAMERA ANGLE #3—MOVING AVERAGES

One of the most basic technical tools is the Moving Average (MA). MAs are used to signal major changes in direction, and are by far our most important technical tool for evaluating long-term trends.

To take a simple example, a 40-week gold MA is constructed by taking the weekly prices of gold (probably the Thursday afternoon London Gold Fix) each week for the last 40 weeks, adding them up, then dividing by 40. This would give you the average price of gold for the last 40 weeks. You then place a dot at the appropriate point on the chart. You make the average "move" each week by dropping the oldest week and adding in the new week, recomputing, putting another dot on your chart and connecting it by a line. You do this week after week, creating a moving line on your chart, a 40-week Moving Average. See the dashed line (-----) on Camera Angle #3 chart.

Moving Averages have a lot of uses, including smoothing out the chart lines on wildly volatile price swings so you can detect a coherent pattern.

When MAs are overlayed on a chart of the actual price movement of the investment, as in the Camera Angle #3 chart, they can tell you some very important things. The most significant gold MAs are the 11-week, 40-week and 68-week.

Camera Angle #3—MOVING AVERAGES

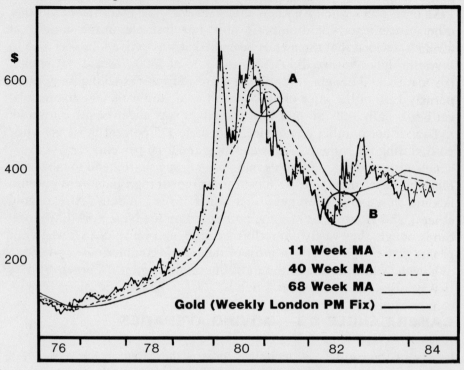

GOLD MOVING AVERAGES

The dotted, dashed, and thin solid lines are Moving Averages. During bull markets, gold (dark, solid line) is above them, and in bear markets, gold is below them. Their behavior can give us very useful buy and sell signals.

We use more than one Moving Average because we want to see how they interact with each other and with the investment we are studying. For example (see chart), during the explosive part of the bull market of 1976–1980, the shorter MAs were higher than the longer MAs. The 11-week MA was above the 40-week, which was above the 68-week. Gold was above all of the MAs. This is classic bull-market action.

Shortly after the top of that market at $800, in late 1980, as you can see also in the chart, gold fell below the 11-week MA, but failed to break the 40-week MA. It rebounded to $750; then, at about $650, it had broken both the 11- and 40-week MAs and the averages began to "invert," switching places relative to each other (circle A). The 11-week fell below the 40-week, which fell below the 68-week. This accurately confirmed a long, expensive bear market. During most of that bear market, from early 1981 until mid 1982, the short-term averages were lower than the long-term averages, and gold was below all the averages. As long as that chart formation persisted, I was uninterested in gold.

At the bottom of the bear market in 1982, gold began to rise through all the MAs, and they again began to invert, switching places to their more normal relationship (circle B), and what appeared to be a new bull market began.

Two of our most important confirmations of a primary uptrend occur when: (1) the price of the investment is above the longest-term basic MA, which in the case of gold is the 68-week MA; and (2) the shorter MAs are higher than the longer MAs. When an investment in a bull market drops below any one of its MAs, it's a sign to be cautious and check some of the other Camera Angles, which we will explain in Appendix I. When it drops below two MAs, I liquidate some of my positions, taking some profits. When it drops below its basic long-term MA (68-week in the case of gold), I'm completely out.

When the MAs start crossing each other, and other Camera Angles confirm, it means "sell," and that's what happened in late 1983.

After giving us our clearcut buy signals in 1982 (see circle B, Camera Angle #3 chart), and some dandy profits, in early 1983 gold fell through its 11-week average, its 40-week average in May, and finally in October broke through its 68-week MA. Also, the averages began to invert again, and the 11-week and 40-week MAs dropped below the 68-week MA. We were taking profits all along the way because the MAs told us that the bull market we thought we were experiencing was a very unusual critter. It could be either the first phase of a new bull market, which began in June 1982, the final gasp of a long bear market, which began in 1980, or simply a false start, giving us an unprecedented investment event. I had never seen a decisive bull-market Moving Average formation reverse itself in such a short time, certainly not in gold, where the cycle tends to last several years once a bull market begins.

I then looked at some fundamental Camera Angles to try to figure out what was happening. As the picture became clearer and the evidence accumulated, I concluded that gold had gotten off to an early false start because investors had been anticipating an immediate rekindling of inflation, which did not materialize because interest rates had remained high and there was a huge, potentially deflationary international debt crisis to be resolved. Inflation was postponed, and gold would have to back off and make another start, as discouraged inflation-hedge investors were selling in the absence of a rising Consumer Price Index. We used many indicators in drawing this conclusion, but the behavior of the MAs was the most helpful.

We sold our gold and silver shares with the lion's share of our profits intact and went to the sidelines in a money market fund to wait it out. We are still waiting as this is written, although the picture may have changed by the time you read this—another reason to send for the free update before you act.

As the chart makes clear, the MAs won't give you the very top and the very bottom of an investment cycle, but they will give you most of it. It was Baron Rothschild who said, "You can have the first 20 percent and the last 20 percent of the market, and I'll take my 60 percent out of the middle." Exact tops and exact bottoms are very difficult to identify. They are signaled only by the most sensitive short-term indicators, which usually don't tell you much about the long-term trend and tend to give too many false trend signals. Our objective is to catch the biggest chunk out of the middle of a bull market and to stay out of the bulk of the declines. To try to grab it all is greedy. There's an old saying on Wall Street, "The bulls make money, and the bears make money, but the pigs go broke."

OPTIMUM MOVING AVERAGES

Each investment has its own personality, and the "optimum" MAs for one investment may not be the same for another. The 68-week MA seems to be the most dependable primary trend indicator for gold, but it might be totally inappropriate for charting the Oil Industry Group Index or the Dow Jones, for example. It takes a lot of experimentation (and a personal computer) to sort out which MAs are ideal. That's one of the functions we perform for you through the *Financial Success Report,* but you can do it for yourself on your personal computer with the help of Chapter 13, "Pac-Man Takes On the Malarial Economy."

Moving Averages can also be used to give dependable automatic buy and sell signals. That strategy has been pioneered by such people as Dick Fabian, who publishes the *Telephone Switch Advisory Newsletter* (see Appendix II). He utilizes the 39-week Moving Average on all the no-load mutual funds. You simply buy when the investment moves above its 39-

week MA, and you sell when it and the Dow averages drop below it. No-loads are generally ideal for this trading strategy because there is little or no cost as you switch in and out, once you've made your initial investment. This has proven to be very profitable over the long term.

An automatic signal takes the emotion out of investing. It gives you a strategy, it helps you to be disciplined and, if you follow the rules, you are forced to be patient. Remember, strategy, discipline and patience are essential to success in the investment markets.

THE ELDRIDGE STRATEGY

Paul Eldridge, one of my resident technical geniuses, has developed a fascinating Moving Average strategy that utilizes the same principle used by *Telephone Switch Advisory Newsletter,* but there are some special features that make this uniquely ours, and far more profitable.

The Eldridge Strategy works best with stocks, mutual funds or commodities that tend to have long primary trends that last several years and come around at regular intervals. It is ideal for investing in the Malarial Economy, but it only works if you never deviate from the strategy.

The Eldridge Strategy will tell you whether to buy or sell, and when, and at what price. When the market goes against you, it will take you out automatically with minor losses. It will keep you fully invested in every major upward move. It takes about fifteen minutes of work per week.

Using our computer, we have tested Moving Averages from two weeks to one hundred weeks to see which of these MAs best fits the personality of each investment. We want an MA that is sensitive enough to touch the price of the investment often enough to get you into the major moves when the price of the investment moves above the MA. It also has to get you out in time to miss any major declines when the price drops below the MA. The MA must follow the investment closely enough to not miss the major moves, yet not hug it so closely and touch it so often that it gives you too many false signals.

We studied United Services Gold Fund (U.S. Gold) from its inception as a "pure-play" gold-shares fund in July 1974. It fits our requirements perfectly in that it is cyclical and very successful, and its cycles last long enough to give you major bear- and bull-market movements. U.S. Gold also fits nicely into the Malarial Economy cycle.

We calculated the MAs that give the optimum automatic buy and sell signals that make you the most money over the cycle. We went clear back to July 1974 to get enough data to accurately assess the true personality of the fund and find the optimum MAs which most accurately reflected all the major price movements. We observed the fund through two bear markets and two bull markets. We checked each potential Moving Average from 2 weeks to 100 weeks, examining the number of trades, the largest percentage of loss in any single trade, the largest cumulative percentage of loss of original capital at the lowest point and the total profit to date.

Our studies showed us U.S. Gold had two optimum MAs, a 70-week bull market MA and a 31-week trading MA.

This makes the Eldridge Strategy completely unique, a quantum leap ahead of the simple 39-week MA strategy used by the pioneers like Dick Fabian (for whom we have great respect).

If you had just bought U.S. Gold at the beginning of the study, when it became a "pure play" gold fund, and hung on until the end of the study, you would have made 46 percent on your money. Not bad! But you would have made 766 percent following the Eldridge Strategy, using the optimum MAs for buy and sell signals.

The buy-and-hold investor would have had a paper loss at the bottom of the bear market of 77 percent. Instant breakdown! The Eldridge Strategy trader, using the 70-week and 31-week MAs for buy and sell signals, at the lowest point would still have had a cumulative gain of 7.76 percent!

Look at the Eldridge Strategy chart. The bold solid line is U.S. Gold, the thin solid line is the 70-week MA and the dotted line is the 31-week MA.

The price of U.S. Gold crossed the 70-week MA only five times in nine years. No other MA had fewer than seven crossings. *The 70-week MA is the optimum long-term MA. When the price of U.S. Gold is above the 70-week MA, we are in a bull market. When it is below the 70-week MA, we are in a bear market.*

An Eldridge Strategy buy signal is triggered when the price of U.S. Gold rises above the 70-week MA, indicating it is probably in a bull market. We hold until it falls below the 31-week MA or below the 70-week MA, whichever comes first. We buy again when it rises above the 70-week MA or above the 31-week MA, with one exception.

Since one prime objective is to keep losses small, we do not buy U.S. Gold when it rises above the 31-week MA if the 31-week MA is below the long-term-trend 70-week MA, because this is likely to be only a bear-

UNITED SERVICES GOLD FUND OPTIMUM MOVING AVERAGES

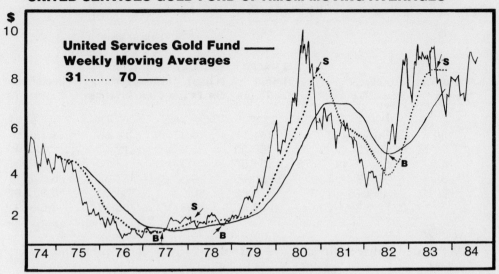

THE ELDRIDGE STRATEGY

This chart illustrates the strategy of buying or selling automatically based on an investment moving above or below optimum Moving Averages. The arrows indicate some of the buy (B) or sell (S) signals. This strategy from the first buy signal in 1977 through late 1983 produced a 766% return, or 127% per annum.

market rally, which will probably be short-lived and produce losses. The 31-week MA *must be above the 70-week MA to use the 31-week MA to trade the fund.*

To clarify things, look again at the Eldridge Strategy chart. The arrows pointing up are "buys," and the arrows pointing down are "sells."

Let's see how using the 31-week and 70-week MAs together can increase profits and reduce trading (see U.S. Gold Eldridge Strategy table on page 192). As of Friday, December 16, 1983, a strategy using both 31-week and 70-week MAs since July 1977 (when U.S. Gold first broke above the 70-week MA) would have produced a total return of 766 percent (including interest earned when out of the market and in a money market fund), for an average annual rate of return of more than 127 percent! No trade ever showed more than a 5.07 percent loss, and there was *no* cumulative loss in 75 months!

U.S. GOLD: THE ELDRIDGE STRATEGY
Using the 70-Week and 31-Week MAs ($1,000 Capital)

ROUND TRIP TRADES	BUY/SELL TRADE DATES	$ PROFIT/ (LOSS) ON TRADE	% GAIN/ (LOSS) ON TRADE	CUMULATIVE % GAIN/ (LOSS) INCLUDING MONEY MARKET FUND INTEREST	INVESTMENT CAPITAL (a)
1	7/15/77–3/17/78	$227.84	22.78	22.78	1,229.53
2	3/24/78–4/7/78	(61.17)	(4.97)	16.83	1,186.61
3	6/23/78–6/30/78	(60.23)	(5.07)	12.63	1,129.49
4	7/14/78–11/3/78	(51.87)	(4.59)	7.76	1,095.30
5	1/26/79–1/2/81	3,280.50	299.51	337.58	5,528.11
6	9/3/82–8/5/83	3,318.83	60.04	784.69	8,861.52
7	8/12/83–9/23/83	(209.55)	(2.37)	765.97	8,694.95

We traded fourteen times (buys and sells). Moreover, by using the 70-week MA and the 31-week MA, we had four losing trades out of seven, but the four losses were very small, and the three winners were huge.

By comparison, an investor who held on to U.S. Gold from the sell signal on January 2, 1981, until we got a new buy signal on September 3, 1982, had lost 34.6 percent of his money. At the same time, those following the Eldridge Strategy would have made 26 percent in 20 months in a money market fund—a swing of over 60 percent.

GIMME ACTION!!

Some people trade for the action, for the excitement inherent in active trading, and would rather trade and lose than not trade at all. However, a disciplined, limited trading strategy is where the profits are, and profits give me all the excitement I need. We are long-term investors going with the primary trend. Nevertheless, as a specific trading technique for those who choose to trade and for those who have the essential patience and discipline, the Eldridge Strategy, when used consistently over a long period of time, can produce spectacular results. (Also, you could safely take time off to go on an African safari for two months, leaving only a few simple instructions with someone you trust.)

For this system to be effective, you must act on *all* signals. No exceptions! For convenience, use Friday's closing figures. You can do your charting over the weekend and call in your order first thing on Monday. If you use only no-load mutual funds which have telephone-switch privileges, you save all commission costs and can act quickly.

Even though the commission charges will reduce the profitability somewhat, the Eldridge Strategy can also be used on any stock which has a long cycle, especially if you have an account with a discount brokerage house like Schwab, or if you negotiate a commission discount with your broker. Most brokers will give you one when pressed.

You can do your own charting (which is cheapest), or rely on us for signals (which is easiest).

For most traders, taking a loss is a painful experience and to be postponed. The small "untaken" losses turn into big real losses, which take these traders out of the game, or make it hard for them to come back. The Eldridge Strategy forces you to take losses while they are still small.

One last point. The Eldridge Strategy profits were usually long-term rather than short-term gains, which is important from a tax point of view, such as the 299 percent profit from January 1979 through January 1981.

One caution. If you should get a buy signal, then a quick sell signal, and take a loss as a result, the IRS may deem it a "wash sale." If within a period of thirty days on either side of a sale you acquire substantially the same stock or securities, a resulting "wash sale" loss is generally not deductible for tax purposes. (Traders and dealers are exempt from "wash sales" provisions.) See IRS Code Section 1091, or your accountant. It's not likely you'd get the buy and sell signals that close together, but it is possible, and the "wash sale" rule may or may not apply to you.

Buying and selling using the Eldridge Strategy creates taxable events which can diminish profits, but those are offset by the fact that the losses are usually tax deductible, and the gains are long term, at more favorable tax rates. (See Chapter 12, "Taxflation.")

Another point is that you should not try to trade a no-load fund with less than $2,000. Most of them have a minimum requirement of $1,000, and if you took some losses early in the game and your account balance fell below the minimum, you could have to commit more capital to stay in the game.

The optimum MAs for United Services Gold Fund (See Appendix II for address and phone) are the 70-week and the 31-week.

For gold, there are two choices. You can trade just the 68-week MA and do very well, or you can use the 40-week and 11-week MAs exactly the same way we used the 70-week and 31-week MAs on U.S. Gold, and make even more money. In the past, the first strategy (trading the 68-week MA), however, produced only long-term gains, while the second strategy (using the 40- and 11-week MAs) produced short-term gains, and taxes somewhat offset the larger profits. There were also a lot more trades using the two MAs, which meant you had to watch a lot closer, and you also spent more on commissions.

We are still accumulating research on optimum MAs for several other investments, including silver, ASA and all the no-load funds, and we will keep people posted in the *Financial Success Report* and in the free one-time-only update. Until then, you can trade U.S. Gold or gold bullion, using the above strategies.

When you send for the one-time free update, if you specifically request the Eldridge Strategy MA charts and data, we will send you the current updated charts and a table of optimum Moving Averages for U.S. Gold Fund so you can pick up your own charting from there.

Remember—strategy, patience and discipline! This simple but effective rule can protect your behavior from your emotions—fear and greed—and can vastly increase your profits over those of the usual buy-and-hold investor.

The objectives of the Eldridge Strategy are to cut your losses short when the market goes against you, and never to miss a major move. The only way you could have done better than the Eldridge Strategy would have been with luck, buying at every low and selling at every high. In fact, "luck" is not a strong enough word. You would have had to be clairvoyant and omniscient.

The Eldridge Strategy isn't the only strategy that works, and it doesn't work with all investments, but it is an important new weapon in the battle for middle-class financial success.

There are many other technical Camera Angles with which you should have at least a nodding acquaintance. They require some real study. I've put them in Appendix I so you won't get stalled at this point. Once you've finished the book, you can then decide whether you want to get really serious about the technical Camera Angles. If so, Appendix I will also show you just how to start your amateur charting career. Then load up on all the books on the subjects listed in Appendix II. Good luck, and happy charting!

CHAPTER
12

TAXFLATION

Why is it that, for most people, books on making money are exciting, but books on keeping it cause eyes to glaze over? To me it is bizarre that people will risk so much and work so hard to make investment or business profits or wages, and then give most of it to an ever more rapacious tax man out of ignorance and a stubborn refusal to do the most basic homework—just because it is considered dull.

More than 70 percent of all federal revenue is not spent for the general welfare: things like roads, courts, defense and so on, which benefit us all. The majority of tax revenue is simply "transferred" (translation: stolen) from producers to nonproducers.

That's immoral (see Chapter 15, "The Spiritual Roots of the Malarial Economy"), so I feel no compunction in using every legal strategy possible to reduce my taxes. It's my war against theft. I'm not joining the confrontation-type tax rebels, nor am I willing to break the law or cheat. I don't need to—not when I can beat the tax game within the law. You can be an aggressive tax avoider and survive an audit.

As Judge Learned Hand pointed out many years ago, ". . . nobody owes any public duty to pay more [taxes] than the law demands."

There are three ways to lose money in the Malarial Economy. The first two I have already discussed, but will repeat just to keep them fresh in your mind.

1. You can lose purchasing power to inflation without actually losing dollars.

2. You can lose actual dollars to the market by being on the wrong side of the investment cycle.

You can avoid losing through (1) and (2) and end up losing to the tax collector. Any investment portfolio which does not give equal consideration to all three risks is doomed to fail. When I make investment buy and sell recommendations, I have no idea what your tax situation is, your tax bracket, or your gain or loss situation. You have to apply these factors to your own situation, and it may lead you to different conclusions from mine. Never ignore the effect of taxes on your decision. Investments that produce only income are not only exposed to inflation, but most are also fully exposed to taxation.

You can be a little early or a little late in the chills or fever cycle and still make some money, but you won't keep it unless you do some tax planning. You must protect yourself from the tax consequences of your success, which will be penalized by Uncle Sam. If you have even modest income or profits, you are now forced to consider tax planning and tax shelter.

Riding the Malarial Cycle creates tax problems for the investor. When you move out of one class of investments to another as the cycle changes, you create taxable events. Tax factors should affect your buy and sell decisions.

MATCHING CAPITAL GAINS AND LOSES

Here is how capital gains and losses impact upon your taxes.

When it comes to taxes, the capital investor has four taxable events to consider: (1) a long-term gain; (2) a long-term loss; (3) a short-term gain; and (4) a short-term loss.

Long-term gains are profits from the sale of capital investments held longer than one year, although Congress is considering reducing the holding period to six months, which they may have done by the time you read this. Check with your tax adviser. Only 40 percent of the income from a long-term gain is taxable; the other 60 percent is exempt from taxation.

Short-term gains are profits from the sale of capital investments held one year or less, and are fully taxed at ordinary income-tax rates. When you file your tax return at the end of the year, however, you do not treat each transaction separately. You have to go through a three-step matching process to determine your taxes.

1. First, you must match short-term gains and short-term losses and net

them out. If you had $10,000 in short-term gains and $5,000 in short-term losses, you netted $5,000 in short-term gains.

2. You must next match long-term gains and losses and net them out. If you had $20,000 in long-term losses, and $5,000 in long-term gains, you netted $15,000 in long-term losses.

3. You then match up your net $5,000 in short-term gains against your net $15,000 in long-term losses, giving you a bottom line net of $10,000 of long-term losses, of which $5,000 or 50 percent is an allowable deduction.

If the net result had been short-term losses, 100% would have been deductible.

Now, the problem is that capital losses are only deductible against your ordinary income up to a total of $3,000 in any one year, so, in the above example, you would end up with $2,000 in nondeductible losses, although you can carry them forward indefinitely. Obviously, if you are on top of the situation, as you get down toward the end of your tax year, you might decide to take a $2,000 long-term gain before year-end to offset your net-loss position. In the above example, that gain would be tax free, because of the offset.

If you had a net gain, you might take a year-end loss to balance against it and reduce or eliminate taxes. As you get toward the end of the year, you must make buy and sell decisions that will match up to your best tax advantage. Even the best-managed portfolio has losses as well as gains. You must keep careful track of both gains and losses along the way so you know where you stand while there is still time for year-end transactions, or there will be some unpleasant tax surprises next April 15. That's no time to find out.

You may not need to invest in sophisticated tax shelters if you do some basic tax planning. Any investment strategy that ignores tax consequences is doomed. Tax planning is for all middle-class Americans, not just the rich; and next April 15 is not the time to do it.

FIRST THINGS FIRST

Tax planning requires finding out where you stand now with regard to taxes, and what tax liability will result from taxable transactions. Then you will need a plan of action to reduce, eliminate or postpone that tax liability.

You must analyze the tax consequences of a transaction before you conclude a sale, purchase or lease. This can guide you in making decisions on timing, buying or leasing, and recognizing or postponing gains or losses.

DETERMINING YOUR TAX BRACKET

You must first know your marginal tax bracket, which is the highest level of your income subject to tax. If your taxable income for 1983 is $35,000, and you are married and filing a joint return with your spouse, your bracket is $29,900 to $35,200. For every dollar in taxable income over $29,900, you must pay thirty cents (30 percent) to Uncle Sam. If you add state income tax, you could easily approach 40 percent. Knowing your tax bracket allows you to determine the effect of tax-saving decisions.

Check last year's tax return or consult your tax preparer. Be sure to allow for increases in income this year, and the effect of any tax cuts or increases enacted by Congress.

You must always have some idea of your current federal and state tax liability. You should also know what "carry-forwards" you may have from last year's return, and a darn good idea of what next year's income and deductions will be. Also be aware of tax code changes that may affect you. Many sections of the 1982 tax law (TEFRA) include changes that are being phased in over the next few years.

Tax planning usually does no good *after* a transaction or contract is completed. Once you have sold something and received full payment, it is impossible to consider the installment-sale method or a tax-deferred trade.

Understanding your alternatives is also important. For example, if you are borrowing, you might consider having your interest rate reduced by paying "points" up front, thus increasing your current-year deductions.

Knowing the effects of taxable events beforehand enables you to make much better decisions regarding timing of purchases or sales, and whether or not to defer income or accelerate deductions for the current tax year.

TIMING

Most of us are cash-basis taxpayers and therefore recognize income for tax purposes when we receive it. Conversely, we can deduct expenses only when we actually pay them. Therefore, timing of investment transactions, payments of deductible bills, and receipt of income can be crucial near the end of a year.

Deferring income from one year to the next gives you another year's use of the tax money for investing. Likewise, an acceleration of a deductible expense into the current tax year would, in most cases, save taxes this year, if you have the cash to pay some bills early.

Many businesses are on the "accrual" basis for tax purposes. They recognize income when earned, rather than when received, and deduct expenses when incurred, rather than when paid. If you have a small business and can legally involve it in a given transaction, consider the accrual basis for timing of income or expense. You can't, however, mix cash and accrual accounting for tax purposes. It's either one or the other.

DEFERRING INCOME AT YEAR-END

If, after getting a handle on your current tax situation, you find it would be to your tax advantage not to have any more income this year, here are a few suggestions.

1. If you have a Christmas bonus coming, consider deferring it until next year.

2. If you are selling an asset at a profit, consider an installment sale. You may wish to receive no cash at all this year. Installment gains are taxed only as they are received.

3. If you are self-employed, you could delay completion of services or contracts, or defer billings.

4. Delay the sale of profitable investments (this timing is also important in short-term versus long-term gains decisions) until next year. Tax considerations are important, but don't let them prevent you from realizing gains that may vanish next year. Weigh tax considerations against market-timing considerations. Also, tax considerations should not be the only factor in taking losses that may show promise of becoming gains.

5. Delay receipt of retirement benefits.

6. Delay payment of property taxes until the new tax year, but weigh the tax savings against interest and penalties.

ACCELERATING DEDUCTIONS

1. Complete losing transactions this year to recognize deductible losses.

2. Consider making charitable contributions before year-end.

3. Prepay state income taxes this year with an estimated payment. They are deductible from your federal return.

4. Make large purchases this year where sales taxes apply. They are deductible. If the purchase is for business purposes, this will trap possible investment tax credits and depreciation deductions into this year.

5. If you can show medical deductions above 5 percent of your adjusted gross income, accelerate dental work or buy that new pair of eyeglasses this year.

See your tax adviser for your specific deductions.

TAX-FREE INCOME: MUNICIPAL BONDS

What about tax-exempt municipal bonds? Not a good idea!

You would be making a dangerous tradeoff of inflation protection for tax-free income and exposing yourself to the municipal bond market's vulnerability to a major default and potential capital losses. The Malarial Cycle has increased the risk of a large borrower going down the tubes (such as WPPS, the huge Washington State nuclear development that took bondholders down for $2½ billion when it defaulted). The rest of the "muni" bond market can be adversely affected because of "guilt by association."

There are also market-price risks. In an era of strained municipal budgets, a shrinking urban tax base and rising social burdens, you could wake up one morning and find your AAA muni bond has been downgraded to A—and the market price will fall accordingly. This recently happened to Chicago. There are real market risks even in AAA-rated munis.

Also, as you now know, a rise in interest rates during the fever would give you capital losses that are only partially recovered during the chills.

IRA AND KEOGH PLANS

Several years ago Congress created two new tax-sheltered vehicles—the IRA (Individual Retirement Account) and the Keogh plan. The IRA was for employees and the Keogh plan was for the self-employed.

With these new vehicles, each person is permitted to set aside certain amounts of his earned income with an approved trustee, which can be deducted from your total income before computing your taxes. This tax-deferred money can be left in that account to be invested and grow without taxation until age fifty-nine and a half, at which time you can begin to withdraw the money. It will then be taxed as ordinary income.

The IRA permits each wage earner to set aside $2,000 annually, and an unemployed spouse can set aside $250 every year.

Before January 1, 1984, the Keogh plan permitted the self-employed to contribute up to $15,000 each year, but from 1984 on, that limit was removed, creating even more incentive to become "self-employed," a subject I will discuss later.

During the time the money is in the account, any profits from investment will accumulate tax free. This means that buy and sell transactions, interest earnings or dividends in the IRA or Keogh plan are not taxable events.

As soon as Congress liberalized the rules, huge advertising campaigns were mounted by financial institutions trying to get their hands on this money, as it was dependable long-term investment money with which they could make long-term lending plans.

Millions of Americans went for IRAs and Keoghs, creating a fascinating phenomenon which has been little noticed and certainly underreported. It forced Americans to become very conscious of long-range financial planning and retirement at a much earlier age.

The IRA and Keogh plans are the greatest inventions since cheese nachos (available at 7-Eleven stores. Don't see Appendix II. Just checking to see if you're still awake). The only drawback is that the Congress inserted a provision in the 1981 tax bill, clause 314b, which made it illegal for you to put "hard assets" such as gold, silver, antiques, diamonds, collectibles or "anything the Secretary of the Treasury shall deem to be a collectible" in IRAs, Keoghs or any "self-directed" retirement plan (although this restriction will probably not apply after January 1, 1984, to a Keogh plan amended to become a "qualified retirement plan" with you as your own trustee, as explained later in this chapter). This "special interest" provision was written by the Savings Bank Association to recapture money going into collectibles, and Free the Eagle has been fighting to have it repealed, but so far, it still applies.

The other common pitfall of the typical IRA or pre-1984 Keogh is that the trustee usually has the independent right to decide where that money will be invested. Strangely enough, the trustee tends to feel that the best place to put that money is in the institution that employs him. If you start an IRA or a Keogh with a bank or a savings and loan, your money will always be in a CD.

There is, however, the "self-directed" IRA offered by brokerage houses, "families" of mutual funds and some banks, where you can make the decision on how and where the money will be invested (with the exception of the 314b restriction).

You now know that in the Malarial Economy you must be able to switch investments with the cycles. If you are going to keep your tax-sheltered retirement money within the framework of this philosophy, you have to have a "self-directed" IRA and/or other retirement plan and pick investments that don't just produce income but also beat inflation. Here are three of my favorites:

1. A family of mutual funds, as long as that family allows "no-load" or "low-load" switching from one fund to another. You can open your plan with that mutual fund family, putting the money temporarily in their money-market fund. When you believe precious metals are about to go up, that the fever is beginning, you can move into their gold fund. If you believe growth stocks are the place to be, you move into their growth fund. When it looks as if interest rates are at their peak and bonds are depressed, you switch to the bond fund. Usually, all this requires is a phone call. The switching fee is usually nominal (about $5) if you select the correct fund.

Here are five acceptable fund families which have an acceptable mix of funds.

Bull & Bear Group
11 Hanover Square
New York, NY 19005
800-942-6911

Lexington Group
580 Sylvan Ave.
P.O. Box 1515
Englewood Cliffs, NJ 07632
800-526-4791

Fidelity Group of Funds
82 Devonshire Street
Boston, MA 02103
800-225-6190 (call collect)

United Services
P.O. Box 2098
Universal City, TX 78148
800-531-5777
512-696-1234

* Strategic Investors
Available from brokers or financial planners.
See Newcastle Financial Group, Appendix II

For a complete listing, write for the current Directory of No-Load Mutual Funds: No-Load Mutual Fund Association, Inc., Valley Forge, PA 19481 (215-783-7600). Send $1.00 to cover cost of mailing.

2. Some real estate funds are strongly oriented to capital appreciation but uniquely designed for tax-exempt investment. A typical fund will yield around 10 percent currently with additional tax-free interest equal to 75 percent or more of the appreciated value of the real property. This "bonus" amount is payable when the property is sold, and is a hedge against inflation. It is not mortgage-financed, as leverage is a no-no for IRAs.

3. Oil and gas income funds. A typical fund will consist of several limited partnerships providing investors with regular quarterly income from producing oil and gas properties. Each partnership is structured to enable IRAs to receive tax-deferred income and offers an opportunity for high current returns with the ability to parallel inflation.

The above IRA instruments are usually available through brokers, financial planners or, in the case of the mutual funds, from the fund itself. Newcastle Financial Group (see Appendix II) stays on top of all the new offerings in this area.

* Strategic is a "load" fund, charging a sales commission up front. It is usually sold by brokers or financial planners, while the other "families" are "no load," or "low load," and shares are bought directly from the fund by mail. Strategic's gold fund has been such an outstanding performer, however, that its performance more than offsets the commissions, and it has the same low-cost switch privileges as the other funds.

THE TAX-FREE SWINGER

We recently did a study to determine the best kinds of investment for your tax-sheltered retirement plan. The conventional wisdom says that you should simply put it in an interest-bearing account, such as a CD at the bank. The argument is that capital gains are already taxed at very favorable rates, so why have any capital gains transactions in a tax-deferred plan? Settle for interest.

The conventional wisdom, however, comes up against the reality that these plans, by their very nature, are long-term plans, and the Malarial Economy is a long-term reality. Even though taxes are not a factor, inflation is, and you have to have capital gains to beat inflation during the fever, although, during the chills, the lack of taxation on the earned interest does tend to lengthen the periods during which earned interest gives you a positive return.

If an IRA makes up the bulk of your retirement investment program, you ought to take a very conservative approach and ride only the long tidal waves of the Malarial Economy according to the recommendations I have already made.

If, however, your IRA represents only a small portion of your total investment program, and you have some speculative money you use for swinging in the markets, it is a terrific place for your trading account, as long as you avoid leverage. If you're going to be trading growth or penny stocks, and assume that you will have profits (which you should assume or you shouldn't be doing it), use your IRA for that purpose. Then you don't have to agonize over whether or not you dare hold a weakening investment long enough to get a long-term gain, or worry about matching up gains and losses. You can do what the market dictates without regard to tax considerations, as all profits are completely tax-sheltered until you start withdrawing the money. When you begin withdrawals, you are taxed at ordinary income rates, but because you have been able to invest the money that you would have paid in taxes over the years, you should have a lot more money. With proper planning, you should be sufficiently tax-sheltered to soften or completely eliminate the tax impact of your withdrawals upon reaching the required-withdrawal age.

BETTER THAN AN IRA?

As I mentioned earlier, the new expanded Keogh rules have made it very advantageous to become "self-employed," because, along with the other tax benefits of having your own business, you can shelter from taxes far more income than the $2,000 annual IRA pittance, although you now can and should keep your IRA too. The new rules allow up to $30,000, or 25 percent of compensation, whichever is the lesser, in defined *contribution* plans. Defined *benefit* plans, under certain conditions, can be even more generous, especially if you are over forty-five.

Every employed person is really in business for himself, selling his personal services to his employer. Many of you should make it official by immediately establishing "independent contractor" status and beginning to reap a cornucopia of legal tax and tax-free pension benefits.

The steps that should be taken by a presently employed person before he can become "self-employed" are as follows:

1. Establish independent contractor status with your present employer.
2. Decide whether or not you should form a corporation, a Subchapter S corporation, a partnership or a proprietorship.
3. Contract with your newly formed business entity for your personal services, thereby making your time and talent the chief assets of the newly formed business.
4. Your business then contracts with your employer to provide the services that you are now providing as an employee.
5. Your employer pays your salary to the business, which then gives you a salary and bonuses and forms the juicy pension plans presently allowed under tax law. You can even employ other members of your family and pay them salaries, if it is to your advantage to have some of your income transferred to their 1040s to get it into even lower tax brackets.

BECOMING AN INDEPENDENT CONTRACTOR

Before you can change your employee status to "self-employed" if you presently receive much of your income from wages, you must first become an "independent contractor." That's the only way you can convert your wages to business income.

Authors, athletes, entertainers, doctors, dentists, lawyers and people who operate a going business, such as a hardware store or convenience market, are already independent contractors. But what about the engineer who works for an engineering firm? Can he become an independent contractor to take advantage of the best tax shelter still available—his own business? The answer is, "Maybe."

Since 1960, the IRS has fought efforts to establish "independent contractor" status. They know better than anyone the tax benefits you can have by doing so, so they have tried to make it harder, but they have not yet succeeded in making it impossible. In fact, in 1982 Congress clearly defined two categories of nonemployees. For tax purposes, independent real estate agents and direct sellers are not employees, and the people for whom they work are not employers.

As for other occupations, Congress ducked the issue, continuing indefinitely the current ban on further IRS rule-making. The law is murky, but if you follow these guidelines and get your employer to agree, you can be an independent contractor:

1. You must control the number of hours you work and your schedule.

2. Your compensation must be calculated on the basis of productivity, sales commissions, project completion or anything *except* the number of hours worked.

3. It helps if your home or other property is the principal place of business. If the work must be performed on another's premises, arrange to pay a fair rental (compensation can be adjusted accordingly).

4. All these details must be in a written contract that also states you will not be treated as an employee for federal tax purposes. Also, make sure the contract describes services not usually performed by an "employee."

Control is the central issue: Does the employer have the right to determine how you perform the task, or does he only control the end result? Trusted employees are often given the freedom to come and go as they please, as long as the job gets done.

How do you persuade your employer to let you become an independent contractor?

First, calculate your cost to your present boss. Include your salary and fringe benefits, which might include a health plan, life insurance, a retirement plan and the employer's share of Social Security and unemployment taxes. These benefits usually cost more than 30 percent of your gross salary.

Now, figure your tax and financial picture if you took the same money, ran it through your business and set up your own retirement and fringe-benefit program; and compare it with the same picture as an employee.

To make it more palatable to your employer, offer to contract for your services at less than your employer's present total cost. Just be sure that you come out ahead.

Most very large companies won't cooperate, but smaller firms will often be willing to pay equal or less money to your new business, just to keep you happy. The result could be a large tax deduction.

CORPORATION BENEFITS

Once you have established yourself as an independent contractor, you must weigh the relative merits of incorporating. Generally, if your income is more than $50,000 you must at least consider a corporation.

Look at the federal income-tax rate for corporations and the comparable rate for individuals.

CORPORATE TAXES		PERSONAL INCOME TAXES	
TAXABLE INCOME	TAX RATE	TAXABLE INCOME	TAX RATE
$0 to 25,000	15%	$0 to 23,500	11%–28%
25,000 to 50,000	18%	23,500 to 55,300	28%–45%
50,000 to 75,000	30%	over 55,300	50%
75,000 to 100,000	40%		
Over 100,000	46%		

As you can see, corporate tax rates are lower across the board. Personal income gets into the higher brackets at much lower income levels.

Corporate stockholders are not taxed individually on earnings that are retained in the business. The decision as to what will be paid out or retained is up to the directors (you and your family), who are elected by the stockholders (guess who?).

If the corporation is sold or liquidated, cash that reflects earnings which have been kept in the corporation and not paid out to stockholders (you and your family) will probably be taxed at the lower long-term capital gains rate, a maximum of 20 percent.

There is potential for double taxation. First, the corporation is taxed on its profits, then the owner is taxed on the dividends received from the corporation. In the worst case, with bad planning, the owner of the corporation could end up with as little as 27 percent of the corporate pretax income over $100,000. However, proper planning should eliminate this problem, which can be offset by a lot of the deductible benefits a corporation can give you, things which would not be deductible for an individual. For example:

You can pay out most of the income to yourself in salary and bonuses, which are deductible for the corporation. However, consult your tax adviser regarding unreasonable compensation penalties.

You can borrow from the corporation in one tax year and wipe out the loan by declaring a bonus in the subsequent tax year. That way you can determine in which year the taxes will be paid, a not inconsiderable advantage.

Your corporation can buy life insurance for you up to a face value of $50,000, deduct the premiums, and they are not taxable to you. You cannot now deduct your insurance premiums.

The corporation generally gets the same deductions as individuals, but this does not apply to purely personal deductions, such as medical expenses or alimony payments, and the corporation cannot offset capital losses against other kinds of income as an individual can. The corporation also cannot take a deduction or credit for political contributions, but can deduct 85 percent of dividends from other domestic corporations.

The corporation can provide medical and disability insurance and reimbursement of all uninsured medical expenses. These are tax-deductible corporate expenses, and not taxable income to you, as long as you do the same thing for all employees. As you or your family are the sole employees, that works out fine as long as they are not officers and/or shareholders.

The corporation can have a different tax year from you as an individual, creating opportunities to shift income from one year to another legally.

The corporation can also protect you from some legal liabilities. In theory, a corporation can go broke and leave large debts while the owners are untouched. This can be a considerable advantage in a product-liability case, which could involve big bucks.

However, as a practical matter, when a small corporation borrows money, the lender usually insists on a personal guarantee by the stockholders, so this liability protection does have its limitations. Also, doctors and lawyers, who are especially vulnerable to malpractice suits, had better keep their personal malpractice insurance current, because they could be personally liable for negligence judgments in excess of the policy limits.

If your corporation should lose money, you cannot deduct the losses against other earnings on your personal tax returns, although the loss may be carried back three years and forward against corporate profits for up to fifteen years. This disadvantage can also be overcome by using a "Subchapter S" corporation, where the losses can pass through to you for tax purposes. If you are merely using the corporation as a "personal service corporation" and you know you will have net positive income, this is not a consideration.

For example, if you are starting a business that you expect to show losses for a year or two before it gets off the ground, then it might be to your advantage to keep that business outside your corporation and have your corporation acquire it later when it is profitable, so that those early losses will be fully deductible, assuming you have other income to offset them.

The advantages of incorporating will often outweigh the disadvantages. You can decide what activities will be left in your corporation or kept outside your corporation, and have it either way.

Start-up costs vary widely but need not be significant. You must also be conscientious and scrupulous about corporate resolutions, minute books and board and stockholder meetings. The IRS will constantly be looking for evidence that you are not acting like a corporation, and not only can you lose the tax benefits but you could be hit with penalties and interest.

PENSION PLANS FOR THE SELF-EMPLOYED

It's in the area of pensions that being in business for yourself really pays off. Because of the 1984 liberalized pension rules, this applies to incorporated and nonincorporated businesses.

You can set up liberal pension and/or profit-sharing plans. Both the money contributed to the plan and the investment profits are deferred from taxation until retirement, as with an IRA, but contributions are far more generous and flexible than under an IRA or the old Keogh plans. In some instances, business owners have been able to put more money into these plans than they took in salary. If you now have a Keogh plan, you should "amend" it to take advantage of the new, more liberal rules.

As of January 1, 1984, the following tax and retirement benefits are now open to regular corporations, "Subchapter S" corporations, proprietorships and family partnerships.

1. IRS-approved retirement plans. This fringe benefit gets my unequivocal endorsement. You get a guaranteed 100 percent tax deduction for each year's contribution. Earnings accumulate tax deferred, and with some creative planning your pension plan can be free from estate taxes at your death. It is also shielded from creditors.

In 1984, Keogh plans will die, but they will be resurrected in more generous form, so your present Keogh can be amended to give you the same retirement benefits as corporate plans, including the removal of the $15,-000 limit. And you can be your own trustee.

Qualified retirement plans come in several varieties—defined contribution plans, defined benefit plans and combinations of both. If you plan to retire at sixty-five and are under forty-five, a Defined Contribution Plan will probably allow you to set aside more money. Above forty-five, however, a Defined Benefit Plan will generally allow you to set aside more money than a Defined Contribution Plan, and hence more money sheltered for retirement.

2. Cash or Deferred Compensation programs. These programs offer great flexibility for you and your employees (if any). They are expressly blessed by Internal Revenue Code Sections 401(k) and 402(a)(8). Employees can reduce their present salaries and funnel the reductions into the company's retirement plan. The money contributed to or earned in the pension fund escapes federal taxes. The monies are deemed to be employer contributions, although they must be held in a separate, nonforfeitable account for the employee.

A "cash option" plan participant can withdraw sums from his personal account in case of "hardship." Second, he can withdraw his accumulated funds at retirement as part of a lump-sum distribution from the qualified plan, and use a special ten-year income-averaging option for lump-sum distributions. You can't do that with an IRA.

You can also do something with a corporate retirement plan that you can't do with an IRA or a noncorporate plan. You can borrow from it up to $50,000, or half of the vested pension, whichever is less. The pension plan defers taxes on the interest it receives on the note; at the same time you are deducting it on your personal income tax return.

GET MOVING

I am astounded at how many sophisticated people have not taken advantage of independent contractor status. All you need as an excuse is the right kind of job and a moderately high tax bracket.

You can set up your own business format or use an attorney to set up a professionally structured form that suits your individual needs. Whichever you decide to do, you should read up on the subject so you know enough to do it properly or to understand fully what your attorney and accountant are doing.

The best known do-it-yourself book on incorporating is *How to Form Your Own Corporation Without a Lawyer for Under $50,* by Ted Nicholas. *Inc. Yourself,* by Judith McQuown, is another.

Al Lowry's book *How to Become Financially Successful by Owning Your Own Business* has an outstanding section on small-business formats and is a must for the small-business owner. Also consider the American Entrepreneurs Association Incorporation kits (see Appendix II).

The best, most complete word on setting up those wonderful pension benefits is in the *Howard Ruff Financial Planning Home Study Course* (see Appendix II).

Your accountant and attorney may have advised against those strategies. Make them defend their reasons.

The contest between taxpayers and tax collectors will go on forever. As they plug one loophole, we'll find another legal one that will hold up when the IRS audits you. If the stakes are high enough, you would be foolish not to give it your best shot. A business of your own is a worthy piece of ammunition in this ongoing warfare.

STILL NEED AN IRA?

Even if you have a fine business plan, you are also allowed to have an IRA, and you should, even though the amounts you can shelter are comparatively small. Two thousand bucks a year is still two thousand bucks, and for most of you, that's a lot of money. That IRA is well worth having.

TAX SHELTER

You should also consider buying investments that will give you tax shelter and are economically sound for the Malarial Cycle.

The term "tax shelter" is both gimmicky and inaccurate. A better term would be tax-advantaged investment. Merrill Lynch labels its deals "tax investments." Paine Webber refers to them as "tax incentive investments." These terms focus on the most important aspect of tax shelters— the investment.

A properly structured tax shelter will throw off more deductions than income, giving you paper losses that can be used to offset your income from your job, dividends, interest, etc., but it must also be a sound investment with good prospects for profits in the Malarial Economy.

Many tax shelters also carry serious legal risks. The IRS is fighting an all-out war against "abusive" tax shelters, and now has dictatorial powers to define "abusive." A lot of shelters you used to get away with no longer pass muster.

Until 1983, many tax-shelter investors looked only for tax savings, ignoring sound economic fundamentals. They assumed that even if the IRS disallowed the shelter, it would be three or four years before they had to pay the tax, together with simple interest at 12 percent, which was tax deductible. If the taxpayer was in a 70 percent bracket and the IRS shot down his high-flying tax shelter, his net interest cost amounted to 4 percent per annum. In the interim, his tax money would have been invested elsewhere. The "audit roulette" gamble was worth it.

This logic no longer holds up. The interest rate for tax deficiencies will now be determined twice yearly and compounded daily. The current rate is 11 percent! With the maximum tax rate now at 50 percent (down from 70 percent), the reward for a winning tax gamble is less than it used to be, and the penalty for a loser is much greater.

But there's more. The Economic Recovery Tax Act of 1981 (ERTA) added two new negligence penalties and a whopper for overvaluation of tax shelters. That mislabeled abortion called The Tax Equity and Fiscal Responsibility Act of 1982 (TEFRA) added another penalty for taking "questionable" tax positions in your return and a special penalty aimed at the promoters for "abusive" tax shelters.

The IRS now has broader powers of discretion to define "abusive." The rules are ever-changing. In the government's never-ending pursuit of more and more money, it becomes more and more repressive and reaches for more and more Gestapo-like power, and it is getting it. Congress authorized hiring five thousand new agents under the last tax bill who are strictly compliance types, going after "abusive" tax shelters and "tax protestors." In the constant running battle between democracies and their citizens over who gets to keep the money, the government has taken a big leap forward in its power to confiscate your earnings. Any novel tax scheme that hasn't been tested in tax court, or passed an audit, should be left for someone else to experiment with. (See Chapter 10, "How Not to Get Ripped Off," for a discussion of tax-shelter scams.)

Even with these hazards, many tax shelters can beat the IRS within their own rules. I like (1) residential real estate; (2) certain research and development projects (R&D); (3) hydroelectric projects; (4) oil and gas drilling; and (5) equipment leasing—all of which I will discuss shortly.

If all the advice I gave you earlier in this chapter still won't save you from a big tax bill, don't panic into buying the first tax shelter that comes along, even if you do get a "free trip to Bermuda, just for listening." The tax-shelter peddlers tend to proliferate at year-end, looking for buyers who are running out of time to avoid paying large tax bills. Remember, tax savings are only part of the justification for tax shelters.

Savings are achieved by deducting operating "losses," including "depreciation." "Investment tax credits" are also a major factor. Generally, tax shelters are also highly leveraged, giving the taxpayer the advantage of minimum investment in comparison to the amount of tax benefits. Any profits are deferred until future years and are usually taxed at capital gains rates, not as ordinary income.

With all these advantages, it is no wonder many investors have jumped into shelters without looking, particularly when, in some cases, you can wait until the last few days of the year to invest and still receive the benefits of a full year's depreciation and investment tax credit.

Before you can really understand the tax shelter principle, you must understand the magic of "depreciation" and investment tax credit (ITC). Let's use income-producing real estate as an example.

DEPRECIATION

Under our present tax laws the government allows you to assume that the "improved" portion of your real estate investment, that is, the building (not the land on which the building sits), is losing value every year. You are allowed, within certain limits, to assume a "life," over which time the investment will become worthless. That's "depreciation." You can depreciate any capital investment used in a trade or business or held for the production of income. Items that cannot be depreciated are inventory, land, and such capital investments as stocks and bonds. Some properties are "amortized" rather than depreciated.

You can then deduct from your income as an expense that percentage of the depreciation to which you're entitled each year.

If you use a fifteen-year life, each year you could then deduct about 6 percent of the "cost basis" of your building from your income on your tax return, using a separate form 4562.

Your "basis" is the purchase price of the building (again, not including the land), plus the cost of capitalized improvements.

For practical purposes, depreciation is a legal fiction. In an inflationary environment, the value of the property is actually going up. Depreciation is a deductible "expense" for which you do not actually have to lay out any cash.

The magic of depreciation allows you to buy a piece of property, have a positive spendable cash flow and yet show a substantial loss for tax purposes.

Depreciation, when added to interest costs and other deductible business expenses, generally gives you enough excess losses in a residential real estate investment to have deductions against your ordinary income—about $4,000 tax shelter for every $100,000 of income property you own.

All tax shelters utilize the depreciation concept. Congress has enacted special provisions in the law that give certain investments faster depreciation schedules. You get larger deductions if Congress feels there is some social or economic benefit from granting this special privilege. This includes buildings of historical value that you have refurbished.

Oil and gas exploration and mining throw off "depletion allowances," which work much like depreciation. You are allowed to assume that the oilfield or mine is being "depleted," so you deduct the depletion allowance from the income.

INVESTMENT TAX CREDIT (ITC)

Investment tax credit, or ITC, is a more powerful tax benefit than depreciation. Depreciation is a tax deduction. It is deducted from income before computing taxes, and the value of a tax deduction depends on your tax bracket. If you are in the 30 percent tax bracket, any additional deduction is worth thirty cents on the dollar.

ITC, however, is deducted directly from your bottom-line taxes. It is worth one hundred cents on the dollar! Unlike depreciation, which goes on year after year, ITC pays off in the year the tax shelter is purchased, unless it reduces your taxable income to less than zero, in which case you may carry the ITC forward.

Some good tax shelters will give you both ITC and depreciation, along with other deductions.

Investment tax credits have been enacted into the law by Congress to encourage businessmen and investors to buy certain kinds of equipment, generally for the purpose of stimulating a particular industry.

Generally, when a businessman buys a new piece of equipment or machinery for business purposes, he is given an investment tax credit. This includes trucks, airplanes, drill presses, computers and so on.

The combination of high leverage, ITC and depreciation can create tax magic—tax savings in the first year of an investment that exceed the amount of money you actually invest, although the IRS and the Congress are making that more difficult all the time.

If you put 10 percent down on a tax-sheltered investment which is subject to ITC, and the ITC is 10 percent, your down payment actually costs you nothing.

Among my favorite tax shelters that generally produce ITC are hydroelectric projects and equipment leasing.

There are other tax credits that apply to specific investments, such as—in the case of hydroelectric projects—an energy tax credit of 11 percent.

There are also energy tax credits available to homeowners for installing energy-saving devices or systems such as solar heating and insulation.

RECAPTURE

One hazard of depreciation and investment tax credit is that if the investment is disposed of or converted too soon, the IRS will "recapture" the tax savings.

In the case of depreciation this is how it works: You have "depreciated" the property down to a "basis" considerably less than your original basis, and you dispose of or convert the property. Any gains on the difference between what you paid for the property and what you sold it for will not be taxed as they would be with most investments. Instead, you will pay taxes on the difference between your *depreciated* "basis" and what you sold it for. This, in effect, "recaptures" the depreciation benefits you received from the investment and treats them as ordinary income.

That makes it very advantageous to trade, rather than sell, an inflated equity in a depreciated building for an equity in a larger building in a tax-deferred exchange, which is allowed under IRS Code Section 1031. That way you have an adjusted basis in the new building, and you avoid having to shell out cash in the form of taxable-gains taxes.

In the case of investment tax credit, the recapture can be pretty painful. Each year for five years, 20 percent of the tax credit becomes "nonrecapturable" if the asset is sold or otherwise disposed of. For example, if you bought a truck and sold it after two years, 60 percent of the ITC you claimed would still have to be paid back to the IRS.

If you decide to buy another truck, you have a new ITC; however, you are not allowed to offset the new ITC against the recapture. They are considered separate tax events and must be treated separately. You have to pay the recaptured ITC with hard-earned, after-tax dollars.

Because the amount of ITC you must recapture depends on how long you hold the investment, a tax-shelter investment should be a long-term deal, which means it must be a sound investment.

Now let's examine my favorite tax shelters.

1. Residential income property. The ideal tax shelter will enjoy most of the tax benefits described above, plus, it will also be inflation-hedged, providing capital growth, rising income distributions, or both. Improved income-producing real estate is the ideal tax shelter for most amateur investors because it is a fine inflation hedge, the principles are simple, and there are no restrictions on using the paper losses from real estate to offset other income, unlike many other tax-sheltered investments which have such restrictions.

Income-producing real estate makes sense through both the chills and fever phases of the cycle. During the fever you get capital gains as prices go up, and during the chills you'll probably lose only about half the paper profits made during the fever—ten steps forward and five steps backward. During both the chills and the fever cycles, however, you receive income from rentals, and you get tax shelter from deductible expenses, interest payments and depreciation. You need tax shelter during the chills because then you have taxable ordinary income through earned interest from bonds and money market funds. During the fever, you have capital gains, plus ordinary income from dividends (mining stocks, oil stocks and so on) to be sheltered.

You should have some depreciable real estate investments in your portfolio before you consider other tax shelters. If you don't want to buy and manage property yourself, then buy into a good public or private syndication (see Chapter 8, "Real Estate").

2. R & D partnerships. Fortunes have been made recently in high-technology companies introducing high-growth products. Witness the astounding growth of Northern California's "Silicon Valley." However, individual investors have been all but excluded from investing in these companies at the early stages when growth potential was greatest. Most of these companies have been financed by venture capitalists, who in turn

drew their capital from large tax-exempt investors such as pension plans and university endowments. By the time individuals got a chance, much of the growth potential was history, and picking the right stock was a low-odds bet.

Recently, however, a new investment vehicle has emerged. Research and development (R&D) partnerships give sophisticated individual investors an opportunity to invest in new technology with attractive tax benefits—if they can avoid the hazards. The tax structure of R&D partnerships is so attractive that they have proliferated, all too frequently with dubious economic consequences. Also, some partnerships are organized for tax reasons only, with little or no regard for the economic soundness of the project or the skills of management. Tax advantages have turned into huge writeoffs—real losses of real money.

If carefully selected, however, R&D partnerships can offer a unique combination of tax benefits with high return potential. The age-old problem is: How do you separate the wheat from the chaff? The following guidelines should help.

R&D partnerships rarely fail because the technology fails—financial management and marketing inadequacy are far more frequent causes of failure. Always keep in mind the following priorities, in this order: management, marketing and technology. Here are some specific criteria:

(A) Management capability is necessary in (1) the general partner who manages your investment; (2) the research organization; and (3) the marketing and manufacturing entity. Here there is no substitute for experience—lots of it.

(B) It is much easier to enter a growing market with a new product than it is to enter a stable, stratified market where established companies are fighting tooth and nail for market share and survival.

(C) Avoid consumer products such as toys or household gadgets. Successful fads like Rubik's cubes and Cabbage Patch Dolls are few and far between.

(D) An independent general partner should protect the limited partners. His rewards should be the same as theirs, not skimmed off the top.

(E) Invest in improvements or advances in proven technology. The same tax benefits are available for developmental work as for unproven widgets. When a prototype already exists and only needs additional work to reach the market, it's a much better risk than basic research. Successful revolutionary products are extremely rare.

A project offering improvement in an existing, growing market is a much safer investment than one proposing to revolutionize an industry.

(F) The project should reach commercial readiness in no more than eighteen months to two years because cash flow will not begin until then.

(G) Avoid excessive leverage. Most tax-shelter deals involve investing some cash up front and signing a recourse note committing you to pay more money in the future. If you put up your money this year and the note requires payments in subsequent years, you probably can't get the full tax write-off that you would have gotten had the money all been paid in the year in which the initial cash was paid. Something between all cash and very little cash is reasonable.

Excessive leverage is usually bad economics. In order to pay off the loans, you are relying on income from the new product, which is already carrying a heavy debt load, probably limiting the growth necessary to provide a return. Excessive leverage can also prompt the IRS to shoot down your entire deduction, adding a stiff penalty to boot.

(H) The income is generally based on royalties, which should be a percentage of gross sales rather than net profit. "Net" is too difficult to define. Royalties should probably range between 5 percent and 9 percent. Higher royalties may cripple the project. A lower rate will stretch the return too far into the future.

(I) Are the sales needed to generate the expected returns really achievable? Projects which produce millions of dollars in sales in a short time are few and far between.

Sound R&D partnerships can reasonably offer an immediate deduction of between 80 percent and 90 percent of the first year's investment, and a conversion of ordinary income to capital gain. They also offer an opportunity to share in the profits, excitement and personal satisfaction of being involved in new technology.

(J) If you consider only the potential tax deductions, and ignore basic soundness and economic prospects, you could lose money and tax benefits.

3. Hydroelectric projects. Hydro projects are only economically feasible because of two comparatively recent developments.

Federal law, and in some instances state laws, now require that utilities buy privately produced power at rates determined by state utilities commissions. This was originally intended to encourage developers of home power units, such as windmills. Because these rates are set by the utilities commission and tend to rise with inflation, the income is inflation-hedged.

The second development is technological. Many years ago, when most of our big power projects were built, high dams with a large fall of water from a major river were required. Now small, economical power-producing units can tap power from streams that are comparative trickles. Generally it's not even necessary to build a dam.

Many experts are forecasting severe electrical power shortages in the 80s. In spite of the current surpluses, demand for power will probably exceed supply, and rates paid for power will rise and provide an excellent inflation hedge for private power producers.

In addition, such projects can provide big tax benefits. Most of the costs should qualify for both the 10 percent ITC and the 11 percent energy tax credit—direct dollar-for-dollar offsets against your bottom-line tax bill. In addition, most of the cost of development is expected to qualify for a five-year life—a beautiful, fast depreciation write-off.

Investment opportunities are generally available at two stages of development—when (1) the initial engineering and feasibility studies are being done, and (2) at the point of actual development.

In the first stage, the risk is greater because power-sale contracts cannot usually be obtained until all feasibility studies and government permits have been issued—but tax benefits and cash distributions tend to be much greater.

In the second stage, the risk is less when permits have been issued and a power-sale agreement has been obtained, but the potential rate of return is usually less.

This industry is unusually attractive because it is still in its infancy.

4. Oil and gas drilling. The United States will be heavily dependent on oil and gas in the foreseeable future. The 1982–83 downturn in prices is attributable to the worldwide recession, high production levels by some exporting countries desperately needing foreign exchange, and lower heating-oil demand during the mild winter of 1982. Most of those factors are behind us, and the present high levels of price-depressing inventories cannot continue much longer. This industry will rebound.

Despite synfuels, windmills, geothermal and solar energy, the domestic oil and gas industry will remain our largest source of energy for a long time. Well-chosen oil- and gas-drilling partnerships are among the finest, soundest tax shelters.

The basic value of oil- and gas-drilling partnerships is, in part, to be found in the balance between costs of production and the price of oil. If costs drop faster than crude-oil prices, even during an oil glut, you can still make money. Well-structured drilling partnerships were hot in 1980–81 and were economically good investments then. They can be even better today. While it's true that the price of oil is down, the cost of producing a barrel is down even more. In 1981, it cost about $14 to find that barrel of oil. Today it's close to $9. During the last ten years, the price of oil has escalated 650 percent, but the production costs have increased only 300 percent. Profits per barrel are still high, even if oil drops to the more pessimistic estimates of $22 per barrel. That's why oil-drilling partnerships are still good deals.

What about the price of oil over the next two to five years? No one really knows for sure, but one thing seems clear. Unless prices fall drastically, investors in oil- and gas-drilling projects aren't likely to be hurt. And if prices go up—which is likely during the next three years—you will have that much more to gain. A return to 1979 consumption levels alone would wipe out the 1983 surpluses in a hurry.

The tax laws provide for full deduction of "intangible" drilling and development costs as they occur. They can run as high as 70 percent to 80 percent of the initial investment. These are the costs incurred for drilling a hole in the ground in preparation for locating and producing oil and gas. If you leverage your investment by borrowing, write-offs could go as high as three times the cash invested.

Other costs are capitalized and deducted over a period of five years. The equipment (pumps, piping and the like) might also produce an investment tax credit. If successful, your drilling partnership will produce a partially tax-free stream of income, because the income is offset by a "depletion allowances" deduction of 15 percent.

5. Equipment leasing. Equipment leasing is a multibillion-dollar industry involving a vast array of equipment ranging from computers to jet aircraft, boxcars to cable TV, oil tankers, shipping containers, medical equipment, farm machinery and more. Much of the investment in equipment leasing is done through limited partnerships which pool investors' money to take advantage of the tax opportunities.

The typical equipment-leasing transaction occurs in two phases:

(a) A leasing company purchases equipment and leases it to a corporation or other business entity which will use the equipment in its business.

(b) After a few years, the leasing company will usually sell the leased equipment, resulting in a loss of the tax benefits to the leasing company.

Now, how do you become involved? You invest in a limited partnership or trust which buys the equipment and then leases it out. You get depreciation, interest expense deductions, investment tax credits in some cases (in the first year) and the residual value of the equipment. Your deductible tax benefits are limited by the amount you have invested or for which you are "at risk."

An equipment-leasing deal can give you multiple write-offs. The partnership can leverage its investment in the first year to produce tax losses two to four times greater than the original cash investment by borrowing 50 percent to 80 percent of the equipment-purchase money. Additional paper losses can be produced in the second and third years, if the deal is properly structured.

Equipment-leasing deals have always been thought of as tax shelters for only the very wealthy. This is no longer true. Some require as little as $10,000.

For $10,000, it is not uncommon in a short-term lease to get an investment tax credit (a direct offset against your income tax) of as much as $1,600, and tax-sheltered income over a five-year period. Some equipment-leasing projects can give three to four dollars in deductions for each dollar invested. For high-bracket taxpayers, this frees up tax dollars for other investments. If you put those liberated tax dollars into a solid real estate investment, the result is a higher net worth.

However, equipment tax shelters limit your tax benefits to the amounts you have invested or for which you are "at risk," which usually means the financing will have to be done with a "full recourse" note, meaning you are personally liable for the note if the deal goes sour and the sale of equipment doesn't generate enough cash to pay off the financing.

EVALUATING TAX SHELTERS

Where do you look for a good tax shelter? Major brokerage houses and financial planners all sell them. Newcastle Financial Group (see Appendix II) does a super job of "due diligence" research and screening, and is totally in tune with the Malarial Economy philosophy.

When looking at tax shelters, get help from a good accountant. If you do your own planning and research, here are some pointers in evaluating a tax shelter:

1. Would you consider this a good investment without the tax shelter?
2. Is the tax benefit greater than the possible negative cash flow? (You'll need to know your tax bracket to figure this.)

3. Will you be "at risk" for the leveraged portion of the investment? With many shelters, if you're not, the IRS may disallow tax benefits. That's not true of real estate, where your liability is usually limited to the property, and your other assets are not at risk.

4. Does it have a true business purpose, that is, to produce income, or has it been formed just to sell tax benefits? If so, the IRS will shoot it down.

5. What and where are the assets of the tax shelter, and how are they valued?

6. Could you withstand an economic loss if the shelter's projected scenario turns out wrong?

7. What are the chances the IRS might determine the tax shelter to be a sham? Have similar projects survived an audit or been upheld in tax court?

8. What is the inflation-protection potential? Will the investment appreciate? Will the income grow with inflation?

9. Examine the "pro forma." Most tax-shelter salespeople will show you a "pro forma" statement of how the shelter will benefit you for tax purposes. Compare the assumed tax bracket with your own and be sure you understand the tax-recapture consequences of dropping or selling the shelter after only one or two years.

The best tax shelters are those that are perfectly legal, pass all the IRS tests, give great tax benefits and beat inflation. They should be sound long-term investments and should require only the initial investment.

10. Beware of overinflated residual values. Many times, particularly in the case of equipment leasing, the entire case for the shelter rests upon assumptions about the asset value at the end of a stated period of time, say three years. In other words, the asset must be disposed of or traded at an assumed, future "residual value" in order to make the shelter economically feasible.

If you are not knowledgeable about the particular equipment, spend a few bucks and ask an expert.

As my friend Bob Allen says in *Creating Wealth,* "If you think education is expensive, try ignorance." This chapter is just the beginning of your tax-shelter education, but there is enough here to keep you away from 90 percent of the pitfalls, if you put it into practice. Your biggest mistake, however, would be to take no action. You then lose to the IRS by default. I think we should make them fight for their money. After all, you had to fight to get it in the first place.

PAC-MAN TAKES ON THE MALARIAL ECONOMY

Investing in active public markets is vigorously competitive. For every winning trade, there is a loser on the other side of the trade. The consistent winner had the knowledge and the appropriate temperament, but in the 80s, the consistent winner will also need a new set of skills to give him the winner's edge over his competition. He's going to have to know how to use a personal computer if he really wants to be among that 10 percent of investors who make 90 percent of the money. Investors who refuse to buy computers and learn to use them will be as obsolete as if they had refused to use telephones, automobiles or airplanes. They will lose some of their money to the investor who has a computer. If you are in a significant tax bracket, your computer can ensure you don't goof up those year-end tax decisions described in the previous chapter. Those mistakes could cost you much more than the computer. And besides, your computer and its software are tax-deductible purchases.

More than 20,000 programs have been written for microcomputers, some of which can do a crackerjack job of helping you manage your investment portfolio and helping you plan and keep track of your taxes—but only if you own one and use it.

I hope, by demystifying the subject, that I can motivate you to buy a personal computer and learn how to operate it.

Electronic portfolio management—using a computer to help you keep track of and analyze investments—provides one important advantage: speed. You can evaluate the performance of your current portfolio, obtaining sophisticated reports with little more than a few key strokes. You can play complex "what if" games, trying out various strategies, shuffling and reshuffling the data. You can track dozens of sophisticated variables on hundreds of stocks—and do it in just minutes. If Chapter 11 and Appendix I inspire you to become a chart technician, a computer isn't just nice to have; it's indispensable if you value your time.

Computers are great drudgery reducers. They can vastly increase your ability to explore and evaluate new investments. Because you can respond faster and with more sophisticated analyses, you can successfully manage more investments with higher volatility, giving you better diversification and higher profit potential. Your computer will pay for itself, and then some!

Some programs can keep your short- and long-term gains figured up-to-date so you can make intelligent year-end buy or sell decisions, as well as other tax decisions.

If you're currently spending five to ten hours a week managing or analyzing your portfolio (or should be and aren't), you are a prime candidate for a personal computer. A computer will greatly increase the amount of investment information you can digest, and will slash the time you need to spend at it.

If you haven't made investments because you don't have the time to educate yourself about the markets before committing your money, you need a computer. You can quickly sift through years of financial data on almost any investment, or sort out vast libraries of financial articles in seconds, entering only a key word or phrase, such as "gold," "Dow Jones" or "interest rates." Try that at your local library!

If your portfolio is complex and/or highly diverse, a computer will give you a bird's-eye view you can get in no other way.

A computer is nothing if not a powerful information-gathering resource. You can use it to sort out years of financial data on almost any investment in minutes, or to search libraries of financial newspaper and magazine articles.

You may presently own a personal computer but will rely mostly on your broker and people like me to provide you with investment information. I appreciate the vote of confidence, but all your broker or I can do is point you in the right direction and give you examples of investments to consider. A computer can give you the edge in exploring the markets we suggest and finding real money-makers of your own.

GETTING STARTED

Automating your portfolio requires you to learn what computers can do, and their jargon, "Computerspeak." You must know what you want your computer to do and shop for a computer that fits your requirements.

COMPUTERSPEAK 101: HARDWARE

Let's learn the basics of computer hardware.

Central Processing Unit (CPU): This is the "main box," housing the guts of your computer.

Microprocessor: This is the heart of the CPU. It's the gadget behind the personal-computer revolution. Computers acquire "input," then process that input, and "output" the result, all on a chip the size of your thumbnail.

Disk Drive: "Record player" for the floppy disks that contain computer programs. It reads input or stores output.

Modem: The device that lets your computer talk on the phone with other computers, such as Dow Jones News/Retrieval. Modem speed is measured in "baud." The higher the baud, the faster the modem (sounds vaguely obscene!).

Printer: The device the computer uses for printed or drawn output. Dot-matrix printers form characters with small dots and are not suitable for producing typewriter-quality printing, but they do graphics well. Typewriter-quality printers produce higher-quality characters, but are more expensive.

Expansion Board: A printed circuit board that gives the computer enhanced capabilities. It usually provides additional memory and allows the computer to connect to a printer and a modem.

RAM (Random Access Memory): 64K RAM, for instance, means approximately a 64,000 "byte" memory capacity. A "bit" is one "letter." A byte is eight bits, or one computer "word." Computers have "internal memory," which determines how much room the microprocessor has to operate a program, and "external memory" for input and output storage.

SHOPPING FOR A COMPUTER

A "personal" computer is a scaled-down version of a large computer, while a "home" computer is usually a scaled-up version of a video-game machine. Buy a personal computer. Personal computers have names like IBM and Apple. Home computers have names like Atari and Coleco.

The two most popular machines among investors are the Apple II and the IBM PC, for one simple reason: far more programs that are useful to investors are being written for these two computers than for all the rest combined.

There are many other fine computers, some of which are more technologically advanced than either the Apple or the IBM, but these two companies basically control the software industry. And as you will see in a moment, a computer is absolutely useless without appropriate software.

This situation could change, or some new advance could make another brand of computer more useful than either of the above, but both also have one other advantage; in an exploding industry with a lot of high flyers that crash and burn (such as Osborne, which went broke), Apple and IBM are financially stable companies that will be around five years from now, and parts and service are widely available for both, and will continue to be available.

If you're interested in a lightweight portable, the Kaypro portable will run most software, and the Compaq is billed as "the IBM PC that travels."

All in all, however, I'll stick with the two front-runners for the reasons mentioned above.

Before you can automate your portfolio, you're going to have to know something about hardware and software. There are several fine books on the subject, some of which are listed in Appendix II, but in the interest of encouraging you to get your investment program into the computer age, let's clear up some of the computer fog now.

The first question to be answered is, "Where should I buy my computer?"

SURVIVING IN THE DEALER JUNGLE

My staff visited several local computer stores and found that your friendly computer salesperson is pretty ignorant about software. The prevailing attitude is "Buy the machine, any machine, and we'll look for software later." The computer-sales industry is shamelessly guilty of selling the bottle rather than the wine.

Look for a dealer and a manufacturer who will provide after-sale support. The large retail chains are probably safest. ComputerLand is the largest, with five hundred outlets, followed by Entré with fifty, and Sears Business Systems Centers with forty-five.

Don't overlook well-established local stores. The most customer-service-oriented outfit we found was locally owned.

Avoid unauthorized dealers. Although they may be cheaper, service can range from bad to nonexistent.

TAKING THE PLUNGE

Buying a computer is like buying a car back in the 50s. For $2,000 you could drive it off the lot, but if you wanted paint, upholstery and carpet, that was extra.

Here's what you'll need:

1. The basic computer. Microprocessors come in two speeds, 8-bit and 16-bit. A lot of the new software is being written for 16-bit processors.

2. Maximum internal memory—the more the better.

3. Two disk drives. A lot of programs require two instead of one.

4. Graphics video monitor. Black-and-white is okay, unless your software requires color graphics.

5. Printer with graphics capability. A dot-matrix printer is fine, unless you're going to do word processing, in which case you might want a letter-quality printer. It all depends on who is going to see the finished product.

6. A 1200-baud modem. It will save money when accessing data bases because it's faster, and data bases charge by the minute.

The Apple II series currently has the bulk of existing software on its side. However, most new software is being written for the IBM. I own both but prefer the IBM, even though it costs a bit more.

COMPUTERSPEAK 102: THE PROGRAMS

Here are a few terms you need to understand before you can communicate with a computer salesman.

Software: Computer hardware requires "programs" of instructions to make it work. These programs are called "software."

Interface: This means that software and hardware are compatible with and can talk to other software and hardware.

Floppy Disks: Floppy disks look like the old 45-rpm records, only they're pliable. They are inserted in the disk drive, where information is either stored on them or retrieved from them.

Operating System: The computer needs a master program to tell it how to run other programs. One of the most popular is CP/M (Control Program/Microprocessor).

Applications Software: The general name given to programs aimed at specific jobs, like "portfolio management" or "spread-sheets."

Data Base: A large body of information on someone else's computer, such as market quotes, financial information, and newspaper and magazine articles. Your computer can access it directly by telephone line, through a modem. You pay a fee based on the time your computer is in communication with the data base.

User-Friendly: This means that you don't have to be a genius to use it. Explanations are right on the screen so you can understand them.

INVESTMENT SOFTWARE

A computer is little more than a high-tech flowerpot unless it has software to put it to work.

Ironically, many people don't buy computers, or don't use them when they do buy them, because all computers have a modified typewriter keyboard, and the buyer doesn't know how to type. If that describes you, the first program you should load into your disk drive is "Typing Tutor," so your computer can teach you how.

An investor needs some combination of portfolio-management software that will provide the following:

1. Portfolio listing. This is a current inventory of your investments. You type in the basic information or access it from a data base by telephone. Your program sorts it out and organizes it for you as you regularly update it.

2. Profit/loss statement. You can keep track of your gains and losses. The P&L is instantly recomputed for you whenever the market prices change, or when you record a buy or sell.

3. Category/Cross reference listing. You can isolate specific groups for review, such as dividend-paying stocks, or gold shares.

4. Record of sales. Useful for record keeping and taxes.

5. Access to data bases. You should be able to update your portfolio automatically from a market-information data base.

Two outstanding programs are Personal Investor (PBL Corp) and Portfolio Management System (PEAR). Personal Investor produces gains and losses reports, a dividends report and a unique tax report. It uses the Dow Jones News/Retrieval data base for its automatic updates and can also access other data bases. It even integrates with other software.

The Portfolio Management System package is geared more toward the professional and the really serious investor. With PEAR, you can easily set up model portfolios and test "what if" strategies. It provides one of the best income statements we've seen. It uses the Dial data base (IBM PC computer) and Dow Jones News/Retrieval (Apple series computer) for updates.

FOR THE TECHNICIAN

Look for the following in a good technical-analysis package:

(1) Preprogrammed indicators. You should be able to select basic indicators, such as moving averages, rather than having to program the formula.

(2) User-defined variables. You should be able to use home-grown indicators of your own.

(3) Scale compression/expansion. It should be able to expand or contract the time scales of charts easily.

(4) Data base access. It must access the data bases you need, and allow you to define the ground rules for searching them.

Two good packages are Market Analyst (Anidata) and Technical Analysis (PEAR). Market Analyst contains all the reports recommended earlier, while allowing the use of several excellent investment-history data bases, like Dial.

Technical Analysis does not have a portfolio-management module, but makes up for it with its evaluation report. You can define a trading strategy (like the Eldridge Strategy) and then analyze its profit-and-loss performance all the way back to 1961. This package is for the serious technician.

FUNDAMENTAL ANALYSIS

You can get fundamental data by "accessing" a data base by phone and paying the user charges by the minute, or you can purchase a software package that provides a monthly market update by mail on a floppy disk.

Two excellent choices with their own update services are: Micro PMS (The Boston Co.), and Stock Pak II (Standard and Poor).

Micro PMS lets you define your own ground rules for searching. Each update disk contains about fifty data items on 1,500 of the most widely traded stocks on the New York and American exchanges. Many over-the-counter stocks are also included.

Additionally it provides portfolio and transaction listings as well as charts of overall portfolio performance. You may even measure your portfolio's performance against the Dow, the S&P 500 and two other indices of your own choosing. It will also accept multiple portfolios, which means you can run your own theoretical sample portfolios to test trading strategies.

A really nifty feature is "The Enhancer/Analyzer" It will use your investment objectives and existing portfolio to screen stocks, and then suggest trades! The program accesses the Dow Jones News/Retrieval data base and can also talk to other software, like electronic spread sheets.

Stock Pak II is an upgrade of a popular package originally available for Radio Shack computers. It is now available for the Apple series computer and the IBM PC. Like Micro PMS, it uses a data diskette of about fifty items on each of 1,500 companies. You can choose whether you want all 1,500 on the New York Exchange, the American Exchange, Over-the-counter (2,200 companies) or a composite of all three. The software will generate an additional fifty data items using those provided, giving you a total of one hundred items per company. It will also do several types of charts for easy comparisons. The monthly update diskettes will cost $250–$300 a year ($500–$600 a year with the over-the-counter diskettes). This package will not do portfolio or transaction listings, nor does it interface with data bases.

DATA BASES

Investors with an appetite for exploration should consider software that will access data bases like Dow Jones, CompuServe and Dial. For instance, if you're interested in options, Dow Jones and CompuServe have current quotes, while Dial has quotes that go back to at least 1968.

Dow Jones News/Retrieval is actually a series of data bases. You can obtain several types of financial data, plus financial news, sports, weather and even movie reviews.

With CompuServe, you can get current commodities information, shopping catalogs, games, programming languages, electronic bulletin boards, electronic mail and a huge library of newspaper, magazine and newsletter articles.

Last but not least, the Dial data base is the most comprehensive for market quotes.

Data bases will also let you do other exciting things, like send overnight mail to anyone in the U.S. even if he doesn't own a computer. You can take college courses at your own pace, as data bases are always "open," and you can even make computer conference calls where several computers are linked together in a network. Hale Systems, via its Remote Computing Division (PEAR Systems), operates Dial and has designed the Portfolio Management System and Technical Analysis software, discussed earlier, specifically to interface with Dial.

GETTING HELP

There's an enormous amount of misinformation and downright misrepresentation in the retail microcomputer industry. Too many retailers are more interested in moving inventory than serving people.

To pilot you through these treacherous waters, Personal Touch Computer Service, a consumer-oriented computer consulting service, can make your transition into the computer age as painless as possible.

Terry Jeffers runs Personal Touch and was my partner and president of Target during our first five years. He supervised our computerization. He can help you become "computer literate" and save you many times the cost of his service in discount purchases, then provide telephone advice when you are stymied by your new machinery or its software.

He will not only help you choose software, but also get you large discounts. I have no financial interest in Terry's service.

RESOURCES

CONSUMER INFORMATION/SOFTWARE CONSULTING

Recommended!

Personal Touch Computer Service. 10 Crow Canyon Ct., Suite 210, San Ramon, CA 94583. (415) 831-9104.

BOOKS

Automating Your Financial Portfolio. Woodwell. Hands down, the best book available. Highly readable; packed with information. $19.95.

Computer Selection Guide. Poynter. An absolute must before you enter the dealer jungle. Everything from basics to hardware surveys. Includes checklists of things to look for. $11.95.

Both books are available from Target Publishers, Inc., P.O. Box 25, Pleasanton, CA 94566. Add $1.50 handling, and sales tax where applicable.

NEWSLETTERS

Computerized Investing. American Association of Individual Investors. Norman Nicholson, Editor. Bimonthly. $22 per year, members; $44 per year, nonmembers. AAII 612 N. Michigan Ave., Chicago, ILL 60611. Up-to-the-minute information on investment software and electronic portfolio management.

DATA BASES

Dow Jones News/Retrieval Service. For information call 1-800-345-8500, ext. 5. CompuServe. For information call 1-800-848-8199. Ohio 614-457-8650. Dial. Remote Computing. For information call 1-800-645-3120 or 212-895-3810.

TABLE 1
DATA BASES—YOUR WINDOW ON THE MARKET

CATEGORY	DOW JONES	COMPUSERVE	DIAL
Stock data	To '78	To '74	To '68*
Options prices	Current	Current	To '68
Warrant prices	To '78	To '74	To '68
Mutual fund data	Current	To '74	To '68
Debt securities data	Current	To '74	To '68
Commodities data	No	Current	To '68
OTC quotes	Current	To '74	To '68
Exchanges	NY, Amer, MW, Pac.	All Major	All Major

* Some categories back to 1961.

TABLE 2
SOFTWARE FOR YOUR HARDWARE: COMPARISONS

	APPLE II SERIES	IBM PC
Portfolio Management		
Personal Investor	$145	$145
Portfolio Management System (PEAR)	$695	$695
Technical Analysis		
Market Analyst (Anidata)	$395	$495
Technical Analysis (PEAR)	$995	$995
Fundamental Analysis		
S & P Stock Pak II	$245	expected soon
Micro PMS	$595	$450
Data Base Access		
Dow Jones News/Retrieval	$9–$108/hr	$9–$108/hr
CompuServe	$5–$35/hr	$5–$35/hr Dial
Data (commodities)	5¢/quote— plus monthly chg	5¢/quote— plus monthly chg

NOTE: An expansion board is available from Quadram Corp. that will allow the IBM PC to run most Apple-compatible software.

TABLE 3
THE FRONT-RUNNERS GO HEAD TO HEAD: COMPARISONS.
(Price data as of October 1983. Prices subject to changes and dealer discounts)

ITEM	APPLE IIe	IBM PC
Basic System	8-bit computer, video monitor (monochrome), one disk drive (140K) 64K internal memory (expandable to 128K) $1,995	16-bit computer, one disk drive (320K) 64K internal memory (expandable to 512K) $2,105
Video Monitor	included	USI PI-3 (monochrome), $249. Graphics card, $244
Numeric Key pad	$159.95	included
Operating System	included	$40
Programming	"BASIC"	"BASIC"
Language Internal Memory Expansion	included To 128K at time of purchase $170	included Multifunction board: 256K internal memory, modem and printer hook-ups, clock: $595
Second Disk Drive	140K Memory $395	320K memory $529
Communications Hardware	Super Serial Card, $195 Hayes Smartmodem 1200B. 1200 baud $599	Hayes Smartmodem-1200B, 1200 baud $599
Communications Software	"ASCII Express" $129.95	"Crosstalk" $195
Printer	Epson MX-100 with graphics (dot matrix) $795	Epson MX-100 with graphics (dot matrix) $795
Printer Hardware	Printer hook-up, card and cable $145	Cable: $55
Totals	$4,583.90	$5,406

Prices provided by ComputerLand of Dublin, Ca.

CHAPTER

14

BASIC SURVIVAL: THE WORST CASE

Now it's time to deal with my most controversial recommendations. This easily misunderstood issue has been at the root of most of the media criticism I have had over the years, particularly the "Prophet of Doom" stuff.

These are the first steps that all of you should take to protect yourself against the "worst case" scenarios that you don't really expect will ever happen, but are at least possibilities. "Worst cases" have happened throughout history. They are almost always unexpected. In the volatile world of the Malarial Economy, anything can happen, and with amazing speed.

A portion of your personal and financial resources should be set aside to deal with these unexpected possibilities. After you have done that, forget about it and live your life positively.

There are three basic worst-case steps to be taken, all to meet the most basic of human needs: (1) you should own a home—free and clear if possible; (2) you need a food-and-commodity storage program; and (3) the right kind and adequate amounts of life insurance.

Do you have to be a "Prophet of Doom" to consider these steps?

Actually, "Prophet of doom" is an honorable profession, that is, if I get to define "Prophet of Doom."

The classic prototype of the Prophet of Doom is Jonah in the Old Testament.

It seems that Jonah was told by God to go to Nineveh, and deliver this message: "You are so wicked that God is going to destroy you." Jonah didn't think going to Nineveh was such a red-hot idea, so he decided to go elsewhere. After he had some interesting adventures, he informed the Lord that He now had his attention and he would now go to Nineveh.

When he got to Nineveh, he climbed on the wall of the city and delivered his simple message. "You are so wicked that God is going to destroy you."

To Jonah's utter amazement, the King of Nineveh, along with all of his subjects, believed his message and repented right on the spot ... in "sackcloth and ashes," whatever that is.

Because of their repentance, God didn't destroy them, which personally offended Jonah. After all, his credibility was at stake. Jonah literally demanded that God destroy them. Of course, God did not. He could not, because they had repented.

I've concluded from this story that it is the function of a "Prophet of Doom" to prevent the doom he prophesies.

I plead guilty to being deeply concerned about the ultimate adverse consequences of the Malarial Cycle, but I must also prepare for them while wielding what influence I may have to prevent them, because they are clearly possible. My only weapon is the pen.

My worst-case forecasts are all "This is what could really happen if ..." It's the "if ..." part that motivates my survival advice and my political activities. But even while I'm thrashing away at the political windmills, I must be prepared for the distinct possibility (which may even be a probability) that even though we win some battles, we will lose the war, and a "worst-case scenario" could materialize.

That scenario includes such possibilities as a runaway inflation triggering severe labor problems, nationwide strikes and a breakdown in the distribution of vital commodities, such as food, an "uncontrolled substance" to which I am addicted. If I go without food for very long, I get severe withdrawal symptoms.

Another factor that could disrupt the distribution of the necessities of life is the mere fact of inflation.

Our entire commodity-distribution system, from the farmer down to the consumer at the supermarket, depends upon the easy and smooth functioning of the credit system. The farmer borrows money to pay for seed and tractors. He then sells grain on credit to the elevator operator or the wholesaler, who sells to the miller, who sells to the baker, who sells to the supermarket—all on credit. They then sell to you at the supermarket, accepting your check virtually without question.

It is a system based on trust—trust that the money is stable and will not "go broke" between the time they extend you the credit and receive payment.

In a runaway hyperinflation, the credit system breaks down and makes normal commerce difficult, spotty or, in the *worst,* worst case, even impossible, for unpredictable periods of time.

Minor food-supply problems could be compounded by panic. There are numerous instances in the past where fear has triggered panic buying, the most notable being the day President Kennedy announced the frightening Cuban missile crisis. In Denver, where we lived, within hours the local supermarket looked as if a swarm of locusts had gone through it.

Shortages of food are not a certainty, but they are a distinct possibility. Consequently, my "worst-case scenario" protection program begins with the storage of food.

You can't just store any old food, because you have to consider problems of shelf life and nutritional balance, especially if you might have to depend on those supplies over several months or years. It could be a time of great stress, so you need an antistress diet, as stress is a destroyer of health.

I've covered this at great length in *How to Prosper During the Coming Bad Years,* and I suggest you get your hands on a copy. If you can't find it in a bookstore, it's available from Target Publishers, P.O. Box 25, Pleasanton, CA 94566; (415) 463-2200 for $3.95.

You can also refer to the Recommended Vendors, listed in Appendix II under "Food Storage," who sell the commercial food-storage programs I designed years ago. I have no personal financial interest in that recommendation, but I give it a high priority.

I'd like you to know the difference between this recommendation and the "head for the hills" hard-core survival crowd.

This group of undoubtedly sincere people (and I have friends among them) have essentially given up on the American system and now assume that nothing can prevent a holocaust. They have built retreats in the mountains, stocked not only with food but with guns and ammunition. These groups believe that:

1. There will be a total collapse of society.
2. There will be mob rule and looting in the streets.
3. It will spread to the countryside, and even to the mountains.
4. The only ones who "survive" will be those who are willing to kill without hesitation.

I think those positions are excessive and unlikely, but not impossible. Hard-core survivalists are really talking about the end of the world as we know it. I don't know how to prepare for the end of the world, so my preparations have been much less radical.

I have chosen to live in a part of the country that has a tradition of civil order, neighborly helpfulness and food storage. That's just one of the reasons I chose Utah. If the "worst case" materialized, it would be far more likely to do so in New York, Baltimore, Los Angeles or Detroit than in Provo, Utah.

I wouldn't have moved near Provo for that reason alone, however. I moved here because I love this valley. I went to BYU. My children have also gone to BYU, and some are still attending. I love the low-crime environment, the neighborly trust, the fishing, the skiing, the clear air, BYU football and the old-fashioned values that predominate in this community. But the sense of safety and security in a potentially disrupted world was one factor in my decision. My "survival" precautions probably would have to be a bit more extreme than yours because I have high visibility, and if a worst case did materialize, it would probably occur to someone that "Howard Ruff has food."

I also vividly remember those dark days in 1968 when Kay and I and the kids were grateful for our stored food. Such little local and personal tragedies are becoming far more frequent as a result of the Malarial Economy.

I live my life on the assumption I'll never have to use my stored food and, of course, will be thrilled if I don't. I hope that my investment in food is totally wasted—and the odds favor that being the case.

Of course, we rotate this food, using and replacing it as we go along. Before my stored food reaches the end of its shelf life I contribute it to a local church or charity to feed the poor, take a tax deduction for its purchase price and use the tax savings to help finance my restocking.

After I have my food stored, I work hard politically to ensure that I will never have to use it. I also try to look for positive investment opportunities in the current financial environment, whatever that might be. I do not dwell on "survival." It is something to be prepared for and forget about.

RISK-FREE INVESTING

I also recommend the wholesale purchase, in bulk, of other commodities you use on a regular basis. Not only would this be essential in a worst case, but it can save you lots of money. Store at least a six months' supply of toilet paper, spark plugs, hunting ammo (not for shooting the "starving hordes," but either for barter or for hunting), Kleenex, feminine hygiene supplies, paper towels, diapers, soap, toothpaste, razor blades, automobile parts, an extra set of tires. . . . You can let your imagination run wild. Anything you now buy and use up on a regular basis could be added to your list.

Rotate these supplies. The worst thing that could happen to you is that you would end up using them in 1986 or 1987, having paid 1984 prices. It is a nontaxable capital gain. It's the equivalent of buying an investment, having guessed right about its direction, selling it for a profit, paying the taxes and buying these commodities on an "as needed" basis. It's also a lot less trouble. The main differences are that (1) Uncle Sam doesn't get his piece out of the middle, because you realize the profit on your investment by consuming it at higher prices; and (2) you took zero risk.

This is the only totally riskless advice I have ever given, yet more of my subscribers will probably buy highly volatile stock options based on my short-term buy signals than go for the commodity "sure thing." Sure things just aren't very exciting.

I've already discussed your basic core survival holdings of gold and silver coins. I could very well have put the information in this chapter, but it made more sense to discuss it along with precious-metals investment. Still, you should not think of those coins primarily as an investment. Buy them now at the current price, and don't keep adding or subtracting from your net worth as the value of those survival coins goes up and down. If we experience a worst case, a silver dime will be precious. It will take all the argument out of barter negotiations. If we don't have a worst-case scenario, but only continued rising tides of fever during the Malarial Economy, you will have made a lot of money on that investment.

If my whole Malarial scenario is wrong, and the price of gold and silver goes down, write it off as a necessary expense, the equivalent of having paid a life-insurance premium and not having been lucky enough to cash in big by dying prematurely.

LIFE INSURANCE

Speaking of insurance, over the years I've incurred the wrath of the insurance companies by being publicly and loudly negative on most of their services, particularly the ones that were the most profitable for them. Among these were the typical cash-value, whole-life policies and annuities, which were lousy investments during the fever cycle, generally yielding only 2 to 6 percent. Now it's time to reconsider.

Insurance is usually considered boring because of its complexity, but it is so essential to a sound financial plan that I must tackle it here. Besides, the insurance industry is in the midst of such a revolution that the odds are very high that your present insurance policies are inadequate or much too expensive. A new and bigger policy would probably improve your finances. Let's see if we can't breathe a little romance into a usually dull subject. I'll try to be brief and concise.

Insurance is fundamental to a financial survival plan. However, after that self-evident statement, you get lost in the jungle of obsolete policies and the proliferation of "new and improved" insurance plans, some of which I find pretty interesting, despite my previous insurance broadsides. Here are some of the new developments:

1. A forty-year-old man, in 1979, could purchase a $100,000 term policy for $372.58. Today, a forty-year-old man can purchase the same policy for $161 to $211.58 less. The 1979 price of $372.58 will buy $200,000 worth of insurance today, even though he's four years older.

In 1979 a whole-life policy for a forty-four-year-old man was about $20 per thousand. There are similar policies today for around $8 per thousand.

2. Policies that weren't even on the drawing board in the 70s are available now; for example, a tax-sheltered fund that can provide liquid emergency reserves and pay for term insurance with before-tax dollars. More about this later.

3. Insurance has become more competitive as an investment. (I'd like to think we helped push the companies in this direction.) Some widely sold policies still aren't cost-effective, but the industry has taken giant steps forward because of the following factors:

Interest rates. Insurance companies now earn higher interest on their investments, and the consumer has become high-yield-conscious, forcing the companies to pass on the profits. Many insurance policies are currently yielding 11 to 12 percent, compared to the previous 2 to 6 percent.

Mortality cost. People are living longer, so insurance companies can spread the risk over a longer period of time, reducing the premiums. Until a couple of years ago, insurance companies based their rates on a 1958 mortality table. Rates on most new policies are based on a 1980 mortality table, which shows a three-years-longer life expectancy for a forty-five-year-old man. The "time value" of money for the company over those three extra years makes a significant difference in cost.

Sharing risk and profit. This is the biggest change. Insurance companies have always offered guarantees of premiums, death benefits, cash values, settlement options and so on, requiring hedges to be built into the cost. Some companies now let the policy owner share in the upside potential.

If the company's assumptions are met (10 percent return on investments, for example), the rates and values of a policy will remain as quoted. If the company does better, profits will be shared with the policy holder.

If these assumptions are not met, however, the insurance company now reserves the right to increase the premiums, reduce the coverage, or both. The insured shares some of the investment risk as well as the profit. If the company performs well, premiums can be much lower; if it performs poorly, premiums could be higher; but there is usually a contractual lid on the premiums at about the same amount as it would have been if the company provided guarantees.

Some policies are now much more cost-effective. For example, let's say that you have a term policy with a premium of $1,000 per year, and you're in a 50 percent tax bracket. You actually have to earn $2,000 to have $1,000 after taxes to pay the premiums. Some companies have developed a tax-sheltered fund, under IRS Code Sec. 101. Your funds are liquid, provide a pretty good rate of return (10–12 percent) and can even be invested in a family of mutual funds with nontaxable switching privileges.

You can request your insurance company to charge the $1,000 term premium against your tax-sheltered earnings in the fund. Not everyone is in a 50 percent tax bracket, but the concept is still valid, no matter what your bracket, if you pay any taxes at all. You have tax-sheltered liquid reserves, and you pay your premiums with before-tax dollars.

There are several different versions of this concept, such as Universal Life or Variable Life. Rates, values and benefits vary, so shop around.

Consider these new programs if:

1. You have at least a five-year need for life insurance, not just a temporary need, such as to pay off a short-term note.

2. You have enough discretionary money to put in the tax-sheltered fund to earn enough interest to pay the premium.

3. You are in at least a 25% bracket.

If you have not reviewed your life insurance recently, you should do so now, as the odds are you are probably wasting money.

One key to buying insurance, however, is to use an independent agent who can do business with any company, so she or he can shop for the best deal. Some companies are cheaper for younger people and more expensive for older folks, or vice versa. Some may charge a higher premium but have a far better investment-yield track record. Newcastle Financial Group (see Appendix II) helped me double my insurance coverage at half the cost I had been paying.

Most of you are underinsured, poorly insured or too expensively insured. Get that part of your financial house in order.

SLEEPING WELL

The worst-case survival position, including life insurance, is insomnia medicine. It gives you a sense of security in a volatile and uncertain world when you know all contingencies are covered. You also have a lot of flexibility. You can be as extreme or moderate as you wish. You must do whatever helps you sleep well. As far as I'm concerned, you can be a hard-core survivalist if you wish, as long as you don't do it in the street and scare the horses. Whatever gives you happiness and security in an unpredictable world is okay with me.

I'm not going to put down the hard-core survivalists. After all, what if they're right? But in the meantime, I feel more comfortable with my more moderate position, and suspect that most of you will be also.

CHAPTER
15

THE SPIRITUAL ROOTS OF THE MALARIAL ECONOMY

The U.S. Bureau of Printing and Engraving, which is now running three shifts twenty-four hours around the clock, has just purchased three new high-speed presses which can triple the rate at which money is printed. Not only that, but the bill they're printing the most of today is the $20 bill. It used to be the $10, and before that it was the $5, and before that, the $1. They are printing as many $100 bills as they were printing $20s ten years ago. Ten or fifteen years ago, nobody had a $100 bill in his pocket. Now it's common. Grocery checkout clerks don't even blink when you flash a $100 bill. Ten years ago they would have thought you were crazy. This is a tangible symptom of inflation.

Can we stop the presses?

The older I get, and the more I try to understand the root causes of negative economic trends, including the Malarial Economy, the more often I come up against the bedrock spiritual concepts that are common to most religions. All human behavior has its roots in spiritual principles, and I'm not using "spiritual," in just the religious sense.

John Adams said, "The Constitution of the United States was designed for a moral and religious people, and is inadequate for the government of any other kind."

I'm sure John Adams wasn't using the word "moral" just in the sexual sense, or the word "religious" solely in the sense of being a member of an institutionalized religion or a follower of any particular brand of theology.

243

He was talking about the blessings and the dangers of freedom, particularly the potential for abuse of freedom.

The Constitution of the United States was not an exercise in government, but an exercise in freedom from government. Thomas Jefferson said, "Government is a singularly dangerous beast and must be chained." The Founding Fathers chose to chain it with the Constitution. The underlying assumption was that a free and enlightened people could govern themselves for the most part, and as long as there is a basic consensus about behavior and principle among the majority of the people, then a minimum of government is required. If people restrained themselves by the practice of sound moral and ethical principles, there would be little reason for the government to restrain them. Democratic government, whether it is a pure "democracy" in which the people directly create the laws, or a "democratic republic" where we elect the people who make the laws, has one inherent flaw that makes it immensely vulnerable to the weaknesses of human nature: if they choose, the majority of the people can legally plunder a minority. Inherent in the exercise of freedom is the assumption that the majority will never decide to do so.

The Constitution works only if the people are also willing to work. If the majority of the people decide not to work, the Constitution is inadequate to protect from plunder the hard-earned resources of those who do.

Freedom requires free markets. No free society can exist without free markets and a free flow of capital.

Laws are not required to regulate wages and prices if the people understand that wages and prices are best controlled by the almost mystical interplay of supply and demand, which rewards performance and ingenuity and hard work, and punishes slothfulness, selfishness and greed.

For example, if I invent a brand-new widget that will improve the lot of a large number of human beings, I am free to build it and sell it, and to become wealthier in the process, assuming that I know how to tell the world that I have created this wonderful contraption. If I become greedy and charge too much because I am the only manufacturer of this essential widget, others will eventually begin to covet my profits and plot to get a piece of the action. They will go to work to invent a better widget so they can circumvent the patent laws, or to invent something that does what my widget does, only faster and cheaper. The greedier I am, and the more money I make, the more attention I attract from others who may be equally talented. They will try harder and harder to do me one better.

Soon there is another widget on the market, or something that makes my widget obsolete. I now have to spend money to improve my widget, and I now have to advertise and hire salesmen as more widget manufacturers move into the marketplace. Now price becomes a competitive factor and I can no longer charge what I wish. Sooner or later, the price of widgets comes down, and I find myself, along with the rest of the widget makers, making the 5 to 7 percent return on investment that eventually becomes the norm in almost every industry.

In a truly free-enterprise system, government does not need to make official moral judgments about my greed and attempt to control me by governmental action. The free-enterprise system acknowledges that human greed exists, and pits one man's greed against another's, and neutralizes excessive greed through competition. Soon the competition has created a reasonable balance between supply and demand, and the customer benefits.

This is the kind of free society John Adams and Thomas Jefferson envisioned.

The America that Adams saw is founded on certain old-fashioned concepts: that free societies produce the most good and the least evil; that theft is wrong; that work is noble and expected of everyone; that a man should be willing to stand on his own two feet; that he should be free to succeed or fail and keep the fruits of his labors; that it is ignoble to accept that which you have not earned; and that when we are successful we have responsibilities to share our wealth with those who, because of youth or age or sickness or incapacity, cannot take care of themselves—especially our own families.

Until fairly recently, it was accepted virtually without question that the state owed you absolutely nothing but an opportunity. It didn't owe you a "decent standard of living," "dignity," "an education," "a cheap government-subsidized loan," a "serene and worry-free old age," or "a safety net" to protect people who failed from the consequences of their failure.

We were expected to love our country and give it our support in time of trouble, and to give our lives if necessary in defense of its freedom and its principles.

It was less than a quarter century ago when we all agreed without reservation with the ringing words of John Kennedy, "Ask not what your country can do for you, but ask what you can do for your country."

Now, nearly all of the above principles are not just being challenged but are in disorderly retreat.

Is this a failure of government? There are those, and unfortunately they are now in the majority in both political parties, who believe that the solution is more government, more laws, more regulation, more taxes and more benefits from the public treasury.

If the majority of Americans reject those bedrock principles of personal character, the Constitution will be inadequate to maintain social order and a stable prosperous society. Even more laws and regulations will be created to fill the vacuum created by this failure of Americans to discipline themselves.

When the invisible, unconscious consensus, which manifests itself in mass behavior and economic cycles, swings from individual responsibility to the abdication of responsibility to an all-powerful omnipotent government, then there are no additional laws, regulations or political movements that can save free institutions from destruction. That doesn't always mean the collapse of society, but it can mean the collapse of freedom.

The greatest threat to freedom today is not Communism, but government itself. It is growing exponentially, as it fills vacuums, totally out of control, with no effective opposition to the trends. "We have met the enemy, and he is us."—Pogo.

Even Ronald Reagan, when he proposed his 1983 budget, announced proudly that nothing had been done to disturb the "social safety net," and we have all heard him brag on television about how benefits to the "truly needy" have been increased under his administration.

As I look back over my life, especially those experiences which I shared with you at the beginning of this book, I realize that if in 1968, when I had fallen, some agency had been standing there to protect me from the consequences of my failure, if someone had kept the wolf from my door, I would not have been motivated by sheer desperation to succeed. In those painful weeks and months in 1968, if there had been unemployment insurance available for small businessmen who go broke (there was not at that time), it would have been so easy to surrender to dependence, and something good and noble within me might have died.

The corollary to success is failure. Human nature is such that if we eliminate from our society the consequences of failure, we eliminate the greatest incentive to succeed, and we wipe out from our lives one of the most important drives that has fueled human progress—sheer desperation.

Now let's take a look at the specific bedrock principles of human growth and progress that have been profoundly violated and that must be "repented of" before we can solve the problems that have created the Malarial Economy. "Repentance" means making a fundamental, permanent change of attitude and behavior. Until that happens, the Malarial Cycle will not be controlled.

The economic and political marketplace of ideas and mass behavior is rooted in the attitudes, fears, weaknesses and strengths of the masses of people, especially in a free-society democracy. When I try to analyze what kind of changes in our society are necessary to stop an adverse trend, it's like peeling an artichoke. First I blame "the bureaucracy" for some dumbheaded action. Then I realize that Congress created the agency that houses the regulatory bureaucracy. So let's blame Congress—"the politicians."

But who instructs the politician through lobbying and elections? The people. So let's blame "the people."

But why did the people act as they did?

Aha! There's the heart of the artichoke, the root of the problem.

Almost always I discover that correcting the problem requires changing mass human behavior in the same areas that inspired Old Testament prophets to cry "Repent!"

This is not a pulpit, so I will confine my comments strictly to the financial and economic impact of the massive and almost universal violation and abandonment of what Christians and Jews would consider God's commandments and what humanists who share these values would consider "useful taboos" that are the heart of the artichoke. Several of God's "Top Ten" best illustrate the point.

"Thou shalt not covet." You don't often hear a lot about that one, compared with "Thou shalt not kill," or "Thou shalt not steal," not even in church. What does "Thou shalt not covet" have to do with finance and economics?

Debt is the root cause of inflation. Covetousness is the root cause of debt.

You coveted your neighbor's boat. You didn't have the guts to steal it from him, but you're going to steal from your kids. You're going to borrow money to buy the boat; the Fed will have to monetize the debt, which will add to inflation, which will come to roost on your children's backs. You didn't realize you were stealing from your kids, but you were. If you did not covet that boat, and instead practiced all the old-fashioned nineteenth-century virtues, you wouldn't think of buying the boat until you saved up the money for it. Perhaps in a simpler age you would have made your own.

We also covet services from government we aren't willing to pay for, which is the cause of inflationary deficits.

When the human race is willing to "repent" of its covetousness, then inflation will come under control. That leads me to the next violated principle.

"Thou shalt not steal." Ben Lichtenberg defined democracy as the state of affairs in which you consent to having your pocket picked and elect the best man to do it. The whole transfer-payment process, which is 70 percent of the federal budget, involves stealing from one person to give to another through the taxing power of government (less 40 percent for handling, which has to be monetized). If we resist this theft, we are not considered "compassionate."

Rising resentment of this process is stirring a growing tax revolt, ranging from outright confrontation with the IRS, on the basis of principle, to simple evasion and a growing underground economy.

I visited Sweden not too long ago. Their tax burden is heavier than ours, but strangely enough, there isn't as much resentment over taxes in Sweden as there is here. Most Swedes believe that the money that they give to the government is given back to them in the form of benefits, such as lengthy paid vacations, health subsidies, day care, maternity and paternity leave, and so on. Being a homogeneous society, with no visible, militant underclass demanding more and more, there is far less resentment.

This nation is not Sweden, and our taxpayer class does not perceive itself as getting back as much in benefits as they are paying in taxes. We know we are involuntarily forced to support nonproducers. This is the stuff of which class warfare is made. So far, the weapons used in this war have been mostly rhetorical, but it is class warfare just the same, and when the plundered producer class digs in its heels and says, "No more!" it could become violent.

When government plays Robin Hood, robbing from the rich and the middle class to give to the poor, we must remind ourselves that Robin Hood was not necessarily a romantic hero who looked like Errol Flynn. Robin Hood was a thief.

I find nowhere in any religious literature justification from God or the Prophets for theft on the basis of the fact that the person from whom you stole had more money than someone else.

There is a legitimate case to be made for paying taxes for national defense, for the roads we all use, for the police and firemen who protect us all, for the schools, the courts and so on. But money taken involuntarily from one person to benefit another is stolen goods. The out-of-control aspect of the federal budget monster that is devouring us is the "entitlements," a name that seems to mean that a lot of people I don't know are "entitled" to the fruits of my labors.

Theft is not only bad for the victim, it is soul-destroying for the thieves and the beneficiaries of the theft. The chances that they will ever be productive are pretty slim.

I have little hope for a universal change in our thieving and covetous ways, because of one simple statistic: *56 percent of the people in this country get a regular check from some level of government.* They have been bought, hooked and corrupted. And if you include those who benefit from government contracts, and their employees and dependents, and their suppliers, and *their* employees and their dependents, you're talking about 77 percent of the U.S. population's depending on some form of transfer payment. They are receiving plunder—money extracted involuntarily from others. As naturally as night follows day, and with few exceptions, these people are unfailingly liberal advocates of more and bigger government.

In early 1983 the White House threw in the towel on trying to cut spending to balance the budget. An unnamed White House spokesman said, "There is no constituency for reducing government spending." No one is seriously considering cutting the entitlement programs. Remember, if you qualify, you're "entitled," and there are no ceilings on the total payout.

"Thou shalt not covet" and "Thou shalt not steal" head my list of national sins, but they are not the only basic human failings that have led to the Malarial Cycle. Next comes:

"Thou shalt not kill." If the people of the world decided that killing was morally wrong, armaments spending could be eliminated, and inflation would tumble almost immediately. A large part of the federal deficit is attributable to our defense budget. I'm not proposing unilateral disarmament, because the Russians' combination of growing military power, improving technology and aggressive amorality scares me to death. When you've got a bully in your neighborhood, you don't protect yourself by demonstrating you're weaker than he. But in a more perfect world, if the majority of the people, and especially those in power, were to decide that killing is unthinkable, our economic woes would shrink almost overnight.

"Thou shalt love thy neighbor as thyself." Most everyone agrees that we have a horrendous welfare mess, with second- and third-generation welfare recipients who know no other way of life. They have become a permanent underclass, trapped and seduced into dependency, now believing welfare is their permanent right. This costs the producing-taxpaying class untold billions of stolen and printed dollars. The system, by penalizing success with confiscatory taxation (the bigger the success, the higher the tax penalty) and rewarding dependency, creates built-in incentives to expand the tax-consuming class at the expense of the tax-paying class.

This welfare mess couldn't have come into existence until our failure to "love thy neighbor as thyself" left a vacuum into which government willingly moved, as it was the classic opportunity for politicians to buy the loyalty of millions of voters by pandering to their "wants" until the narcotic of dependence turned "wants" into "needs," then "rights."

If most Americans had routinely accepted the responsibility for brothers, sisters, parents, children and cousins who had temporary financial difficulties, were handicapped, or blind, or mentally or emotionally disabled, our public-welfare programs would then be needed only for people with disabling handicaps and no close family, or for victims of catastrophic illness beyond the ability of relatives to finance. If churches and volunteer organizations loved "thy neighbor as thyself," soup kitchens and shelters for the indigent would not need public funding.

On the other side of the ledger, if the people who have temporary difficulties also loved "thy neighbor as thyself," they would practice a rather old-fashioned virtue. They would detest their dependence on others and tolerate it only as long as it took to get back on their feet. They would consider such dependence to be demeaning and would want to escape that condition as quickly as possible. In all fairness, some do feel this way, but they are an ever-shrinking minority.

Because welfare comes from "government," and is not visibly stolen from the purse or wallet, millions of people are willing to accept this impersonal money with no pangs of conscience.

Politicians use the foolproof buzzword "compassion" as justification for their sick appeal to this human weakness. Because private compassion is an endangered species, official public compassion has become the order of the day. The temptation for the politician to buy votes, and for the voter to vote himself benefits from the public treasury, is just too irresistible. And as government has so completely assumed the role of Uncle Nanny, the average guy on the street feels no need to involve himself in the welfare of others. Besides, Uncle Nanny has taxed away the money that he might have given to charity. As taxes have risen, charitable giving has shrunk, despite the tax deductibility of private charity.

Another justification for this theft is the doctrine of "equality," a concept that has been perverted until it would be unrecognizable by Thomas Jefferson or Benjamin Franklin, were they to rise from the grave. "Equality of opportunity" has been twisted to mean compulsory "equality of result." This attempted leveling of society by theft—compulsory transfer of wealth—is an enemy of freedom. It is the essence of Communism, which has only succeeded in distributing the poverty more equally, while bringing to a screeching halt the dynamic creation of wealth that flourishes where markets are free and success and failure are both permitted.

We can be free, or we can be equal. We can't be both.

If we repented of this one great sin of omission, the positive impact on taxation and inflation would be huge.

"Honor thy father and thy mother." If we practiced the old-fashioned virtue of accepting responsibility for the financial and emotional needs of parents, they might not be tucked away in a shabby state-supported "rest home" somewhere in Arizona or Florida, trying to make it on an inadequate pension check. We would have more three-generation households, which throughout history have been an important link in passing values and traditions from one generation to the next. There would also be more family closeness and love.

But because we have failed to accept personal responsibility for our elderly, the Social Security program has grown into an inflationary monster of unimaginable proportions.

Then there is the flood of printed money that will be necessary to fund the $7.5 trillion Social Security "unfunded deficit," the gap between what will be collected from the assembly-line worker's paycheck and what will have to be paid to a population which is growing older. Soon we will have only two workers supporting each retiree. "Honor thy father and thy mother" is a big one.

"Thou shalt not lie." That brings me back to Social Security. The whole jury-rigged system is built upon several lies.

Lie #1: The FICA money that was taken from your paycheck is saved for your old age.

Nothing could be further from the truth. The money that was taken from you under false pretenses has already been spent to support pensioners who reached their "golden years" before you did. The money to support you will be ripped off from some poor working stiff.

Lie #2: Social Security is an earned "pension."

Actually, it's a "transfer payment." Remember, a "transfer payment" is money which is taken from someone to give to someone else. Social Security is really in the same class as welfare, Aid to Dependent Children and food stamps. The fact that they took FICA taxes from you over the years to give to someone else doesn't mitigate the fact that your "pension" is a transfer payment, nor does it give you the moral right to take it from someone else. In both cases, it is theft. But because most people believe the lie, even very wealthy retired people, who wouldn't think of taking food stamps, feel morally and ethically at peace when they accept their Social Security payment. I know many good people making $100,000 a year from investments who, without even a twinge of conscience, cash their Social Security checks. They have swallowed the big lie.

Lie #3: The Social Security program has been "saved" by the recent political compromise. There is no need to make basic, significant changes in Social Security.

Remember, compromises are a great way to come to agreement, but not a very good way of arriving at truth. The truth is that the Social Security Commission understated the size of the problem by $7.5 trillion, deciding in a compromise agreement that there was a $150 billion problem, and then proceeding to solve it. The temporary remedy, which is woefully inadequate and dips into the Treasury for the first time, is the first breach in the Treasury's defenses against raids by Social Security. It has only begun.

The $7.5 trillion deficit is very close to the value of everything that everyone in America owns. It can't be paid, except with huge mountains of printed money, which will destroy the purchasing power of the very funds retirees are counting on. Social Security, all by itself, guarantees a hyperinflation.

There are lots of other lies, such as "we owe it to ourselves," which is often quoted in defense of a large national debt. Actually, we owe about 40 percent of our short-term debt to the Arabs, the Germans and the Japanese. If the truth were told, we would have to admit that all of the national debt is ultimately owed by our children, and will come due when they become workers and taxpayers.

"Ye shall know the truth and the truth shall make you free." There can be no freedom when dishonesty in government is an automatic reflex, and when we refuse to face the truth about the realities of the world around us. If we won't honestly and unflinchingly define the problem, we will never find the solutions. Don't hold your breath.

"Thou shalt not commit adultery." I discussed at some length in *How to Prosper During the Coming Bad Years* ("Sin Tax" Chapter 11) the economic impact of broken homes (with adultery still the chief cause of divorce), couples having children without the formality of marriage and then breaking up, leaving the mother and children dependent upon the city or county. I came up with a price tag of about $500 to $2,000 per taxpayer to support the shattered products of the sexual revolution, so I need say no more about that one.

When human beings as a group are not compassionate, charitable and can't postpone gratification, when they do not save and invest wisely, or voluntarily contribute to the general welfare, a nation is in deep trouble. Laws, regulations and new tax policies are merely symptomatic treatment, while the underlying disease rolls on unchecked, perpetuated by greedy or ignorant politicians who remain in office by pandering to the basest of human weaknesses. Until such time as this nation is ready to "repent" of these moral, ethical and economic sins, we can only expect more of the same. The prognosis is terribly discouraging.

THE HAIR OF THE DOG THAT BIT US

What could cause such repentance?

I refer you back to my miserable experience in 1968. It took the loss of a child and the destruction of my business to traumatize me to the point where I was willing to make radical changes in my behavior. Perhaps the nation and the world will have to undergo similar shocks before we become willing to make such radical changes.

Generally, humans don't make basic behavioral change unless it becomes apparent to them that continuing on their present course will produce such unpleasant results that they'd rather not go through it. Usually they have to have a taste of it.

The alcoholic or the drug addict rarely kicks the habit until it creates such misery, fear, pain and suffering that he decides that the misery, fear, pain and suffering of going through withdrawal is the lesser of the two evils. We seem to have to reach some low point in our lives before we make basic changes.

The early character of America was formed in the misery of the Valley Forge winter. We became a permanently united nation out of the agony of the Civil War.

The miserably, painfully traumatic Great Depression of the 30s had long-term beneficial effects on the national character. Perhaps the strength, resilience and character that enabled us to fight World War Two on two fronts and win, with unity and a sense of national purpose, was molded in the 30s.

The foundations of the prosperity of the state of California were laid by the flood of migrant workers who fled the dust bowl. Had we had extensive welfare and unemployment funds, I'll bet we would have three generations of welfare parasites in Oklahoma and Texas. They would have been frozen in place by the dole, just as millions of workers in obsolete smokestack industries are paralyzed into immobility in Detroit, Pittsburgh and Cleveland by unemployment, inflation, welfare and food stamps.

The sexual behavior of the nation, as reflected in its entertainment—the movies particularly—went from the wildly permissive days of the roaring 20s before the Depression, to the highly conservative behavior of the 30s and 40s after the Depression. I don't think that's coincidental. Trauma builds character.

Inflation will end only when society reverses the growth of debt. That requires bankruptcy, debt repudiation on the national and international level, or rapid, disciplined debt repayment at all levels. This process is inseparable from depression, deprivation and widespread suffering. Perhaps that is the only experience that will bring us to our senses. As miserable as it might be, the end result could be a happier, stronger country—just as I have enjoyed my happiest years since the misery of 1968.

The lesson of history is that individuals and nations generally must experience severe trauma before they make dramatic changes, and anything less than radical dramatic change won't work here. Our behavior, our values, our thought processes, even our instinctive responses to problems must change.

Sometimes I feel, when Free the Eagle fights this or that law, that we are only attacking symptoms. There's an old adage that says, "For every person who attacks the roots of evil, there are hundreds flailing away at the leaves." The sentiments I have just expressed are aimed at the roots.

Perhaps enlightenment in the midst of ignorance will help some. I know a lot of well-intentioned liberals whose hearts are in gear, but whose heads are in neutral. They don't understand that when they vote to take money out of someone's pocket to give to someone else, their highly principled intention to help someone is offset by the highly unprincipled position of forcibly stealing from another person.

I'm sure that many good-hearted liberals who honestly think of themselves as "compassionate" would feel a whole lot different if it dawned on them that the symptoms they are alleviating today with the public printing press are nothing compared to the misery that will be created tomorrow because of the burden of debt and inflation that will come to rest on the backs of the next generation.

I've had especially interesting experiences with schoolteachers, who, as a whole, are probably one of the most liberal groups in America. The National Education Association had hundreds of delegates at the Democratic National Convention in 1976. They provided the votes that gave Jimmy Carter the nomination. The NEA stance on almost every conceivable social and political issue could only be characterized as ultraliberal. These are the people who are teaching our children. They look upon conservatives who say "no" to further government spending as totally lacking in compassion. My experience with teachers who subscribe to my newsletter, however, has been that when you can teach a teacher sound economics, he or she realizes that alleviating today's symptoms only leads to tomorrow's terminal disease. I've seen these teachers turn 180° and exert a powerful, positive influence on the economic and political thinking of young people.

Perhaps the problem isn't solely the willful violation of basic moral and ethical principles. Perhaps it's also ignorance of the significance and consequences of those principles, and the bad trade-offs made when principles are apparently in conflict.

Now that you know more about me, you may believe me when I say I would much rather persuade someone of a sound principle than make lots of money. Fortunately, however, I am in the pleasant position of making a better-than-average living, while spending most of my productive time in just such an educational effort. I love it.

HOW TO ANALYZE INVESTMENTS

I told you in Chapter 11 that there were many other technical Camera Angles we use to confirm or deny our fundamental Camera Angles and our Moving Average studies. Here are some of the key ones, including some that are indispensable to the short-term trader.

If you don't intend to do your own charting, don't worry if you don't fully grasp all the details. The degree to which you do understand these, however, can vastly increase the usefulness of any financial newsletter and your own investment judgment, and increase your confidence in the judgments and philosophy expressed in this book.

CAMERA ANGLE #4—TRENDLINES

Trendlines are simply straight lines drawn on the charts, touching the peaks and valleys of the movements of an investment. Those straight lines on Chart #4 represent resistance (line A) on the upside or support (line B) on the downside. When an investment moves decisively through a trendline, we should be alert to further change of direction.

Trendlines are among the simplest and most basic tools, and they give us early warnings of a change in primary trend, as well as preliminary buy and sell signals.

Trendlines all by themselves tell you very little. They are useful only in conjunction with other signals.

CAMERA ANGLE #5—HIGHS AND LOWS

Many things can be learned from the chart pattern of the investment itself. "Higher highs" when combined with "higher lows" (A and B on Chart #5) are usually a very constructive pattern. "Lower highs" when combined with "lower lows" (see C and D on Chart #5, page 258) are generally a destructive pattern.

256

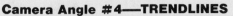

Camera Angle #4—TRENDLINES

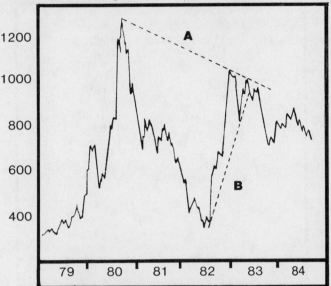

BARRON'S GOLD-MINING GROUP

Trendline A is a "resistance" line. When an investment breaks above a declining resistance line, that's bullish. Trendline B is a "support" line. When an investment breaks below a rising support line, that's bearish.

CAMERA ANGLE #6—POINT-AND-FIGURE

One of the most useful weapons in our battery of investment technical tools is the "point-and-figure" chart. It's not hard to understand, and it's the simplest, least time-consuming chart to keep.

Point-and-figure charts differ from all other charts in two important ways:

1) X's and O's are used in plotting instead of the traditional lines or bars.

2) Point-and-figure charting completely disregards the element of time and is used solely to record changes in price. X's are used to show price increases and O's are used to show price declines. If there are no price changes big enough to trigger a new X or O, even for days or weeks, the chart doesn't change. By the same token, if the market is moving fast, you could get several X's or O's in a day or week.

Let's go over some examples of point-and-figure charts on gold and silver.

Camera Angle Chart #6A (page 259) on gold illustrates several points. Each time gold goes up $10 or more, an X is entered on the chart. If gold rises by only $9, no X is entered.

Camera Angle #5——HIGHS AND LOWS

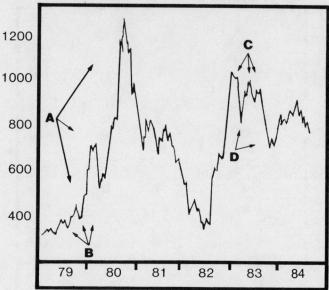

BARRON'S GOLD-MINING GROUP

"Higher highs" coupled with "higher lows" (A and B) usually mean a rising investment (in this case, a whole stock group), while "lower highs" coupled with "lower lows" (C and D) usually mean a falling investment.

Your choice of scale is based on experience. The "optimum" scale is the one that gives the most dependable signals, producing the least false starts while catching the largest profitable swings; $10 tends to give us the best gold signals. This means that before we record an X or an O in a square, prices must move in $10 increments, in accordance with the price scale on this particular chart.

THREE-POINT REVERSAL

Because Chart #6A is a "three-point reversal" chart (3 times $10), in order to change directions from the X column to the O column, allowing us to record an O, gold must decline by $30 or more below the last recorded X. At that time we record three O's (representing the $30 decline), and one O for each additional $10 decline thereafter. The "three-point reversal" requirement keeps us from getting too many false signals.

For example, if gold, after rising to $415, falls to $389, no O's are entered,

Camera Angle #6A—POINT-AND-FIGURE

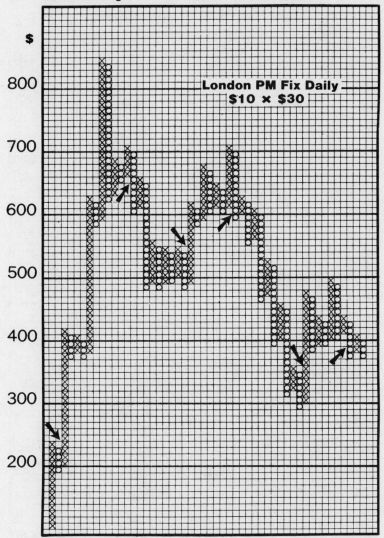

GOLD (June 1, 1977 through December 9, 1983)

A point-and-figure chart records X's when an investment rises, and O's when an investment declines. When an "X" column surpasses the last "X" column, it's a buy signal (see downward-pointing arrows). When an "O" column falls below the last "O" column, it's a sell signal (see upward-pointing arrows).

Camera Angle #6B—POINT-AND-FIGURE

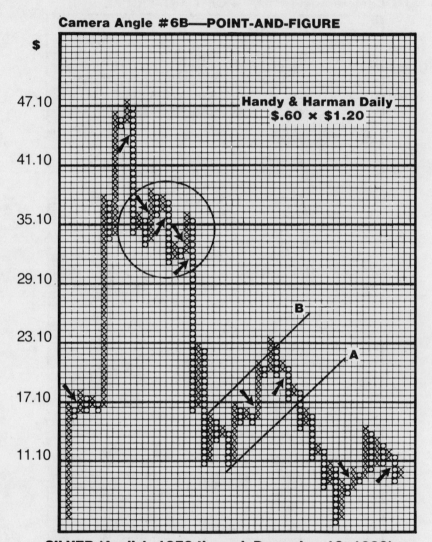

SILVER (April 1, 1978 through December 13, 1983)

As with the preceding gold chart, X's are used for rising prices, and O's are used for falling prices. The downward pointing arrows denote "buy" signals and the upward pointing arrows denote "sell" signals. Straight line B is a resistance line. Straight line A is a support line.

because the last X is at $410, and the price of gold must drop $30 from the last X to get a "reversal." Gold would have to fall to or below $380, $30 or more below $410, before we record three O's. For every additional $10 drop in gold, another O will be recorded.

In order to reverse to the upside again and record an X, it also takes a "three-point reversal," or a $30-or-more increase in gold above the last O. At that point, three X's would be placed on the chart.

We call Camera Angle Chart #6A a "10 by 30" chart—$10 increments, with a $30 reversal.

Although three-point reversal charts are most popular, the variations are unlimited. Camera Angle #6-B, for example, an "optimum" silver point-and-figure chart, uses a two-point reversal (60¢ by $1.20). It is called a "60 by 120" chart. Optimum point-and-figure chart scales are arrived at through extensive trial-and-error experimentation with price scales and reversal amounts.

BUY AND SELL SIGNALS

An "optimum" point-and-figure chart generates buy signals when the X column reaches a higher level than the previous column of X's, and sell signals are given when the O column reaches a lower level than the previous O column (see arrows on Camera Angle 6A and 6B charts).

Note that buy signals (downward-pointing arrows) helped us catch all the major up moves, and sell signals (upward-pointing arrows) got us out before all the expensive declines. The few false signals we received (circle) resulted in only minuscule losses.

A "three-point reversal" can mean $1 by $3, $.50 by $1.50, or $.30 by $.90— any amount, as long as the "reversal" is three times the amount of the first number. A two-point reversal chart uses two times the amount of the first number.

The smaller the increments, the more sensitive the charts, because a smaller price change can reverse the chart. Since $.20 moves occur more frequently than $1 moves, the $.20 silver chart will give a lot more buy and sell signals. We look for the optimum scale that is sensitive enough not to miss a major change, but not so sensitive as to give us too many false signals.

SUPPORT AND RESISTANCE

Conventional point-and-figure analysis uses 45° trendlines to indicate support levels on the downside and resistance on the upside (see support line A, and resistance line B on Camera Angle Chart #6B).

A tentative buy signal is given, for example, when the price rises above a resistance line, and a tentative sell signal is given when the price falls below a support line.

Point-and-figure charts alone don't tell us everything we need to know, but they are one important piece of our "instant replay" puzzle.

CAMERA ANGLE #7—RELATIVE STRENGTH

One of the most valuable Camera Angles is the "Relative Strength" study. We follow 96 stock industry groups, plus the precious metals, the major market averages, commodities and currencies, and after doing the appropriate calculations, weigh them against each other to see what is stronger than what. We want our money to be in the industry groups that are gaining strength relative to other investments. When we decided to go into silver and gold stocks in July 1982, rather than gold bullion (and made a lot more money), we measured their strength against gold through Relative Strength studies, which told us they were much stronger than gold. This turned out to be true.

Another objective of Relative Strength studies is to find emerging investments before they have risen to the top. Every week we rank the top ten to twenty investments in Relative Strength, but we also look further back in the pack to see what is on the way up, the "emerging investment." That was how we caught the oil stocks fairly early in their 1983 advance. As long as these strongest investments stay high in the Relative Strength rankings we will stay with them, assuming all other technical factors are hanging together.

Relative Strength is determined by matching up two investments in the following way.

Let's say we have concluded we're in a fever cycle, and we don't know whether to buy gold bullion or gold-mining shares. We would look in *Barron's,* the weekly investment newspaper that everyone should subscribe to, and get the *Barron's* weekly Gold Mining Group Index figure. We then divide it into the London second gold fix for Thursday of the same week. The resulting number is then represented by a dot on the chart. We do this each week, connecting the dots with a line.

When the resulting line is rising (Bracket A, Chart #7), bullion is stronger than gold shares and is likely to outperform them, so you buy gold. When the line is falling (Bracket B, Chart #7), gold shares are stronger than bullion, and the shares are likely to continue to outperform the bullion, so you buy mining stocks.

We use this technique to look for the strongest stock industry groups or commodities. We compare with each other all the 140 investments and indices we are watching and rank them from the highest to the lowest, and watch carefully for significant changes in these rankings. It might take weeks if done

Camera Angle #7——RELATIVE STRENGTH

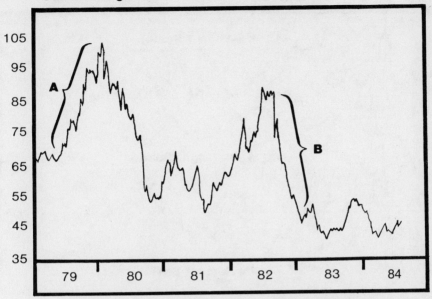

GOLD VS BARRON'S GOLD SHARE INDEX

A rising line (A) means gold is stronger than gold-mining stocks, and a falling line (B) means you will make more money in mining stocks.

manually. Our computer does these calculations in minutes. If we see something starting to move up, we red-flag it. If it continues rising, we then go to work on that investment, applying fundamental analysis, moving average studies, point-and-figure charts and so on. If it meets all of our criteria, it becomes an "emerging group." We then look for the strongest segments of that group.

Relative Strength, in and of itself, has its limitations. If both investments you are comparing are in a bear market, all it will tell you is which one is falling more slowly. You only want investments which are in primary uptrends, so fundamentals and Moving Averages first determine whether or not we're even interested. Relative Strength studies, in conjunction with Moving Averages, should get you into a trend relatively early in the game and keep you there until the trend has run its course.

As Jim Dines, the "original gold bug," says, "A trend in motion will tend to remain in motion until it ends." That simpleminded-sounding statement is a lot more profound than it appears on the surface. It means "stay with a trend until

Camera Angle #8—MOMENTUM

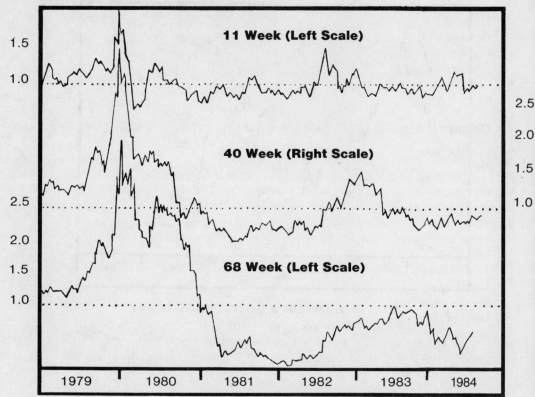

11 Week (Left Scale)

40 Week (Right Scale)

68 Week (Left Scale)

GOLD MOMENTUM (Thurs. 2nd London Fix)

This chart tells you if an investment is gaining or losing momentum, gathering strength or fizzling out. Above 1.0, it is stronger, especially if it is rising. Below 1.0, it is weaker, especially if it is falling.

it runs its course. Don't anticipate the end of a trend. Let the market tell you; don't try to tell the market."

CAMERA ANGLE #8—MOMENTUM STUDIES

One way to gauge the strength of an investment is to measure its "momentum." We measure the momentum of gold, for example, using various time frames for varying degrees of sensitivity, by simply dividing today's price by that of 11 weeks ago, or 40 weeks, or 68 weeks (the optimum Moving Averages), depending on how sensitive you want the measurement to be. You do this each week and chart it, just like the other Camera Angles.

If the resulting number is above 1, and rising, then the price is gaining momentum, like a rocket accelerating from the launching pad, moving faster and faster. We watch first for an 11-week momentum change, then a 40-week and a 68-week, which generate increasing levels of concern or interest. You will notice we use the same time frames as the optimum Moving Average for that particular investment.

CAMERA ANGLE #9—MOMENTUM OF RELATIVE STRENGTH

Now this gets really tricky!

Remember our underlying theme; the big money is made by participating in a primary trend. Since the primary movements of cyclical investments generally last for long periods of time, we want to verify that an investment is in a primary trend. We want to guard against "marrying" a scenario—becoming blind to contrary technical evidence—so we use an indicator called "Momentum of Relative Strength." This is a little tougher to explain.

Momentum, as I just explained, is used to determine whether an investment is getting stronger or weaker. Momentum of Relative Strength is used to determine whether an investment is gaining strength at an accelerating rate in relation to the market in general or to other investments. We want investments that are not only running a good race but also pulling away from the pack.

Let's say you want to determine the Momentum of Relative Strength of gold bullion vs. the Gold-Mining Stock Group. You take this week's Relative Strength figure of gold vs. gold shares, computed as we explained in Camera Angle #7, and divide it by the Relative Strength figure of 50 weeks or 30 weeks, or 13 weeks ago, and chart the resulting numbers weekly. If the line is falling, gold is losing strength relative to gold shares at an accelerating rate. The shorter time frames are more sensitive to change; the longer ones are more dependable in signaling long-term trends. If the line is going up, bullion is strengthening vs. gold shares. If the current figure is above 1 and rising, we can say with reasonable confidence that gold is pulling away from gold shares. You can use this to compare any two investments, or any two industry groups.

SHORT-TERM INDICATORS

The preceding Camera Angles deal with primary trends, but we don't want to catch a primary trend after most of the profit is behind us, or stay with it too long. We must monitor some of the more sensitive short-term indicators to alert us to the possibility of a trend change. Also, short-term traders and speculators, especially if they're trading highly leveraged investments like futures or stock

Camera Angle #9——MOMENTUM OF RELATIVE STRENGTH

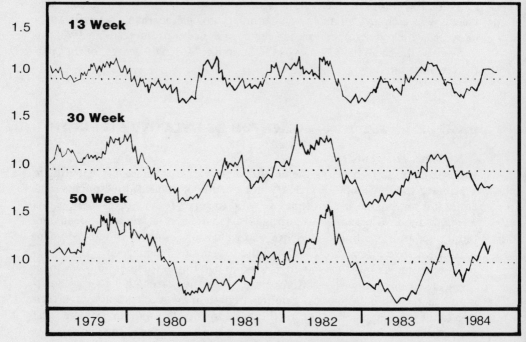

GOLD VS GOLD SHARES

This chart tells you if gold is stronger or weaker than gold-mining shares. If the line is rising, gold is gaining strength, relative to mining shares. If the line is falling, it is losing strength at an accelerating rate.

options, should use technical tools that signal changes in direction with as little time lag as possible.

CAMERA ANGLE #10——MONEY FLOW

One of the most sensitive indicators is "money flow," developed in the 20s by Jesse Livermore, perhaps the greatest of all speculators.

He calculated his money-flow figures by multiplying the day's volume (number of shares or contracts traded in that particular investment) by the price change of the stock or commodity. This indicates whether money is flowing into or out of the investment.

An example of four days' money flow is given in the following table on ASA (an investment trust listed on the New York Stock Exchange, which invests in

ASA MONEY FLOW, MARCH 1983

	Vol		Price Change		Daily MF	Cumulative MF
3/8	552	×	− 1.50	=	− 828(a)	
3/9	507	×	+ 1.37	=	+ 694(b)	−134(c)
3/10	631	×	+ .75	=	+ 473	339
3/11	507	×	− 1.00	=	− 507	−168

South African gold shares). We calculated the money flow using data from *The Wall Street Journal.*

On March 8, 55,200 shares of ASA traded and the stock was down $1.50. We multiply −1.50 by 552, giving us a money flow of −828 (a). We do the same thing the next day and get a money flow of +694 (b). We add them together and get our cumulative total of −134 (c). We then plot that cumulative money flow (dashed line, Chart #10) on the same chart as the stock (black line, Chart #10).

When the money flow line is rising, more money is flowing into the stock than out of it. When it is falling, money is flowing out of the stock. Rising money flow is bullish, and falling money flow is bearish.

In Chart #10 (page 268), sharply rising money flow gave us an ASA buy signal in August 1982 at $27 (two-headed connecting arrows, Chart #10). We held on until the money flow gave us a sell signal in February 1983, and sold out at $78 (see circle, Chart #10). We made fortunes in ASA options.

CAMERA ANGLE #11—MOVING TOTAL VOLUME

Successful short-term technical analysis, just like long-term trend analysis, requires weighing each factor against other evidence. Money flow is most useful when it is used in conjunction with "total volume" studies. We want the two to agree before we act. This keeps the odds on our side.

Experience has shown us that the 12- and 24-day Moving Total Volume figures are the most useful.

"Moving Total Volume" is calculated by adding up the total volume figures for that investment each day for the last 12 days (but *not* dividing by 12, as we do with Moving Averages). You then make the total volume "move" by each day dropping the oldest day, adding the current day and recalculating. You place the dot on the chart and connect it to the previous point with a line. The resulting line is Moving Total Volume (broken and solid lines at the bottom of Chart #11).

Camera Angle #10 MONEY FLOW

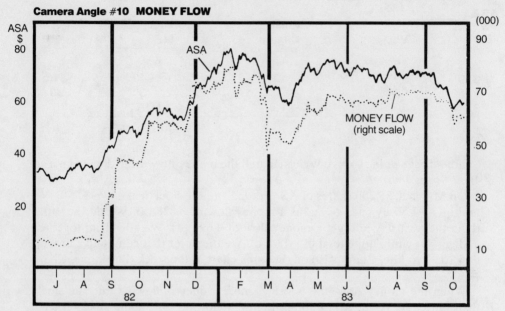

This chart illustrates whether money is flowing into or out of a particular stock or commodity, in this case ASA, listed on the New York Stock Exchange.
Rising money flow (dotted line) is bullish, falling money flow is bearish.

A healthy market will rise on increasing volume. When the market is in a downtrend, volume tends to drift downward with it. A rising market with rising volume and rising money flow is very bullish, as in September 1982 (see oval, Chart #11), when it confirmed what the money flow was trying to tell us. It can also be an early-warning indicator of a major change in trend. Alone it doesn't tell us much.

CAMERA ANGLE #12—PUT/CALL RATIO

The Put/Call Ratio is an excellent short-term measure of speculative sentiment. It helps measure "Contrary Opinion," which is an important short-term investment tool. Contrary opinion can't be used alone, but taken in conjunction with other indicators, it can be very helpful.

As explained in Chapter 9, "Going for Broke," lots of stocks have "listed options," which are a leveraged way of investing in the stock market. People buy call options when they expect the price to go up, and they buy put options when they expect the price to go down. The Put/Call ratio helps to measure the general opinion of investors relative to that investment. When the sentiment is

Camera Angle #11—MOVING TOTAL VOLUME

ASA
$

Moving Total Volume (dashed and solid lines), when used with Money Flow, can be an important confirmation. Rising volume with rising money flow usually means a rising stock (see oval, Sept. 82).

weighted heavily one way, I generally want to bet the other way, not just to be difficult but because the majority is usually wrong.

We obtain the raw data every week from *Barron's,* which shows the volume of each put and each call for the preceding week. We simply add up all the put volume, then add up all the call volume, and divide the total put volume by the total call volume, which gives us a number which we then chart weekly.

We generally use a five-week Moving Average, as the weekly gyrations are erratic, and the MA smooths out the line, making it easier to analyze.

When the ratio is very high, usually after a decline in the stock, pessimism runs rampant. Because the consensus is usually wrong, the stock and its option should turn around and start up. If the ratio is very low, optimism is rampant and the theory of Contrary Opinion would tell you that the stock would tend to turn down. Note on Chart #12 how the put/call ratio line tends to move in the opposite direction from the stock.

In other words, when the ratio is very low, optimism is the mood of the day. If almost everyone is optimistic, they have probably already bought, and we're probably about to run out of buyers. The stock will probably go down. When

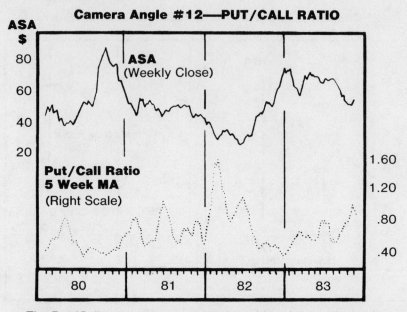

Camera Angle #12—PUT/CALL RATIO

The Put/Call ratio measures bullish and bearish sentiment for the "Contrary Opinion" investor who assumes the majority is usually wrong. A rising lower line means pessimism is increasing, so the stock should soon start up. Conversely, a falling line means optimism is increasing, so a top is probably near. As you can see, the put/call ratio tends to move in the opposite direction from the stock.

the ratio is very high, pessimism is the mood of the day, and that usually means a reversal. If almost everyone is pessimistic, we've run out of sellers. The stock is likely to go up.

I will only buy call options after an extended decline in the stock, when the Put/Call Ratio is high, meaning that pessimism is running rampant, and the Money Flow and Moving Total Volume are also bullish. Options profits are always made by the minority, never by the majority. When the contrary indicator of the Put/Call Ratio is used along with Money Flow and Moving Total Volume, and everything is in synch, I have a high-odds short-term bet. It's not infallible, but it shifts the odds heavily to your side.

The Put/Call Ratio is reliable only when the stocks have had listed options for several years. For example, it works well with ASA, but it isn't worth a hill of beans on Dome Mining. We do, however, use the ASA Put/Call Ratio for option timing on all the other gold stocks, as they tend to move as a complex. We then look to see how much of an option premium there is on each of the stocks to determine which one we choose.

LEFT UNSAID

There is an almost infinite number of combinations of sophisticated technical tools that I could have examined, and there are huge differences of opinion
as to how technical indicators should be interpreted. I've seen equally good
technicians, using the same data, ending up in total disagreement as to the direction of markets, but technical analysis, when combined with both internal
and external fundamental examination, can keep the odds heavily on your
side.

Technical analysis alone is not infallible. I have occasionally had all of the
technical indicators on my side, and not made money. All of these methods,
however, when used together, can reduce the frequency of such unpleasant
events and increase the profitability in the majority of cases when the indicators hold up.

Sometimes the technical signals are so mixed and unclear that you have only
two choices: (1) rely exclusively on the fundamentals; or (2) stash your money
in a money market fund and wait until the technical signals stack up in the
same direction as the fundamentals. This second strategy can cause you to miss
out on some market moves, but I don't total up the money-making opportunities I miss. I do keep careful, close score on the ones I caught that lost money,
because I choose to avoid pain, although an often hostile press will point out
my every blooper in loving detail. I can wait until I get everything on my side,
and I have no regrets whatever about the investments I miss when the picture is
not clear enough to suit me.

APPENDIX

II

RECOMMENDED READING AND PRODUCTS

THINGS TO READ

Although I have tried to give you the essence of each subject covered in the book, in many areas I have barely scratched the surface.

These are the things my staff and I read. I don't agree with everything written in all the listed publications, but I find them all to be useful, provocative, intellectually stimulating and a constant reminder that I don't know everything.

I have no financial interest in any of these products or publications, unless otherwise noted. We do, however, have joint ventures with some newsletter publishers, which interest is disclosed in each case. If not disclosed, no financial interest exists.

As International Paper Company said in a terrific series of ads three decades ago, "Send me a man who reads." The investor who reads will outperform the one who does not.

NEWSLETTER AND ADVISORY SERVICES

TARGET PUBLICATIONS

Howard Ruff's Financial Success Report (Howard Ruff), P.O. Box 25, Pleasanton, CA 94566. Phone: 800-654-4455 (USA), 800-654-4456 (CA), 415-463-2215. $89 for 48 issues. $145 overseas. Also, write to the above address for the free update on this book (one time only).

The Anderson Tax Report (B. Ray Anderson), P.O. Box 25, Department A1, Pleasanton, CA 94566. Phone: 415-463-2215. $145 for 12 issues.

Dads and Moms (Paul Lewis), P.O. Box 25, Pleasanton, CA 94566. Phone: 415-463-2215. $18.75 for 12 issues. Another Target publishing effort. Good ideas for quality family living.

272

Penny Mining Stock Report (Bob Bishop and Jerry Pogue), Box 5100, Pleasanton, CA 94566. Phone: 415-463-2215. $119.00 for 12 issues. This is a Target, Inc., joint venture. We are the publisher. A penny stock bought could be a dollar earned.

INVESTMENTS AND ECONOMICS

The Aden Analysis (Pamela and Mary Anne Aden), Adam Smith Publishing, 4425 W. Napoleon Avenue, Metairie, LA 70001. Phone: 504-456-0040. $250.00 for 12 issues. Technically oriented, but clear, sound and terrific. Their track record is fabulous.

Deliberations (Ian McAvity), P.O. Box 182, Adelaide Street Station, Toronto, Ontario, Canada M5C 2J1. Phone: 416-926-0995. $185 per year.

Dines Letter (James Dines), P.O. Box 22, Belvedere, CA 94920. $150.00 (1 year), 24 issues.

Dow Theory Letters (Richard Russell), P.O. Box 1759, La Jolla, CA 92038. $225 for 26 issues (one year). The best writer in the business. Honest and thorough. Technically oriented.

Forecasts and Strategies (Mark Skousen), Phillips Publishing, 7315 Wisconsin Avenue, Suite 1200 N., Bethesda, MD 20814. Phone: 301-986-0666. $95.00 for 12 issues. Mark is a frequent consultant for our subscribers. Great for the very small investor, especially.

Harry Browne Special Reports (Harry Browne), P.O. Box 5586, Austin, TX 78763. Phone: 512-453-7313. $225 for 10 issues. Consistently well written. One of the original freethinkers of the hard-money movement.

Investing in Crisis (Douglas R. Casey), International Fund Management Inc., P.O. Box 40948, Washington, DC 20016. Phone: 202-298-7381. $195 per year for 12 issues. Outrageously provocative, but terrific.

Jerome Smith's Investment Perspectives (Jerome Smith), P.O. Box 200, Shelbyville, IN 46176. $195.00 for 12 issues.

Low Risk Advisory Letter (Robert Kinsman), 70 Mitchell Blvd., San Rafael, CA 94903. $125.00 for 17 issues (1 year). A good but very conservative performer. You won't get rich, but you probably won't ever lose a dime.

MJF Growth Stock Advisory (Michael J. Funke), New Capital Publications, P.O. Box 879, Mahopac, NY 10541. Phone: 914-628-4203. $195.00 for 12 issues. Another occasional Target joint venture, and a good one.

Myers' Finance and Energy (C. Vernon Myers), 310 Peyton Bldg., Spokane, WA 99201. Phone: 509-747-9371. $200 for 14 issues (1 year) or $110 for 7 issues. The grand old curmudgeon of hard money. He can be a burr under my saddle, but I love his letter.

Personal Finance (Richard E. Band), 1300 N. 17th Street, Suite 1660, Arlington, VA 22209. Phone: 800-336-5407 or 703-276-7100. $39.00 for 24 issues (1 year).

The Reaper (R. E. McMaster), P.O. Box 39026, Phoenix, AZ 85069. Phone: 800-528-0559 or 602-252-4477. $195.00 for 12 issues; 6-month trial subscription for $110.00. Heavy on philosophy, but a brilliant commodity analyst.

Remnant Review (Gary North), P.O. Box 8204, Ft. Worth, TX 76112. Phone: 817-595-2691. $95.00 for 22 issues. Our industry's most solid pessimist, but one of the most consistently helpful publications. Highly recommended.

The Retirement Letter (Peter A. Dickinson), Phillips Publishing, 7315 Wisconsin Avenue, Suite 1200 N., Bethesda, MD 20814. Phone: 301-986-0666. $60.00 for 12 issues. The best in print for the "Golden Years."

Telephone Switch Newsletter (Dick Fabian), P.O. Box 2538, Huntington Beach, CA 92647. $117.00 (1 year).

The Tortoise Report (Robert Ringer), 2001 S. Barrington Avenue, Suite 216, Los Angeles, CA 90025. Phone: 213-477-1955. $95.00 for 12 issues. Making the money to invest. This is a good one.

Wealth Magazine (James Blanchard), 4425 W. Napoleon Avenue, Metairie, LA 70001. $20.00 (1 year), 4 issues.

The Wellington Letter (Bert Dohmen-Ramirez), 745 Fort Street, Suite 1814, Honolulu, HI 96813. Phone: 808-524-8063. $195 (1 year) 12 issues.

World Money Analyst (Mark Tier), 45 Lyndhurst Terrace, 5th Floor, Hong Kong. Phone: 5-416110. Telex: 75355. 10076 Boca Entrada Blvd., Boca Raton, FL 33433. Phone: 305-483-2600. $135.00 for 12 issues. An international perspective.

Young's World Money Forecast (Richard Young), 366 Thames Street, Newport, RI 02840. Phone: 401-849-2131. $475.00 for 12 issues.

The Zweig Forecast (Martin E. Zweig, Ph.D.), 747 Third Avenue, New York, NY 10017. Phone: 212-644-0040. $245.00 per year (published every three weeks) or $145.00 for six months. Marty had the hottest hand in 1982. A fine technician.

DIGESTS

Daily News Digest (W. A. Johnson), P.O. Box 39850, Phoenix, AZ 85069. Phone: 800-528-0559 or 602-252-4477. $95.00 per year (weekly) or six months for $57.00. Endlessly provocative news you won't see elsewhere. Always fun to read.

Hard Money Digest (Richard M. Campbell), 3608 Grand Avenue, Oakland, CA 94610. Phone: 800-327-8456 or 415-444-2800. $137.00 for 12 issues. A summary of what all the gold bugs are saying.

Newsletter Digest (Dr. Al Owen), 2335 Pansy Street, Huntsville, AL 35801. Phone: 205-534-7473. $75.00 for 24 issues (1 year) or $45 for 6 months. A sampling of us all.

Wall Street Digest (Donald Rowe), 120 Wall Street, New York, NY 10005. Phone: 212-344-6676. $150 (1 year) 12 issues.

FROM WASHINGTON

Future File (Jack Anderson), New Capital Publications, P.O. Box 880, Mahopac, NY 10541. Phone: 212-725-2206. $95.00 for 12 issues. Jack is a dear friend, and we sometimes joint-venture in his marketing.

State of the Nation, Free the Eagle, 214 Massachusetts Avenue, NE, Suite 510, Washington, DC 20002. Phone: 202-547-2122. 12 months for $35.00 contribution to Free the Eagle. My personal pride and joy! It's our official political report.

INTERNATIONAL

International Harry Schultz Letter, c/o FERC, P.O. Box 141, 1815 Clarens, Switzerland. Phone: 21-646561. $258 for 12 months. Harry is the granddaddy of us all, and follows an incredible number of investments.

International Investment Letter (Adrian Day), 1300 N. 17th Street, Suite 1660, Arlington, VA 22209. Phone: 800-336-5407 or 703-276-7100. $97.00 for 12 issues.

Investing in Crisis (Douglas R. Casey), International Fund Management, Inc., P.O. Box 40948, Washington, DC 20016. Phone: 202-298-7381. $195 per year for 12 issues. Outrageously provocative, but terrific.

World Money Analyst (Mark Tier), 45 Lyndhurst Terrace, 5th Floor, Hong Kong. Phone: 5-416110. Telex: 75355. 10076 Boca Entrada Blvd., Boca Raton, FL 33433. Phone: 305-483-2600. $135.00 for 12 issues. An international perspective.

METALS

The Coin Dealer Newsletter (Gray Sheet) (Allen Harriman), P.O. Box 2308, Hollywood, CA 90028. $60.00 for 1 year (weekly) or $18.00 for 3 months.

Gold Newsletter (James Blanchard), 4425 W. Napoleon Avenue, Metairie, LA 70001. Phone: 504-456-0040. $95.00 for 12 issues.

Metals Investor (John A. Pugsley), 711 W. 17th Street, G-4, Costa Mesa, CA 92627. $250.00 for 12 issues. Covering strategic metals.

Silver and Gold Report (Daniel Rosenthal), P.O. Box 40, Bethel, CT 06801. $144.00 for 24 issues. A must. Indispensable for all precious-metals investors. Best at exposing scams.

PENNY STOCKS

Penny Mining Stock Report (Bob Bishop and Jerry Pogue), Box 5100, Pleasanton, CA 94566. Phone: 415-463-2215. $119.00 for 12 issues. This is a Target, Inc., joint venture. We are the publisher. A penny stock bought could be a dollar earned.

The Bushnell Penny Stock Advisory (Donna Bushnell), New Capital Publications, P.O. Box 869, Mahopac, NY 11541. Phone: 212-725-2206. $145.00 for 12 issues.

MONEY FUNDS

Donoghue's Money Fund Report (William Donoghue), P.O. Box 540, Holliston, MA 01746. Phone: 617-429-5930. $595 for 52 issues (1 year). The best in its field.

Donoghue's Moneyletter (William Donoghue), P.O. Box 540, Holliston, MA 01746. Phone: 617-429-5930. $87.00 for 24 issues (1 year).

REAL ESTATE

Real Estate Advisor (Robert G. Allen), 145 East Center Street, Provo, UT 84601. $126.00 for 1 year.

Real Estate Intelligence Report (John Gornall), Phillips Publishing, 7315 Wisconsin Avenue, Suite 1200 N., Bethesda, MD 10814. Phone: 800-227-1617 or 301-986-0666. $135.00 for 12 issues.

Winning with Real Estate (Albert J. Lowry), 3390 Duesenberg Drive, Westlake Village, CA 91362. Phone: 213-991-8850. $195.00 for 12 issues. An old friend. A must for all real estate investors.

TAX PLANNING

The Anderson Tax Report, Target Publishers, P.O. Box 25, Department A1, Pleasanton, CA 94566. Phone: 415-463-2215. $195.00 for 12 issues. Another marketing joint venture. B. Ray is the best financial planner I know. He is trustee for my children's trusts.

Tax Angles (Vernon K. Jacobs), 1300 N. 17th Street, Arlington, VA 22209. Phone: 703-276-7100. $33.00 for 12 issues.

COMPUTER ADVISORY SERVICE

Jeffers Personal Computer Newsletter, P.O. Box 5600, San Ramon, CA 94583. Phone: 415-831-9104. $65 for 24 issues (1 year).

RETIREMENT

The Retirement Letter (Peter A. Dickinson), Phillips Publishing, 7315 Wisconsin Avenue, Suite 1200 N., Bethesda, MD 20814. Phone: 301-986-0666. $60.00 for 12 issues. The best in print for the "Golden Years."

DIAMONDS, GEMS AND COLLECTIBLES

Gem Market Reporter (Kurt W. Arens), P.O. Box 39890, Phoenix, AZ 85069. Phone: 602-252-4477. $98.00 for 1 year.

Gemstone Price Reports (J. F. Moyerson), UBIGE s.p.r.l.; Avenue Louise, 221; Brussels 1050, Belgium. Phone: 02-648-07-11. $270 per year, monthly.

Marcum Report, Inc., David Marcum, P.O. Box 30150, Chicago, IL 60630. Phone: 312-282-2459. $120.00 for 1 year.

PreciouStones Newsletter, Phillips Publishing, 7315 Wisconsin Avenue, Suite 1200 N., Bethesda, MD 20814. Phone: 301-986-0666. $177.00 for 12 issues. Indispensable for diamond and colored-stone investors.

SELF-SUFFICIENCY

Mother Earth News, P.O. Box 70, Hendersonville, NC 28791. Phone: 704-693-0211. $18 (1 year) 6 issues.

Self Reliant (Frank Lyons), P.O. Box 1127, Dover, NJ 07801. $12 for 10 issues.

Survival Tomorrow (Nancy Tappan), Personal Survival Center, Inc., 15 Oakland Avenue, Harrison, NY 10528. $60.00 for 12 issues. For the hard-core survivalist.

RUFF RECOMMENDED LIBRARY

All available from Target Publishers, P.O. Box 25, Pleasanton, CA 94566. Add $1.50 postage/handling for first item, 50¢ for each additional item (maximum $6.00).

BOOKS BY HOWARD J. RUFF

How to Prosper During the Coming Bad Years: A Crash Course in Personal Survival, by Howard J. Ruff, Warner Books, 1979. Softcover $3.95.

Survive and Win in the Inflationary Eighties, by Howard J. Ruff, Warner Books, 1982, $3.95. Softcover $3.95.

OTHER BOOKS

BUSINESS

How to Become Financially Successful by Owning Your Own Business, by Albert J. Lowry, Simon and Schuster, 1981, $14.95.

Turning Assets into Prosperity, by Neil Burnett, Valuwrite, 1982, $6.95.

American Entrepreneurs Association, Inc., *Entrepreneur Magazine* and start-up and operation manuals for new and profitable small businesses, 2311 Pontius Ave., Los Angeles, CA 90064. Phone: 800-421-2300 (USA), 800-352-7449 (CA), 213-478-0437.

COMMODITIES

The Commodity Futures Game, by Teweles, Harlow, Stone, McGraw Hill, 1974, $5.95.

Commodity Options, by Terry Mayer, New York Institute of Finance, 1983, $27.95.

The Dow Jones-Irwin Guide to Commodities Trading, Dow Jones-Irwin, 1973 and 1981, $27.50.

The Handbook of Commodity Cycles: A Window on Time, by Jacob Bernstein, John Wiley & Sons, 1982, $44.95.

How to Use Interest Rate Futures Contracts, by Edward W. Schwarz, Dow Jones-Irwin, 1979, $19.95.

COMPUTERS

Automating Your Financial Portfolio—An Investor's Guide to Personal Computers, by Donald Woodwell, Dow Jones-Irwin, 1983, $19.95.

Computer Selection Guide, by Dan Poynter, Para Publishing, 1983, $11.95.

Critical Issues in Software, by Werner L. Frank, John Wiley & Sons, 1983, $25.00.

Investors Computer Handbook, by Rod E. Packer, Hayden Book Co., $11.95.

So You Think You Need Your Own Business Computer, by William Perry, John Wiley & Sons, 1982, $14.95.

DIAMONDS, GEMS AND COLLECTIBLES

The Diamond Connection, by Anthony C. Sutton, R. R. Donnelley and Sons, 1979, $19.95.

The Diamond Book, by Mike Freedman, Dow Jones-Irwin, 1981, $14.95.

The World of Diamonds, by Timothy Green, William Morrow & Co., Inc., 1981, $12.95.

ECONOMIC

How to Prosper During the Coming Bad Years: A Crash Course in Personal and Financial Survival, by Howard J. Ruff, Warner Books, 1979. Softcover $3.95.

Survive and Win in the Inflationary Eighties, by Howard J. Ruff, Warner Books, 1982. Softcover $3.95.

Last Train Out, by Gary North, American Bureau of Economic Research, 1983, $6.95.

Successful Investing in an Age of Envy, by Gary North, Steadman Press, 1982, $14.95.

Wealth and Poverty, by George Gilder, 1981, $16.95.

Wealth for all, by R. E. McMaster, Jr., A. N. Inc., 1983, $14.95. Philosophically deep, but full of real nuggets with great impact.

ESTATE PLANNING

Death and Taxes, by Hans F. Sennholz, 1982, $5.95.

How You Can Use Inflation to Beat the IRS, by B. Ray Anderson, Warner Books, 1982. Softcover $6.95.

INTERNATIONAL

The Swiss Banking Handbook, by Robert Roethemund, Harper & Row, 1980, $19.95.
International Investment Opportunities, by Adrian Day, William Morrow & Co., 1982, $17.95.
Investing Without Borders, by Adrian Day, Alexandria House, 1982, $19.95.

INVESTMENT AND MONEY MANAGEMENT

How to Prosper During the Coming Bad Years: A Crash Course in Personal and Financial Survival, by Howard J. Ruff, Warner Books, 1979. Softcover $3.95.
Encyclopedia of Investments, by Blume and Friedman, 1982, $47.50.
High Finance on a Low Budget, by Mark Skousen, Mark Skousen, 1981, $10.00.
Inside the Financial Futures Markets, by Mark Powers and David J. Vogel, John Wiley & Sons, 1981, $24.95.
International Investment Opportunities: How and Where to Invest Overseas Successfully, by Adrian Day, William Morrow & Co., 1982, $17.95.
Investors Quotient, by Jack Burnstein, John Wiley & Sons, 1980, $16.95.
Never Say Budget, by Mark and JoAnn Skousen, Mark Skousen, 1983, $10.00.
Skousen's Complete Guide to Financial Privacy, by Mark Skousen, Kephart Communications, 1979 and 1982, $17.95.
Strategic Investing, by Douglas R. Casey, Simon and Schuster, 1982, $15.50.
Survive and Win in the Inflationary Eighties, by Howard J. Ruff, Warner Books, 1982. Softcover $3.95.
The Investor's Guide to Stock Quotations, by Gerald Warfield, Harper & Row Publishers, 1983, $13.95.
The Omega Strategy, by William Montapert, Omega Books, 1982, $10.00.

METALS

The Golden Key, by Eli Levine, Sanford J. Durst, 1981, $19.95.
High Profits from Rare Coin Investment, revised 1983, by W. David Bowers, Bowers & Merena Galleries, Inc., 1974 and 1983, $14.95.
Heads You Win, Tails You Win, by Jeffery J. Pritchard, Reston Publishing Co., 1983, $15.95.
The Morgan & Peace Dollar, by Wayne Miller, Adam Smith Publishing Co., $19.95.
New Boom in Silver, by Jerome F. Smith, ERC Publishers, 1983, $19.95.
The New World of Gold, by Timothy Green, Walker & Co., 1981, $15.95.
Platinum, by Anthony C. Sutton, Adam Smith Publishing Co., 1982, $16.95.
Silver Profits in the '80s, by Jerome F. Smith and Barbara Kelly Smith, Books In Focus, 1982, $16.65.
The Strategic Metals War, by James E. Sinclair & Robert Parker, Crown Publishers, Inc., 1983, $17.50.

MONEY FUNDS

Complete Money Market Guide, by William E. Donoghue, Harper & Row Publishers, Inc., 1981, $12.95.

Dow Jones-Irwin Guide to Mutual Funds, by Donald D. Rugg and Norman B. Hale, Dow Jones-Irwin, 1976 and 1983, $17.50.

No-Load Mutual Fund Guide, by William Donoghue, Harper & Row Publishers, Inc., 1983, $13.95.

Successful Investing in No-Load Funds, by Alan Pope, John Wiley & Sons, 1983, $19.95.

The Money Market Fund Primer, by Colleen Sullivan, Macmillan Publishing, 1983, $13.95.

PENNY STOCKS

Canadian Mines Handbook 1983–84, Northern Miner Press, $22.00.

Small Fortunes in Penny Gold Stocks, by Norman Lamb, Penny Mining Prospector, 1982, $14.95.

REAL ESTATE

A Fortune at Your Feet, by A. D. Kessler, Harcourt Brace Jovanovich, 1981, $10.95.

Creating Wealth, by Robert Allen, Simon and Schuster, 1983, $14.95.

Hidden Fortunes, by Dr. Albert Lowry, Simon and Schuster, 1983, $16.95.

How You Can Become Financially Independent by Investing in Real Estate, by Dr. Albert J. Lowry, Simon and Schuster, 1977, $16.95.

How to Manage Real Estate Successfully in Your Spare Time, by Dr. Albert J. Lowry, Simon and Schuster, 1979, $24.95.

Nothing Down, by Robert G. Allen, Simon and Schuster, 1980, $15.50.

RETIREMENT

Retirement Edens Outside the Sunbelt, by Peter A. Dickinson, E. P. Dutton, 1981, $9.25.

Travel and Retirement Edens Abroad, by Peter A. Dickinson, E. P. Dutton, 1983, $12.95.

SELF-SUFFICIENCY

Survival Home Manual, by Joel M. Skousen, Survival Homes, Inc., 1977 and 1982, $19.95.

STOCKS AND STOCK OPTIONS

Commodity Options, by Terry Mayer, New York Institute of Finance, 1983, $27.95.

The Compleat Option Player, by Kenneth R. Trester, Investrek Publishing, 1977, $16.95.

Dynamic Stock Option Trading, by Joseph T. Stewart, Jr., John Wiley & Sons, 1981, $37.95.

How the Average Investor Can Use Technical Analysis for Stock Profits, by James Dines, 1974, $45.00. A classic, timeless work on technical analysis to benefit both novice and sophisticated market student.

How to Buy: An Insider's Guide to Making Money in the Stock Market, by Justin Mamis, Farrar Straus Giroux, 1982, $11.95.

Future Stocks, by Robert Metz, Harper & Row Publishers, Inc., 1982, $13.50.

Options as a Strategic Investment, by Lawrence McMillon, New York Institute of Finance, 1980, $22.00.

Point and Figure Stock Market Trading, by A. W. Cohen, Chartcraft, Inc., 1982, $6.95.

The Stock Market and Inflation, edited by J. Anthony Boeckh and Richard T. Coghlan, Dow Jones-Irwin, 1982, $14.95.

TAX PLANNING

Death and Taxes (revised), by Hans F. Sennholz, 1982, $5.95.

Everything You Always Wanted to Know About Taxes But Didn't Know How to Ask, by Michael Savage, Doubleday Co., 1979 and 1982, $7.95.

How to Avoid Probate!, newly updated, by Norman F. Dacey, Crown Publishing, $16.95.

How to Save 50% or More on Your Taxes—Legally, by B. Ray Anderson, Macmillan Publishing, 1982, $14.95.

Take It Off, by Robert S. Holzman, Ph.D., Harper & Row, 1974 and 1983, $8.95.

Tax Free, by Mark Skousen, Mark Skousen, 1982, $12.95.

Tax Shelters—A Guide for Investors and Their Advisors, by Robert E. Swanson and Barbara M. Swanson, 1982, $32.50.

GOODS AND SERVICES FOR YOUR CONSIDERATION

In some vendor categories, you will note a "Recommended" firm and a list of others which are "Also Reputable." In some instances there is only one "Recommended" firm, and none are listed as "Also Reputable" either because we have not had time to dig any deeper or we are not comfortable with what we have found.

The "Recommended" firms are those which my staff has personally researched, where we have negotiated favorable arrangements for those who choose to take my advice, and which we monitor on a regular basis. As my recommendation provides a substantial portion of the total business of these recommended firms, this gives me considerable clout if any problems arise.

The "Also Reputable" firms have been investigated, but time limitations preclude my monitoring them as closely. These are dependable people who have good business reputations.

This list is subject to change, and I accept no responsibility for any trouble you might have with a firm we have dropped from the list.

Prices are also subject to inflationary change.

VENDORS

COIN DEALERS, BULLION, COINS AND/OR NUMISMATICS

Recommended

Investment Rarities, 1 Appletree Square, Minneapolis, MN 55420. Phone: 800-328-1860 (USA) or call collect 612-853-0700 (MN, AK, Canada, HI).

Deak-Perera, 1800 K Street NW, Washington, DC 20006. Phone: 800-424-1186 (USA), 202-872-1233, (202-872-1630—recorded exchange rates and precious-metals quotes).

Also Reputable

James U. Blanchard & Co., Inc., 4425 W. Napolean, Metairie, LA 70001. Phone: 800-535-7633 (USA), 504-456-9034 (LA).

C. Rhyne and Associates, 110 Cherry Street, Suite 202, Seattle, WA 98104. Phone: 800-426-7835 (USA), 206-623-6900, 206-625-9844 (Hot Line).

Camino Coin Company, 851 Burlway Road, Suite 105 (P.O. Box 4292), Burlingame, CA 94010. Phone: 415-348-3000.

Joel D. Coen, Inc., 39 W. 55th Street, New York, NY 10019. Phone: 800-223-0868 (USA) or 212-246-5025.

Lee Numismatics International, P.O. Box 1045, Merrimack, NH 03054. Phone: 800-835-6000 (USA), 800-842-3000 (NE), or 603-429-0869 (NH), or 603-429-0829 and 603-429-0877.

Manfra, Tordella & Brookes, Inc., Numismatic Department, 30 Rockefeller Plaza, New York, NY 10020. Phone: 800-223-5818 Ext. 621 or 619 (USA), 212-621-9500 Ext. 621 (AK, HI, Local) or 212-621-9539.

Sidney W. Smith & Sons, 2510 Biscayne Blvd., Miami, FL 33137. Phone: 305-573-1200, or 6639 S. Dixie Hwy., Miami, FL 33137. Phone: 305-665-1300.

NUMISMATIC AGENT-DEALER

Judith Kaller/M. Kaller & Associates, Inc., 333 North Broadway, Jericho, NY 11753. Phone: 516-938-6016.

PRECIOUS-METALS CERTIFICATES

Deak-Perera, 1800 K Street, NW, Washington, DC 20006. Phone: 800-424-1186 (USA), 202-872-1233.

Dreyfus Gold Deposits, Inc., 600 Madison Avenue, New York, NY 10022. Phone: 800-223-7750 (USA), call collect 212-935-6666.

Merrill Lynch, Sharebuilder Marketing: see your local Merrill Lynch office, or contact One Liberty Plaza, 5th Floor, 165 Broadway, P.O. Box 520, New York, NY 10080. Phone: 800-221-2856 or 800-221-2857 (USA), 800-522-8882 (NY), 212-709-3932, 212-70⸱-3933, 212-709-3929, 212-692-8600.

SWISS BANK PRECIOUS-METALS ACCUMULATION PROGRAM

Not Monitored

GOLDPLAN A.G., P.O. Box 213-K, 8033 Zurich, Switzerland.

GOLD-SHARE BROKERS AND/OR ADVISERS

Rotan Mosle, a Division of Paine, Webber, Gold-Share Specialist—Barry Downs, 10 E. 53rd Street, New York, NY 10022. Phone: 800-223-5806 or 212-750-0813.

Paine, Webber, Gold-Share Specialist—Gordon Speir, 1600 Broadway, Suite 2200, Denver, CO 80202. Phone: 303-861-2400 or 303-773-2842.

Dean Witter Reynolds, Jon M. Bloodworth, Jack Saunders, 1 Kaiser Plaza, Suite 350, Oakland, CA 94612. Phone: collect 415-839-8080.

PENNY STOCK BROKERS

Recommended

National Securities Corp., Jerry Pogue (Specializing in North American Penny Mining Shares, $3,000 minimum), 500 Union Street, Seattle, WA 98101. Phone: 800-426-1608 (USA), 206-622-7200 (AK, HI, Washington).

Also Reputable

Wall Street West, Donna Bushnell (Specializing in Oil and Gas Exploration Companies), 5340 S. Quebec, Suite 100, Englewood, CO 80111. Phone: 800-525-7598 (USA), 303-740-8444 (CO).

NO-LOAD (OR LOW-LOAD) MUTUAL FUND FAMILIES

Not Monitored

The following mutual funds are subject to changes—depending on the economy.

Bull & Bear Group, 11 Hanover Square, New York, NY 19005. Phone: 800-942-6911.

Fidelity Group, 82 Devonshire Street, Boston, MA 02109. Phone: 800-225-6190.

Investors Research Corp. (Twentieth Century Fund), P.O. Box 200, Kansas City, MO 64141. Phone: 816-531-5575.

Lexington Group, 580 Sylvan Avenue, P.O. Box 1515, Englewood Cliffs, NJ 07632. Phone: 800-526-4791.

United Services Funds (including United Services Gold Shares, Inc.), P.O. Box 29467, San Antonio, TX 78229. Phone: 800-531-5777, or 512-696-1234.

Dynamic Funds Management, Ltd., 330 Bay Street, #1403, Toronto, Ontario, Canada. Phone: 416-363-5621. (Offered in Canada under prospectus only.)

Strategic Investors (a load fund listed because of its outstanding performance), available from brokers, financial planners and Newcastle Financial Group.

MONEY MARKET FUNDS

Recommended

Capital Preservation Fund, 755 Page Mill Road, Palo Alto, CA 94304. Phone: 800-227-8380 (USA), 800-982-6150 (CA) or collect 415-858-2400 (AK, Canada, HI). For information packet 800-227-8996 (USA), 800-982-5873 (CA) or 415-858-3600. Two funds. Capital Preservation I is totally invested in T-bills. This is the one I use.

National Retired Teachers Association/American Association of Retired Persons U.S. Government Money Market Trust; 421 7th Avenue, Pittsburgh, PA 15219. Phone: 800-245-4770 (USA), 800-892-1040 (PA).

Merrill Lynch Cash Management Account, call your local Merrill Lynch office. The best and most versatile of the brokerage house funds.

IRA, KEOGH AND SELF-DIRECTED
RETIREMENT AND PENSION PLANS

Newcastle Financial Group, 1815 South State Street, Suite 450, Orem, UT 84057. Phone: 800-453-1466 or 801-224-9800.

Jon M. Bloodworth and Jack Saunders of Dean Witter Reynolds, 1 Kaiser Plaza, Suite 350, Oakland, CA 94612. Phone: collect 415-839-8080.

Merrill Lynch, call your local Merrill Lynch office.

Most No-Load Mutual Fund Families (see above list).

TAX SHELTERS

Recommended

Newcastle Financial Group, 1815 South State Street, Suite 450, Orem, UT 84057. Phone: 800-453-1466 or 801-224-9800. Newcastle products include real estate, gas and oil, equipment leasing, research and development, energy-related programs, livestock breeding and mining tax shelters and other timely tax-advantaged investments.

FINANCIAL PLANNING AND TAX PLANNING

Recommended

Newcastle Financial Group—provides comprehensive financial, tax and investment services, 1815 South State Street, Suite 450, Orem, UT 84057. Phone: 800-453-1466 or 801-224-9800.

INSURANCE

Newcastle Financial Group, 1815 South State Street, Suite 450, Orem, UT 84057. Phone: 800-453-1466 or 801-224-9800.

COMPUTER COUNSELING

Personal Touch Computer Service, 10 Crow Canyon Court, #210, San Ramon, CA 94583. Phone: 415-831-9104 or 800-356-1122.

REAL ESTATE INVESTMENT TRAINING

Recommended

Robert Allen, Investment Seminars, 3707 N. Canyon Rd., Suite 8-F, Provo, UT 84601. Phone: 801-226-2167.

Albert J. Lowry, Education Advancement Institute, 100 North Westlake Blvd., Westlake Village, CA 91362. Phone: 800-255-6979 (USA), 805-496-4400, or 213-991-8850.

Fortune Seminars (John Schaub), 1938 Ringling Blvd., Sarasota, FL 33577. Phone: 813-366-9024.

Also Reputable

Professional Educational Foundation (A. D. Kessler), Box 2446, Leucadia, CA 92024. Phone: 714-438-2446.

Complete information on various types of real estate seminars is listed monthly in *Creative Real Estate Magazine,* Box 2446. Leucadia, CA 92024. Phone: 714-438-2446.

DIAMONDS

Recommended

Newcastle Financial Group, 1815 South State Street, Suite 450, Orem, UT 84057. Phone: 800-453-1466 or 801-224-9800.

Reliance Diamonds, 484 Lake Park, #19, Oakland, CA 94610. Phone: 800-227-1590 (USA), 800-642-2406 (CA), collect 415-428-0104 (CA, AK, Canada, HI).

COLORED GEMSTONES

Recommended

Investment Rarities, 1 Appletree Square, Minneapolis, MN 55420. Phone: 800-328-1860 (USA) or collect 612-853-0700 (MN, AK, Canada, HI).

FINE JEWELRY

Ounce o' Gold (American Wholesale, 14-carat gold jewelry), P.O. Box 59006, Dallas, TX 75229. Phone: 214-353-0830.

Colonial Diamond Brokers, P.O. Box 674, Frederick, MD 21701. Phone: 301-663-3501.

FINE ARTS

Fine Arts, Ltd. (investment quality prints), 1854 Vallejo Street, Suite B, San Francisco, CA 94123. Phone: 415-775-2722.

Dr. Wesley M. Burnside (consulting & acquisition—American painting & sculpture), Art Department, Brigham Young University, Provo, UT 84602. Phone: 801-378-2281 or 801-378-6204.

STAMPS

M. Kaller & Associates, Inc., 333 North Broadway, Jericho, NY 11753. Phone: 516-938-6016.

FOOD STORAGE

Recommended

Martens Health and Survival Products, Inc., 5365 Avenida Encinas, #F, P.O. Box 725, Carlsbad, CA 92008. Phone: 800-824-7861 (USA), 800-822-5984 (CA), 619-438-0866.

Also Reputable

Grover Company, 330 W. University, Tempe, AZ 85281. Phone: 800-528-1406 (USA); 602-967-8738.

Intermountain Freeze-Dried Foods, 3025 Washington Boulevard, Ogden, UT 84401. Phone: 800-453-9210 (USA), 801-627-1490 or 801-627-7022.

The Simpler Life (Arrowhead Mills), P.O. Box 2059, Hereford, TX 79045. Phone: 806-364-0730. (Shipping Only: 110 South Lawton.) All natural and organic.

Sam Andy Foods, 1660 Chicago Avenue, Building P-1, Riverside, CA 92507. Phone: 714-684-9003.

S.I. Outdoor Food & Equipment by Mail, P.O. Box 1940, 2322 Artesia Blvd., Redondo Beach, CA 90278. Phone: 800-533-7415 (USA), 213-318-2575.

Survival Center, 5555 Newton Falls Road, Ravenna, OH 44266. Phone: 800-321-2900 (USA), 216-678-4000.

Rainy Day Foods, P.O. Box 71, Provo, UT 84603. Phone: 801-377-3093.

Frontier Food Association, Inc., 7263 Envoy Court, P.O. Box 47088, Dallas, TX 75247. Phone: 214-630-6221.

In Canada

Scott's Perma Storage Foods, Ltd., 21 Water Street, Aylmer, Ontario N5H 1G8. Phone: 519-773-2462.

Gary Bikman Distributing, Box 428, Lethbridge, Alberta, T1J 3Z1. Phone: 403-327-5734.

SURVIVAL PRODUCTS (MAIL ORDER)

Recommended

Martens Health and Survival Products, Inc., 5365 Avenida Encinas, #F, P.O. Box 725, Carlsbad, CA 92008. Phone: 800-824-7861 (USA), 800-822-5984 (CA), 619-438-0866.

Also Reputable

Grover Company, 330 W. University, Tempe, AZ 85282. Phone: 800-528-1406 (USA), 602-967-8738.

S.I. Outdoor Food & Equipment by Mail, P.O. Box 1940, 2322 Artesia Blvd., Redondo Beach, CA 90278. Phone: 800-533-7415 (USA), 213-631-6197.

The Survival Center, 5555 Newton Falls Road, Ravenna, OH 44266. Phone: 800-321-2900 (USA) or 216-678-4000.

SECURITY STORAGE VAULTS

Perpetual Storage, Inc., 3322 South 3rd East, Salt Lake City, UT 84115 (mailing only). Phone: 801-942-1950.

Guardian Safe Deposit, 2499 North Harrison Street, Arlington, VA 22207. Phone: 703-237-1133.

SAFES

Adesco Safe, 16720 S. Garfield Avenue, Paramount, CA 90723. Phone: 213-774-0081 and 213-630-1503.

Boston Lock and Safe Company, Inc., 30 Lincoln Street, Boston, MA 02135. Phone: 617-787-3421.

J. Goodman Company, 29 Arden Road, Livingston, NJ 07039. Phone: 201-994-3079.

Southern Securities, 207 Center Park Drive, Knoxville, TN 37922. Phone: 800-251-9992 (USA), 615-966-2300.

Survival Vaults, P.O. Box 462, Fillmore, CA 93015. Phone: 805-524-0286.

Tennessee Business Systems, 1200 Dodds Avenue, Chattanooga, TN 37404. Phone: 615-265-3884.

Warman Safe Co., 1545 Broadway, San Francisco, CA 94109. Phone: 415-776-5350.

EDUCATION AND SEMINARS BY HOWARD J. RUFF

The Howard Ruff Financial Planning Home Study Course, complete with computer analysis of your financial affairs. $395. From Target, Inc., P.O. Box 25, Pleasanton, CA 94566. (USA) 800-654-4455 (Cal.) 800-654-4456.

Howard Ruff National Conventions. Held twice yearly. For information contact Target Travel, International, P.O. Box 25, Pleasanton, CA. Phone: 800-227-2446 (USA), 800-321-5307 (CA), 415-463-2220.

TRAVEL WITH HOWARD RUFF

Howard Ruff Investment and Travel Seminars at Home and Abroad. Contact Howard Ruff Travel Seminars, 6612 Owens Drive, P.O. Box 25, Pleasanton, CA 94566. Phone: 800-227-0703, (USA), 800-642-0204 (CA), 415-463-2200.

TARGET TRAVEL CLUB

Complete personalized domestic and international travel services including frequent special-interest group tours, as well as individual travel arrangements. Contact Target Travel International, Inc., 6620 Owens Drive, Pleasanton, CA 94566. Phone: 800-227-2446 (USA), 800-321-5307 (CA), 415-463-2220.

MISCELLANEOUS BY HOWARD J. RUFF

Howard Ruff National Convention Tapes, available following annual conventions from Target, Inc., P.O. Box 25, Pleasanton, CA 94566.

Howard Ruff Sings—Howard Ruff's record album featuring the Osmond Brothers and the Brigham Young University Philharmonic Orchestra and A Cappella Choir. Songs of Country, Money, Family Love and Inspiration. Stereo record or cassette tape $9.95. What more can I say?

Life is Ruff, a board game using inflation-beating strategies. $12.95 plus $2.00 shipping. Target, Inc., P.O. Box 25, Pleasanton, CA 94566.

INDEX

Adams, John, 243, 245
Alderdice Brothers, 165
Allen, Robert G., 117
American Entrepreneurs Association Incorporation kits, 211
American Gemological Laboratory (AGL), 176
Antiques, 108–9
Austrian School of Economics, 84

B. Ray Anderson's Tax Report (Anderson), 178
Balanced Budget Amendment, 55, 57
Bank of America, 46
Bank stocks, 72
Bankruptcy, 131
Banks
    preference for moderate deficits and inflation, 36–37
    vulnerability to natural and political disasters, 46–47
Bearer certificates, reporting requirements for, 103
Bennett, Senator Wallace F., 18
Better Business Bureau, 179

Bishop, Bob, 96
Black Liberation movements, South African, 91–92
Boiler rooms
    and oil and gas lotteries, 171–73
    and strategic metals, 173–74
Boiler-room-brokers checklist, 159
Bonds, and interest rates, 184
Bonds, municipal, 111
Bonds, Sunshine Mining, 101–2
Bonds, U.S. Treasury
    capital gains possibilities with, 110
    and falling interest rates, 110–11
Bowers, Q. David, 108
Bramble Coins, 169
Brokers' discounts, 170–71
Buffelsfontein, 112
Bull & Bear Group, 202
Bull Run, 93, 95
Bullion Reserve of North America, 165–67
Bureau of Land Management (BLM) and oil and gas lotteries, 171–73
Buy and sell signals, 261

Campbell Red Lake, 93
Capital gains
  matching against losses, 196–97
  treatment of hard assets, 90
Carneal, Jeff, 131
Casey, Doug, 95, 117
Ceramics, Chinese, 107
Certificate of deposit, 64–65
Certificate programs, 87–88
Chamber of Commerce, 179
Charting, 182
Church of Jesus Christ of Latter-day
  Saints, 15–16, 18, 23
Coeur d'Alene Mines, 95
Coin World, 108
Coins, numismatic, 107
Coins, silver, 98–99
Collectibles, 107–8
Commandments, violations of,
  247–53
Commodity Futures Trading Com-
  mission (CFTC), 158–79
Commodity Research Bureau Index
  (CRB), 50
Competition, benefits of, 244–45
Computers, 223–34
  books, 232
  buying, 226–27
  data bases, 231
  equipment needed, 227–28
  hardware terminology, 225
  IBM–Apple comparison, 233–34
  investment software, 228–29
  newsletters, 232
  and portfolio management, 223
  program terminology, 227–28
  selection advice, 231–32
  software comparisons, 233
  and technical analysis, 229
Congressional Budget Office (CBO),
  56
Constitution, U.S., 16, 243, 244

Contrary opinion, theory of, 268–
  69
Covetousness, 247
Creative finance, 122, 123–26
Credit expansion, Federal Reserve
  and, 32–34
Crisis Investing (Casey), 95
Cumulative money flow, 267

Data bases, 231
  comparisons, 233
Deak-Perera, 165–70
  certificate program, 87–88
Debt
  covetousness as root cause of, 247
  encouraged by tax policies, 43–44
  as root cause of inflation, 247–48
Declaration of Independence, 16
Deficits, federal, 49–50
Deflation, 45–48
Democratic government
  Ben Lichtenberg on, 248
  inherent flaws of, 244
Depletion allowances, 214
Diamonds, 108
Dictatorships, and hyperinflation, 47
Dines, Jim, 263
Diocletian, 47
Directory of No-Load Mutual Funds,
  203
Disarmament, unilateral, 249
Discipline, importance of, 77–78
Dome Mining, 93
Dow Jones Industrial Average
  (DJIA), 50
  futures available on, 143
Driefontein Consolidated, 112
Durban Deep, 93

E. F. Hutton, 153
Economic forecasting, in Malarial
  Economy, 50

Economic problems and spiritual principles, 243–55
Economic Recovery Tax Act of 1981 (ERTA), and abusive tax shelters, 212
Eldridge, Paul, 188
Eldridge Strategy
  and U.S. Gold Shares, 189–93
  highest-odds trading strategy, 180
Emerging industry groups, 262–63
Employment growth from small companies, 44
Entrepreneurs, young, 115–16
"Equality of Opportunity," 251
Equipment leasing, 220–21
ERPM, 93
Exxon, 113

Failure, fear of, 130
Failure, as precondition for success, 134–35
Failure management, 130–35
Family, Mormon view of, 15
Famine and Survival in America (Ruff), 24
Federal budget and transfer payments, 248
Federal Reserve
  and the American banking system, 36
  and inflation, 32–34
Federal Reserve Board, 40
Federal Reserve notes, 55–56, 59
Fiat money, 61
Fidelity Group of Funds, 203
Financial advisors, worship of, 12–13
Financial War Room, 26, 28, 162, 179
Fog Index, 29
Food and commodity storage, 235–37
Franklin, Benjamin, 251

Free the Eagle
  and the anti-money fund legislation, 68
  and the IMF/Bank bailout, 25
  and 314b, 201
  Washington office, 25
Freedom, as incompatible with equality, 251
Freedom of the press and the newsletter industry, 55
Fundamental analysis
  computer aids, 230–31
  defined, 181–82
Fundamentals, external and internal, 181–82
Futures, stock index. *See* Stock index futures
Futures contracts, and boiler room brokers, 159
Futures market, 140–42

Gemological Institute of America (GIA), 176
Giant Yellowknife, 93
Gold
  bearish factors and bullish factors, 104–5
  buying guidelines, 85–86
  cheapest way to buy large quantities, 102–3
  coins vs. bullion, 88
  moving averages, 186
  relationship to interest rates, 80
  survival holdings, 85–86
  unique qualities, 83–85
Gold coins, income from, 113
Gold Commission, 58
Gold standard, 57–63
Gold stocks, North American, 93
Gold stocks, penny, 94–98
Gold stocks, South African, 89–93
  dividend yields of, 111–12

"Golden constant," the, 83–84
Gold-silver ratio, 98, 185
Government
  dishonesty of, 252
  threat from, 246
Guidebook of U.S. Coins, The (Yeomans), 108

Hand, Judge Learned, 195
Harmony (gold-mining concern), 112
Hartebeestfontein, 93, 112
Hero worship of financial advisors, 12–13
High Profits from Rare Coin Investment (Bowers), 108
Highs and lows, significance of, 256
Hitler, Adolf, inflation and rise of, 47
Home ownership, 235
Homestake Mines, 93
How to Become Financially Successful by Owning Your Own Business (Lowry), 211
How to Form Your Own Corporation Without a Lawyer for Under $50 (Nicholas), 211
How to Prosper During the Coming Bad Years (Ruff), 23, 25, 237
Howard, Col. George S., 19
Hydroelectric projects, tax benefits of, 218–19
Hyperinflation, 44–45, 47

Impala Mines, 107
Inc. Yourself (McQuown), 211
Income, from gold coins, 113
Income tax, indexing of, 49
Incorporating, 207–11
Independent contractor status, 205–10
  eligibility guidelines for, 206
  how to achieve, 205–7

and your employer, 206–7
  retirement plan benefits of, 205–10
Index of Leading Indicators, 50
Indexing, income tax, 49
Individual Retirement Accounts (IRAs) 201–4
  and collectibles, 201–2
  and mutual fund families, 202–3
  and oil and gas income funds, 203
  and real estate funds, 203
  as trading accounts, 204
  self-directed, 203
Inflation
  bullish for gold, 104
  characteristics of, 30
  chart of historical pattern, 35
  French, 30
  German, 30
  hidden damage from, 73
  how Federal Reserve causes, 32–34
  and interest rates, 35–36, 37
  recent history of, 42–43
  Roman, 31
  as root cause of debt, 247–48
  Spanish, 31
  time lag and, 38
Installment sales, 198
Interest rates
  and home sales, 38
  and inflation, 35–36, 37
  and "inflation premium," 51
  and onset of recession, 37
  relationship of short-term to long-term rates, 50–51
  relationship to price of gold, 80
Internal Revenue Service. *See* IRS
International Gold Bullion Exchange (IGBE), 164–65, 167
International Monetary Fund (IMF), 40

International Trading Group (ITG), and, commissions on Mocatta options, 153
Investment Advisor's Act of 1948, 55
Investment Rarities, 165, 170
Investment Tax Credit (ITC), 214–16
Investments
  analysis of, 180–94
  for inflation hedging, 82
IRS, 55
  and abusive tax shelters, 212
  and 1031 tax deferred exchanges, 175, 177
Italy, tax resistance in, 48

Jeffers, J. Terry, 24
  Personal Touch Computer Service, 231–32
Jefferson, Thomas, 243, 245, 251

Kaller, Myron, 108
Kennedy, Teddy, 47
Keogh plans, 201–2, 205, 210
Kloof, 112

Land, raw, 128
Land-for-gems exchange, 175–77
"Lawful money," 55–56
Leverage, 130–61
  danger signals, 161
  example of, in real estate, 136
  and margin calls, 137
Leverage contracts, 159
Leverage strategies, 135–61
Lexington Group, 202
Lichtenberg, Ben, on democratic government, 248
Life insurance, 239–42
Limited Partners Letter, 178
Linn's Stamp News, 108
Livermore, Jesse, 266
Lockheed, bailout of, 42

Loraine, 93
Lowry, Albert J., 23, 117, 127
Lowry Real Estate Investor Course, 23–24

Making Money (Ruff) update, 12
Malarial Economy, 25–49
  chart of, 35
  economic forecasting in, 50–53
  future of, 39–53
  how to invest in, 75
  and hyperinflation, 45
  inflation as root cause of, 30
Mao-tse Tung, 47
Marriott, Bill, 18
Marriott, J. Willard, Sr., 18
Marriott Corporation, 18
Merrill Lynch, 170
Merrill Lynch Sharebuilder Program, 87, 102–4
Middle class, American, 10–11
Midway, 74
Mocatta Delivery Orders, 103–4
Mocatta Metals, 103
Mocatta Options, 152–53
Momentum of relative strength, 265
Momentum studies, 264–65
Monetary policy and Federal Reserve Board, 40
Money flow, 266–67
Money market accounts, 69
Money market funds, 67–70, 110
Mormon Church. *See* Church of Jesus Christ of Latter-day Saints
Mortgages
  Federal Housing Administration (FHA), 120
  fixed rate, 118, 120–21
  graduated payment (GPM), 121
  second, 71
  shared equity, 118, 122
  variable-rate, 121

Mortgages (*cont.*)
  variable-rate with cap, 121
  Veterans Administration (VA),
    120
Moving averages, 185
  optimum, 188–89
Moving total volume, 267–68
Municipal bonds, 200–201
Murphy's Law, Ruff's Corollary to,
    9, 47

Napoleon, 47
National debt, Terri Lynn Ruff's
    share of, 31
National Education Association, 255
Neolife Company, 23–24
New York City, bailout of, 42
New York Commodity Exchange
    (COMEX), 102
New York Stock Exchange Index,
    futures on, 143
New York Times, The, 55
Newcastle Financial Group, 203
  and real estate syndications, 128
  as evaluaters of tax shelters, 128,
    221
  as insurance agents, 242
Newsweek, 167
Nicholas, Ted, 211
Nimitz, Admiral Chester, 74
Nixon, Richard M., 61
North, Dr. Gary, 46
North American Coin and Currency,
    169

Office of Management and Budget
    (OMB), 56
Oil and gas drilling, 219–20
Oil and gas lotteries, 172
Option Clearing Corporation, 149
Options, commodity, 157–59
Options, Mocatta, 152–53

Options, stock, 144–52
  call, defined, 146
  glossary of terminology, 151–52
  on Homestake Mining, 145–46
  "in the money," 146
  limited losses, 144
  listings in major papers, 145
  most conservative approach, 147
  "out of the money," 146
  put, defined, 146
  risk evaluation of, 147–48
  to reduce risk, 148–51
  writing of, 148
Oregon Metallurgical, 107

Paper currency, 58
Patience, importance of, 77
Paul, Congressman Ron, 58
Penn Central, bailout of, 42
Penny Mining Stock Report (Bishop
    and Pogue), 96
Pension funds, 114–15
Perpetual storage, 165
Platinum, 106–7
Pogue, Jerry, 96
Point and figure charts, 257–61
Precious Metals. *See* Gold; Silver;
    Storage of precious metals
President Steyn, 93, 112
Price controls, 47
"Prophet of Doom," 235–36
Proposition 13, 57
Prudential-Bache
  commissions on Mocatta options,
    153
  strategic metals, 174
Psycho-cybernetics (Maltz), 134
Put-call ratio, 268–70
Pyramiding, dangers of, 174–75

Randfontein Estates, 93, 112
Reagan, Ronald, 39–40, 246

Real estate
  commercial vs. residential, 129
  conventional financing, 122
  creative financing, 122
  how to buy, 120–27
  and inflation rate, 117
  Lowry approach, 127
  reasons to own home, 119–20
  rent controls, 127
  shortfall of new rental units, 118
  syndications, 127–28
  tax-deferred exchanges of, 127–215
  with and without leverage, 136–37
  income-producing, 111
Recession, 37, 120
Regulatory agencies, 55
"Relative Strength" studies, 262–63
Rent controls, 127
Research and development partner-
    ships, 216–18
Retirement, 114–15
Retirement plans
  advantages of independent con-
      tractor status, 205–10
  cash option plans, 210
  deferred-compensation programs,
      210
  defined-benefits plans, 205, 210
  defined-contribution plans, 205,
      210
Ringer, Robert, 127
Risk, use of options to reduce,
    148–51
Rosenthal, Dan, 165–66
Ruff House, 25
Ruff Times, The, 24–25
Ruff, David, 20
Ruff, Deborah, 24
Ruff, Eric, 20
Ruff, Ivan, 20–22
Ruff, Kay, 19, 27
Ruff, Larry, 20

Ruff, Pamela, 20
Ruff, Patty, 26
Ruff, Sharon, 20
Ruff, Terri Lynn, 27, 31
Ruff, Timothy, 24
Ruffpac, 25
Rustenberg (mining concern),
    107

St. Helena, 112
Savings and loan stocks, 72
Savings Bank Association, and 314b,
    201
Savings rate, 43
Saxon, Alan, 165–66
Scams
  gems for gems, 177
  land-for-gems exchange, 175–77
  naive, 167–68
  straightforward, 165
  tax shelter, 177–78
Securities and Exchange Commis-
    sion (SEC), 55, 179
Security Pacific Bank, 46
Sennholz, Hans, 62
Sight draft, 86
Silver
  a mining by-product, 100–101
  least expensive way to buy in large
      quantities, 102
  removed from dimes and quarters
      in 1964, 60
  survival holdings, 85–86
Silver and Gold Report (Rosenthal),
    165–66
Silver certificates, 60
Silver-gold ratio, 98
Silver, junk, 98
Silver-mining stock, 98–100
Social Security
  inadequacy of, for retirement, 114
  lies about, 251–53

Social Security (*cont.*)
  $7.5 trillion in unfunded liabilities,
    42, 114, 251–52
Solarz, Congressman Steven, 90
South Africa, 90–92
Southvaal, 112
Special Olympics, 131–32
Stamps, 107–8
Stamps and Stories, 108
Standard and Poor's 500, futures on,
    143
Standard of Ohio, 112–13
Stock, bank, 72
Stock index futures, 142–43
Stock market
  inflation and, 79
  rallies, and recessions, 78–79
Stocks
  buying on margin, 138–40
  buying with the trend, 138–40
Stocks, oil, 112–13
Storage of precious metals
  fungible, 170
  guidelines, 89
  non-fungible, 89, 169
Strategic Investors, 203
Strategic metals, 174
Strategy, investment, importance of,
    76–77
Sunshine Mining Bonds, 101–2
Support and resistance, 261–62
Survival, 86
Survivalists, hard-core, 237–38
Sweden, tax burden in, 248

Tax Equity and Fiscal Responsibility
    Act (TEFRA), 198
  and abusive shelter promoters, 212
Tax planning, 197–98
Tax policies, 43–44
Tax rate, individual vs. corporate,
    207

Tax shelters, 177–78, 211–22, 250
  abusive, 177, 212
  depreciation, 214
  checklist, 178
  equipment leasing, 220–21
  evaluation checklist, 221–22
  horse breeding, 177
  hydroelectric projects, 218–19
  jojoba beans, 177
  motion picture, 177
  oil and gas drilling, 219–20
  penalties against abusive, 178
  research and development partner-
    ships, 216–18
  residential income property, 216
  sources of information on, 178
  television production and distribu-
    torship, 177
Taxation, confiscatory, 250
Tax-deferred exchanges of real es-
    tate, 127, 198
Taxes
  and municipal bonds, 200–201
  accelerating deductions, 200
  deferring income, 199–200
  marginal tax bracket, 198
  matching gains and losses, 196–
    97
Technical analysis, 185–94, 256–71
  buy and sell signals, 261
  computer aids, 229
  cumulative money flow, 267
  emerging groups, 262–63
  highs and lows, 256
  momentum of relative strength,
    265
  momentum studies, 264–65
  money flow, 266–67
  moving averages, 185–88
  moving total volume, 267–68
  point and figure studies, 257–61
  put-call ratio, 268–70

"Relative Strength" studies, 262–64
trend lines, 256
TEFRA. *See* Tax Equity and Financial Responsibility Act
Telephone Switch Newsletter (Fabian), 188–89
Texaco, 112
Think and Grow Rich (Hill), 134
Tingley, Katherine, 27
Transfer payments, 249
Treasury bills, 70
Treasury bonds, U.S., 70–71
Treasury Gold Certificate, 59
Trend lines, 256

United Services Gold shares, 203
  chart of price history, 191
  Eldridge Strategy results, 192
  optimum moving averages, 190
U.S. Bureau of Printing and Engraving, 243
Utility stocks, 72

Vaal Reefs, 93, 112
Value Line Index, futures on, 143
Venterspost, 93
Von Hayek, F. A., 62
Von Mises, Ludwig, 84

Wall Street Journal, 53, 55
War, as bullish for gold, 104
Watkins, Senator, 18
Welfare mess, 250
Western Deep Levels, 112
Western Holdings, 112
Western Precious Metals, 168–69
Winning with Real Estate (Lowry), 123
World Coin News 108
Worst-case survival, 235–42
  and life insurance, 235, 239, 242

Yeoman, R. S., 108